PICTURE CREDITS

1 Popperfoto/AFP; 2 Rex Features; 3 Diana Walker/Time/Katz; 4 David Kennerly/ Frank Spooner; 5 Associated Press; 6 Official U.S. Navy Photograph; 7 Randy Jolly/ Rex Features; 8 © BBC; 9 Associated Press; 10 Ian Black/Rex Features; 11 Rex Features; 12 Popperfoto/AFP; 13 © BBC; 14 Popperfoto/AFP; 15 Photo courtesy of Armed Forces Journal International, USAF photo by MSgt Timothy B Hadrych; 16 Popperfoto/AFP; 17 Mike Moore/Rex Features; 18 Popperfoto/Reuter; 19 Royal Navy Photo; 20 Tom Stoddart/Katz; 21 Popperfoto/AFP; 22 Rex Features; 23 Ben Gibson/Katz; 24 Popperfoto/Reuter; 25 Ken Lennox/Syndication International; 26 Popperfoto/AFP; 27 Steve Bent/Katz

Published by BBC Books,
a division of BBC Enterprises Limited
Woodlands, 80 Wood Lane, London W12 0TT

First Published 1991
© Benjamin Brown and David Shukman 1991
The moral right of the authors has been asserted.

ISBN 0 563 36304 5

Designed by David Robinson
Maps by Eugene Fleurry

Set in Century Old Style by Ace Filmsetting Ltd, Frome, Somerset
Printed and bound in Great Britain by Clays Ltd, St Ives Plc
Cover printed by Clays Ltd, St Ives Plc

Acknowledgements

Many of those who helped with the research for this book cannot be identified and only agreed to talk to us on that basis. They include generals, pilots, soldiers, intelligence officers, senior diplomats, Whitehall officials and many others. They know who they are and we give them our special thanks. To the Iraqis whose accounts of the war appear in the following pages, we have given false names lest they should suffer reprisals.

We would like to thank public affairs officers in the Pentagon, and at US Central Command in Florida and Dhahran, who are too numerous to mention by name. Particular thanks must go to staff at Strategic Air Command at Omaha, Nebraska; the 37th Tactical Fighter Wing, Nevada, home of the Stealth fighter-bombers; and the 101st Airborne Division, Kentucky.

We are grateful to many in the Ministry of Defence in London, including its public relations staff, and those of the Army, Royal Navy and RAF. Others who have made our task much easier are Paul Beaver of *Jane's Defence Weekly*; John Pike of the Federation of American Scientists; David Isenberg of the Centre for Defence Information in Washington, who allowed us to pore over his files; and Justin Webb, Anthony Beevor and Sarah Maunder. Wendy Holden of the *Daily Telegraph* deserves particular thanks for her hard work on our behalf. Madeleine Lewis, who did much of the research and encouraged us with her tireless enthusiasm, made the book possible.

Heather Holden-Brown and Nicky Copeland of BBC Books provided constant advice and assistance. We also thank our editors at BBC News and Current Affairs, Tony Hall, Chris Cramer and Mike Robinson, for their suggestions and for their permission for us to undertake the project in the first place. A final debt of gratitude must go to our wives, Geraldine and Jessica, for their endless patience and support.

THE CRISIS REGION

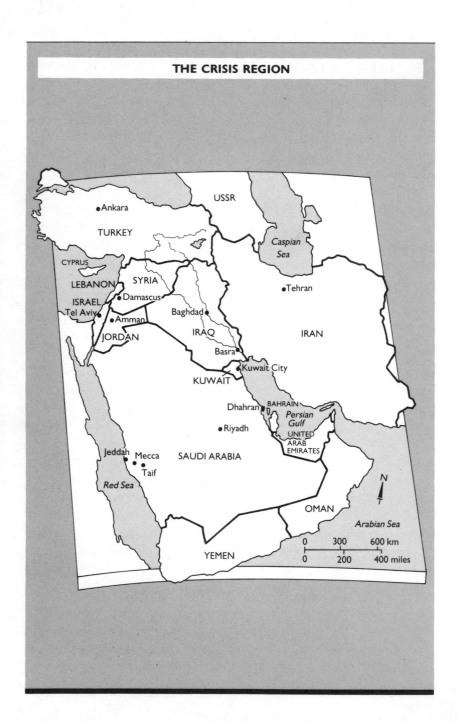

Prologue

I n Florida's sweltering summer heat, General H. Norman Schwarzkopf was hard at work in the trailer where he'd set up his makeshift office. It was parked on the edge of an airfield and was surrounded by dozens of tents used by his staff. In this, the last week of July 1990, United States Central Command was holding a major exercise. About 400 of its officers had moved out of their headquarters in Tampa to two airbases – Hurlburt and Dukefield. Central Command, responsible for all American military operations in the Middle East, was rehearsing for a war in the desert. Most of it was done on paper and with computers: only a few troops were involved. The exercise had been called 'Internal Look' and its scenario was simple – 'Country Orange' had invaded Saudi Arabia and the Americans were trying to drive it back. It would never be said in public but 'Country Orange' was the codename for Iraq.

The exercise was in full flow when Schwarzkopf's intelligence officers decided they had to interrupt him. They walked into his trailer and delivered a startling warning – that the war game he was playing could soon become a reality. They told Schwarzkopf that tens of thousands of Saddam's troops were now massing on the border with Kuwait, poised to invade. Schwarzkopf scoffed at the idea that 'Country Orange' might soon be more than just a computer enemy.

'It's just a show of strength by Saddam,' he said.

By chance the briefing had been overheard by a staff officer. He approached the intelligence men and urged them, despite Schwarzkopf's dismissive attitude, to report it to the deputy Commander-in-Chief. They agreed, and walked down the corridor to see Lieutenant-General C.C. 'Buck' Rogers, whose office was in the same trailer. He saw them in and asked to hear what they had just told Schwarzkopf. Rogers was used to his superior officer keeping important information to himself. The intelligence officers repeated their warning.

'Mmmmm. What was Schwarzkopf's reaction?' he asked.

'Well, he didn't totally explain his reaction,' one of the officers replied. Just like Schwarzkopf to keep his thoughts to himself in front of the intelligence staff, thought Rogers. He decided to go and see his superior immediately.

'What do you make of this thing?' he asked him.

ALL NECESSARY MEANS

'Naaaa,' drawled Schwarzkopf. 'This is just typical Saddam Hussein nonsense, you know. He's trying to strong-arm the Kuwaitis for all the reasons we know, and that's that.' There didn't seem to be any shred of doubt in Schwarzkopf's mind, and no hesitation in his analysis of Saddam's intentions. 'This is another smokescreen – he's not going to do anything. This is posturing,' he told Rogers. 'They're angered by the fact that the Kuwaitis are exceeding their oil quotas. That's driving down the price of their own oil in Iraq. It's a thing they're doing to tell the Kuwaitis they've got to back off and they'd better listen or they're going to get bothered.' Rogers left Schwarzkopf's office with one prediction in particular ringing in his ears: 'It's not going to happen.' It was the advice that Central Command would send to the White House.

A few days later, Buck Rogers arrived at a holiday cottage on Florida's Atlantic coast. It was 11p.m. when the phone rang. The line was not secure so the message had to be cryptic. 'You need to come back right away, sir. The issue that we were worried about has happened.' Rogers knew at once that Kuwait had been invaded. Schwarzkopf had got it wrong.

Five months later, hundreds of millions of people around the world were watching the campaign to liberate the tiny emirate, with wealth out of all proportion to its size or population. What they saw on their television sets looked like a 42-day success story: there were pilot's-eye videos of smart bombs that never missed; there were interviews with troops who said they were going to 'kick ass' and who did; there were briefings from generals who produced charts to show that their tactics were as sophisticated as their weapons. But in this weirdest of wars, nothing was quite as it seemed.

Schwarzkopf, for example, emerged as the conquering hero yet his fellow generals were seriously concerned about the way he ran his War Room. They've told us that his explosive temper created an unhappy atmosphere, where staff were too frightened to make suggestions or to bring him bad news. Relations between the allies were not always as cordial as they appeared either. British commanders were alarmed at the prospect of going into battle with the US Marines, who they viewed as dangerously 'gung-ho' and desperate for glory. At sea, the Royal Navy were livid when the Americans demanded that they clear mines along the Kuwaiti coast in only a fortnight. The Navy said it would take a month and that anything less would put Britain's minehunters in unnecessary danger.

Politically, too, the 'Special Relationship' was occasionally strained. In a New York hotel, Mrs Thatcher quarrelled with the American Secretary of State, James Baker, over whether the allies needed a UN resolution authorising war. London and Washington also argued about how long to keep their embassy staff in occupied Kuwait, and about the risks involved in attacking Saddam's nuclear, chemical and biological installations.

But all this seemed trivial by the end of February, when Downing Street and the White House disagreed about the momentous decision of when to end the war. When President Bush wanted to call a halt after 100 hours, the Prime Minister, John Major, pressed for the campaign to go on. If he had had his way, the shape of Iraq after the war, and the fate of Saddam, might have been very different.

The politicians often claimed that they didn't interfere in the running of the war but once or twice they did. To the outrage of air force generals, London and Washington stopped them from bombing the Baghdad bridges which carried fibre-optic communication cables linking Saddam to his Scud missiles. There were fears that the raids put Iraqi civilians in too much danger, so instead the SAS had to be sent in to cut the cables.

The Special Air Service were already deep inside Iraq, spearheading the 'counter-Scud campaign'. At first, Schwarzkopf had needed a good deal of persuasion to use them. Had he refused, Saddam may have succeeded in provoking Israel into entering the war and shattering the unity of the alliance. We've been told that, contrary to popular belief, allied commanders would have given the Israeli Air Force a free run if they had chosen to attack.

It was the most technologically advanced war in history, and the allies could call on everything from forty satellites in space to SAS men operating on the outskirts of Baghdad. Yet we've learned of astonishing blunders. Reconnaissance photographs were sent to the front, which were either of the wrong place, or, even worse, printed upside down. Telexes from Washington were sent to the wrong address – to Central Command in Florida instead of Centcom in Saudi Arabia. Most important of all, analysts totally misjudged the size of the Iraqi army in Kuwait: it had half the troops they'd claimed.

But whatever the hiccups, no one could doubt that the allied attack was awesome: B-52 bombing raids were so devastating that Royal Navy frogmen felt the sea-bed shudder. After one explosion an SAS man thought that the Americans had 'nuked' Kuwait. It was hardly surprising that Iraqi troops were so desperate to be taken prisoner that some penned themselves into their own PoW camp, even before the allies had arrived.

Nevertheless, at the end of Desert Storm, there were still the same questions there had been before it began. Was it all for oil or was it to stop a new Hitler? Was America playing the policeman again, or was this the United Nations asserting itself at last? Had sanctions been abandoned too early or was war the only way to show that in a new world order, aggression wouldn't pay? Was it a cynical coalition of allies, including some, like Assad of Syria, who were no better than Saddam himself? Or was it a triumph of international solidarity, a rare example of a united world using 'all necessary means' to stop a ruthless dictator?

Chapter I
THE NINETEENTH PROVINCE

'You are a force for moderation in the region and the United States wishes to broaden her relations with Iraq.'

US assistant secretary of state, John Kelly, to Saddam Hussein, 12 February, 1990.

President Bush on the Iraqi army's occupation of Kuwait, November 1990.

'They have committed outrageous acts of barbarism. I don't believe that Adolf Hitler ever participated in anything of that nature.'

No journalists or cameramen were there to spot the number plates of the Kuwaiti ambassador's official limousine as it swept into the grand central courtyard of the Foreign and Commonwealth Office. It was the afternoon of Wednesday, 25 July, eight days before Saddam's invasion. Ironically, the Defence Secretary, Tom King, was in his ministry across the road, announcing controversial plans for deep cuts in Britain's armed forces. As a result, no one noticed the apparently routine visit by His Excellency Ghazi al-Rayes to the Under Secretary for Middle East affairs, David Gore-Booth. The ambassador brought what he considered to be heartening news.

In Gore-Booth's large, cool office overlooking Horseguards parade-ground, the ambassador reported optimistically that the tension between Kuwait and her powerful neighbour, Iraq, now seemed to be easing. According to confidential Foreign Office minutes of the meeting, the ambassador gave an 'upbeat' assessment. He said that energetic shuttle diplomacy by the Egyptian President, Hosni Mubarak, was proving 'highly effective'. Saddam was still demanding control of two Kuwaiti

ALL NECESSARY MEANS

islands, Warbah and Bubiyan, and the eradication of his huge debts, but nevertheless the ambassador had great hopes that Iraq would not now take any military action. Earlier that week, he had met his Iraqi counterpart in London, Azmi Shafiq al-Salihi. The two men had even shaken hands and agreed that the crisis was 'a summer cloud', which would soon disappear.

On the whole, Gore-Booth agreed. He told al-Rayes that he too thought 'the worst was over'. Arab diplomatic activity was helping to take the heat out of the crisis, and so was the prospect of an agreement at an Organisation of Petroleum Exporting Countries (OPEC) meeting in Geneva the next day. All along, Saddam's main bone of contention with Kuwait had been that it was producing more oil than allowed under an OPEC quota; that meant it was forcing down the world price just when Iraq was recovering from its war with Iran and needed to earn as much as possible from its own oil exports. Many diplomats assumed that a deal in Geneva to raise the world price would be enough to satisfy Saddam.

But the minutes record Gore-Booth doubting that an oil agreement 'would be the end of the problem'. Kuwait had been provocative and 'too cavalier' in its oil policy, he told al-Rayes, and would now need to play its oil cards 'a little more carefully'. Gore-Booth went on to tell the ambassador that Saddam 'was prepared to say and do dangerous things'. Al-Rayes was most struck, though, by the warning he was given that Kuwait should show restraint and not send any troops to the border. Gore-Booth told him that the Kuwaiti army should not be mobilised, because that might give Saddam a pretext to invade. 'Don't provoke him' are the words al-Rayes most remembers from the meeting. If his government had ignored that advice from Britain, he believes his country could at least have put up a fight. 'We could have held out for two or three days and given them a bloody nose.' But the conversation that afternoon ended cordially, and the first thing Gore-Booth did afterwards was to draft an instruction to the British ambassador at the United Nations in New York. It told him to raise the Iraq-Kuwait dispute at the next meeting of the Security Council. There was some concern in Gore-Booth's mind, but no alarm.

Much the same could be said of another diplomat who, that very day, had been summoned at one hour's notice to a rather different meeting.

THE NINETEENTH PROVINCE

America's ambassador in Baghdad, April Glaspie, was cabling to the State Department in Washington her report of a now controversial meeting that she'd just had with the man everyone was trying to fathom: Saddam Hussein. It had been an awkward encounter, testing all her experience as one of the State Department's top Arabists. Glaspie, the first female diplomat to head an American embassy in the Middle East, had faced an almost impossible task, with no time to seek instructions. She had to convey a double-message to Saddam: that the United States was concerned by his threats to Kuwait and the other Gulf countries – but that it also wanted to stay on good terms with him. Many officials in Washington were aware of the danger Saddam posed to America's allies along the Gulf and to their pivotal position in the world's oil markets. But the trend over recent years had been to favour Saddam with trade and intelligence. He had turned Iraq into a valuable export market and ensured that it remained a bulwark against the Islamic fundamentalism of Iran. It was never going to be an easy conversation.

Glaspie found him 'enraged' by the previous day's announcement that America was planning joint naval manoeuvres with the United Arab Emirates. This union of little states had been included in the threats levelled at Kuwait, and it looked to Saddam as though Washington was lining up on their side of the dispute. But Glaspie also thought that he was 'conciliatory'. He interrupted their meeting to talk by telephone to President Mubarak and came back into the room with a reassuring message. Saddam repeated to Glaspie what he'd just told Mubarak: that 'he would not solve his problems with Kuwait by violence. Period. He would not do it.' Saddam wanted Glaspie to report that to President Bush.

The conversation didn't end there but its content is disputed. Only the Iraqis had a note-taker present. Glaspie had been summoned at such short notice that she neither had time to bring one nor contact the State Department to obtain new instructions. It was a tragic misfortune. For a meeting that was ultimately to determine whether Saddam's next move would be diplomatic or military, the only accounts available are from Glaspie's memory, leaked extracts from her cables back to Washington and Saddam's propaganda machine.

The Iraqi record quotes Glaspie as saying the United States had 'no opinion on Arab–Arab conflicts, like your border disagreement with Kuwait'. The Iraqis thought that meant Washington wouldn't object if Saddam invaded. But Glaspie, in her later evidence to Congress, said she had added another, vital sentence which the Iraqis edited out. She claims that she told Saddam, 'We insist you settle your disputes with Kuwait non-violently' – and that Saddam said that he would. According to the leaked copies of her secret cables on the meeting, she reported to Washington that Saddam's desire for a 'peaceful settlement is surely sincere'. But the same cables do not portray Glaspie as warning Saddam against war as vehemently as she later claimed. In the event, either her message wasn't strong enough or Saddam didn't believe it, or neither side's account is accurate because, even as Saddam and Glaspie were talking, the Iraqi army was poised in enormous strength on the northern border of Kuwait.

The intelligence was startlingly clear, and had been for at least a week. The satellite pictures could hardly fail to pick out the 100 000 troops massing in the desert and clogging the six-lane highway leading south towards Kuwait. Western defence attachés were regularly leaving their embassies in Baghdad to watch the convoys. What they saw, according to the account given to us by one intelligence analyst, was that the Iraqi army had 'moved beyond the stage of sabre-rattling'. Most or all of Saddam's eight Republican Guard divisions were in place. These were his very best. Unlike the conscripts in the bulk of Iraq's army, Republican Guard troops were regulars, who were given good weapons, good pay and special privileges. Their role was to protect the regime – and act as its spearhead.

The embassy-watchers noted down the markings on the sides of the trucks and tanks. They saw the formidable T-72s of the Republican Guard's two heavy armoured divisions, the Hammurabi and the Medina, along with its mechanised infantry division, the Tawakalna, which had earned its promotion from the ordinary Iraqi army after leading a fierce thrust into Iran. They also spotted the Guard's Special Forces and four more well-armed infantry divisions. To intelligence analysts in London and Washington, it was a warning-sign that 'something very major was going on'. Their view was that Saddam had assembled a force that was too big to keep in position for very long. It had either to be withdrawn or used very soon – and, we have learned, the conclusion was that the Iraqis were 'likely' to invade Kuwait.

Given that analysts tend to use more cautious language, that warning could hardly have been stronger. The officials admitted that they couldn't be absolutely certain but, in repeated messages, they said an invasion was looking more and more probable. On Monday, 30 July, the Pentagon's top Middle East intelligence officer, Pat Lang, is said to have typed a secret electronic message to the head of the Defence Intelligence Agency with this conclusion:

> Saddam Hussein has moved a force disproportionate to the task at hand, if it is to bluff. Then there is only one answer: he intends to use it.

If Lang's words were taken seriously within the Pentagon, their implication never spread outside it. On the day that message was written, the ambassadors of the Big Five, the permanent members of the United Nations Security Council, gathered for a regular closed meeting in New York – apparently unaware of the military appraisal of the danger ahead. As instructed by the Foreign Office in London a few days earlier, Britain's ambassador, Sir Crispin Tickell, raised the dispute between Iraq and Kuwait. The authors have been shown the confidential British record of the meeting. It quotes Tickell as saying that, with the fixing of new and higher OPEC prices, 'the heat appeared to have gone out of the immediate crisis'. But he went on to warn that Saddam's demand for a better oil price was only one source of tension. 'It is right that the five should take notice and exchange assessments,' suggested Tickell.

But even at this stage, no one at the meeting had much to say. The American ambassador agreed that the most difficult problem was Iraq's pressure on Kuwait over their common boundary. The French representative observed that the Arabs wanted to deal with the dispute themselves; the Chinese ambassador didn't know what his government thought about the crisis and had nothing to add; the Soviet ambassador reported that his government had 'received reassurances from the two sides that they would not allow matters to escalate out of control'. It was the most optimistic note in what was described as a 'desultory' discussion.

Tickell had the last word. The confidential record quotes him telling his fellow diplomats, 'if matters degenerated into an armed confrontation, the five would need to meet very quickly to consider a response'. It couldn't have been more prophetic. In as little as 72 hours the ambassadors would indeed have to rush back to their seats around the same table.

By now the warnings from the military intelligence analysts were becoming stronger, almost by the hour. New satellite pictures that arrived at the Pentagon early in the morning on Wednesday, 1 August, showed the Iraqi divisions lining themselves up in attack formation just north of the Kuwaiti border. To those studying the photographs, an invasion now looked inevitable. But their judgement was, quite simply, overruled. Instead, many people in Washington, including the President, George Bush, and his Defence Secretary, Dick Cheney, chose to believe the reassurances they were hearing from their key allies in the Middle East. President Mubarak and King Fahd of Saudi Arabia, in particular, were saying they trusted Saddam's promises that he wouldn't invade. If those two allies were satisfied, why shouldn't Washington be too?

In London, there was no sense of impending crisis either – despite the warnings the military analysts say they were giving. One senior official who was in Number 10 at the time insists none of the reports that reached his desk indicated that an invasion was likely. On the contrary, he says, the intelligence community was 'emphatic' that Iraqi troop movements were only designed to put pressure on Kuwait. In Whitehall, the message was somehow failing to reach those who mattered. Either they weren't grasping the conclusions of the intelligence reports or the reports themselves weren't as clear as the analysts now claim or, more likely, they chose to trust the judgement of their allies in the Arab world.

On the afternoon of 1 August, Mrs Thatcher, then Prime Minister, saw no reason for breaking a long-standing arrangement to fly out to Aspen in Colorado where she was to collect an award and speak at a conference. There was nothing to suggest that her talks with President Bush planned for the next day would be devoted to the single subject of Iraq. At

THE NINETEENTH PROVINCE

RAF Strike Command near High Wycombe, Air Chief Marshal Sir Patrick Hine cleared his desk and set off with his wife for Dover to catch a late-night ferry. Hine had booked a three-week holiday on the Continent; it never occurred to him that he'd soon be the overall commander of Britain's biggest overseas fighting force since the Second World War. Later that afternoon, a senior Royal Navy officer, already away on leave, made a routine check call to his staff at the Ministry of Defence. He was told there'd been 'a bit of flutter' earlier in the day about the possibility of Iraq invading Kuwait but the excitement now seemed to have receded. The conclusion: all was quiet.

It began with the rumble of several hundred tanks surging in an unstoppable wave towards the lightly-defended Kuwaiti border – and then straight over it. The resistance was token, the odds hopeless, and under a moonlit sky the invading army headed with extraordinary speed for the capital. It was 2a.m. local time, 11p.m. in London, and, in the year when East and West had buried the Cold War, the world was about to be immersed in a new and very real conflict.

It was brutally simple. The columns of armour so carefully counted by western intelligence were now rolling down the main highway to Kuwait City. Iraqi jets screamed overhead and Special Forces teams landed by helicopter to seize key buildings. One was the state radio and television station where a broadcaster managed to shout over the air 'hurry to our aid!' before the transmitter was shut down. If another objective was to seize the Kuwaiti royal family, the Iraqis failed. The emir and his entourage had received word of the invasion by telephone and in the time it took the main Iraqi forces to travel the 80 miles to Kuwait City, the al-Sabahs had thrown some belongings into their limousines and raced south for Saudi Arabia. The emir's brother, Sheikh Fahd, manager of the national soccer team, was the only member of the royal family to stay and fight. His reward was to be shot on the steps of the palace shortly before it was attacked with rockets.

Ordinary Kuwaitis had little chance to escape. Many of them woke up to the sound of artillery and machine-gun fire. Others only realised what had happened when they peered out of their windows at dawn and gazed in horror at the menacing sight of Saddam's tanks juddering through their capital. 'It was six in the morning when I rushed to the window,' recalled Amer al-Zuhair, a Kuwaiti film producer. 'It was incredible! Down in the street there were all these tanks. I counted well over twenty-five and I knew they must be Iraqi because we never normally see our tanks in the city like that.' Soon, the Iraqis had the capital completely under control.

With daylight, they set about crippling the diminutive Kuwaiti Air Force – using weapons that Kuwait had once bought for Iraq. The French-made bombs were designed to ruin runways and the Iraqi pilots dropped them at all the main airbases. One of the victims was a BA jumbo making a scheduled stop on its way from Kuala Lumpur to London. By now, the invading army's attacks had become almost pointless. The Kuwaiti Air Force saw no sense in resisting and instead made hasty plans to fly more than half their planes to safety the next day. Other units put up a little returning fire but it wasn't to last long. The sound of shooting died away during the course of the day.

No one was fooled by the Iraqis' absurd claim that they'd been invited in to support an uprising by the Kuwaiti people against the corruption of the ruling al-Sabah dynasty. Soon even Saddam's propaganda machine couldn't be bothered to trot that out any more, and the truth emerged: Kuwait was to become the nineteenth province of Iraq. For the Kuwaitis, and the hundreds of thousands of expatriates trapped with them, terrifying and murderous days lay ahead.

The invasion was first detected by an American spy satellite. High above the Middle East, the unmanned spacecraft, eavesdropping on Iraqi military communications, picked up the order to attack. It was flashed to Washington. The secure phones soon started ringing in the homes of the Defence Secretary, Dick Cheney, the chairman of the Joint Chiefs of Staff, Colin Powell, and the National Security Adviser, Brent Scowcroft. President Bush told them he wanted to make an immediate response. A statement calling on Iraq to withdraw was quickly prepared and lawyers began drafting an executive order to freeze all Iraqi and Kuwaiti assets in the United States. There was talk too of sending fighters to Saudi Arabia. The phones were buzzing all night.

At 2.30a.m. a Pentagon official dialled a number in Florida. It was the home of General Schwarzkopf. He was told that his immediate superior, General Colin Powell, America's most senior serviceman, wanted to see him in his office in the Pentagon at 7a.m. There was a long pause. 'Yes sir, this morning,' said the caller. After another silence, he added: 'Yes, in four and a half hours.' The campaign had just begun for the man who would eventually lead a coalition of more than 30 nations to undo what Saddam had just done.

Kuwait's ambassador in London was also woken with a phone call that night. It was 1a.m., and Ghazi al-Rayes quickly recognised the distraught voice on the other end of the line as that of Suleiman Shaheen, Under-Secretary at the Ministry of Foreign Affairs in Kuwait City. 'They've invaded. They've taken over five of our border posts and they're moving forward,' said Shaheen. As soon as he'd put the phone down, the ambassador rang a special number at the Foreign Office to alert the British government. Throughout the night, al-Rayes got a stream of calls from Kuwait City, detailing the progress of the Iraqi army. The last message was a fax from Suleiman Shaheen, scrawled in his handwriting. 'The troops are now at the gates of the Foreign Ministry,' it said. 'Please do not send us any more communications. You are on your own. Good-bye.'

Out west in Colorado, Mrs Thatcher was being driven to the ranch where she was to stay for the next few days. Her foreign policy adviser, Charles (now Sir Charles) Powell, had gone with her. While he made sure she was comfortable, a team of British government electronics experts was busy setting up her secure communications equipment in 'The Little Nell', a nearby hotel that would serve as a makeshift Number Ten during her stay. It was just as well they did their work quickly because not long after Charles Powell arrived at the hotel, the top-secret apparatus suddenly sprang into life. A 'flash' message was coming through in code. It reported that the Iraqis had crossed the border into Kuwait. Charles Powell immediately rang Brent Scowcroft in the White House, who confirmed it. Powell then called Thatcher.

He thought she sounded 'a bit surprised' since the Cabinet Office view had been that an invasion was unlikely. But her response to Powell's astounding news seemed to him 'very resolute' – one of her first questions was whether Britain could take any immediate military action. Powell said that he would check and later he called the Ministry of Defence in London. It was agreed that two Royal Navy warships, one in Mombasa, the other in Penang, should be sent to the Gulf to join a third warship already there. He also checked with the White House to see whether President Bush would still be coming to Aspen the next day. Yes, came the answer, he would.

At 8a.m. on 2 August in Washington, the President summoned his National Security Council. Just before the meeting started, Bush had a contradictory message for the reporters who were allowed in to see the start of the session.

'We're not discussing intervention,' he declared, but then went on to say he wanted to 'have this invasion reversed and have them get out of Kuwait'.

The Iraqi occupation was hardly 12 hours old and the President was both ruling out American involvement and, at the same time, making a personal commitment to the freeing of Kuwait. It was the first of several mixed messages that he was to send Saddam. But the immediate concern around the table that morning was the likely threat to Saudi Arabia's oilfields. Saddam could all too easily send his 100 000 men another hundred miles south and end up controlling 40 per cent of the world's known oil reserves.

Various ideas for sanctions and for military action were thrown around but there seemed to be problems with them all. Schwarzkopf, who'd made it up in time from Florida, offered two possible responses. One would involve punishment bombing raids by US Navy jets flying from aircraft carriers – but that wasn't likely to achieve very much. The second was to put into action the contingency plan for the defence of Saudi Arabia which, by chance, he and his staff had rehearsed as part of the exercise 'Internal Look' only the previous week. The plan, titled 90-1002, 'Ninety, Ten-oh-two,' had two major drawbacks: it required permission from the Saudis, and then several months to implement. At that moment, neither the approval nor the time seemed to be available. The discussion was inconclusive. In any case, Bush and Scowcroft had to leave for Aspen.

They were 8000 feet up in the Rocky Mountains at the ranch of Henry Catto, the American ambassador to London. There were just four of them: Mrs Thatcher, President Bush, Brent Scowcroft and Charles Powell. It was a meeting arranged by chance – but it would soon prove critical to the construction of a solid alliance against Saddam. Thatcher reminded Bush of Britain's crisis over the Falkland Islands. Like Kuwait, they'd been seized by a dictator and only a resolute hand had freed them, she said. It was a theme she was to repeat many times over the next few days – 'interminably', according to one of those who was present. No one asked her about the war with Argentina. 'They didn't need to; she told them all about it anyway.'

Bush and Thatcher agreed that the priority was to rally world opinion against Iraq. Already the United Nations Security Council had met to condemn the invasion. That was a good start, they thought, but next they had to help defend Saudi Arabia. Some were to say later it was Thatcher who galvanised the President into action. One senior Pentagon adviser even went so far as to call it 'Thatcher's War'. But the British officials who were in Aspen insist that Bush 'didn't need any backbone putting in him', although he did find it invaluable having an ally who thought the same way, and with whom he could 'check his assumptions and bounce his instinctive reactions off'. Privately, Number Ten's verdict was that Thatcher's influence on Bush had been useful, though not critical. 'Left to his own devices, he might have been swayed by other voices.'

Downing Street's view was that if that kind of dialogue had gone through the Foreign Office and the State Department, it could have taken days or weeks. Thatcher's aides were delighted to have 'short-circuited' the usual diplomatic channels and, after meeting Bush, she spent much of that day calling up other leaders to co-ordinate their response, including President Mitterrand of France, Mubarak of Egypt, and the UN Secretary General, Javier Perez de Cuellar. She also talked to Prince Bandar, Saudi Arabia's ambassador to Washington. While the Foreign Office traditionally dealt with the Saudi embassy in London, Downing Street always preferred to discuss things with the Prince – he was their man. Between them, Thatcher and Bush had spoken to most of the key players on the international stage within hours of Saddam's invasion.

When they met again four days later on Monday, 6 August, their talks in the White House's Oval Office were interrupted by a long-distance telephone call that was to change everything. Thatcher had been airing her view that a trade embargo against Iraq would be unlikely to succeed, and that military force would have to be used if Saddam refused to leave Kuwait. Then the caller was put through, and the telephone's loudspeaker switched on. The whole room could now hear the Defence Secretary, Dick Cheney, speaking from the Saudi summer capital of Jeddah, on the Red Sea coast. He'd flown there the previous day to try to persuade the Saudis to accept American military help and now he announced to the gathering in the Oval Office that he had succeeded: the Saudis would accept American forces on their soil.

Cheney had shown King Fahd and his advisers the satellite pictures that highlighted an apparent push towards Saudi Arabia by the Iraqi columns that had just conquered Kuwait. Until then, the kingdom hadn't been convinced that it was under threat. Indeed, during probes into Kuwait, Saudi border scouts had found no sign of the Iraqis. But the satellite photographs had swayed King Fahd and his advisers surprisingly quickly and they agreed to host an American defence force. They hadn't asked how large it would be, so Cheney hadn't told them. But plan 90-1002, under which the troops and planes would be sent, involved deploying as many as 250 000 troops. Cheney had also omitted to inform them about the Pentagon view that the same plan would not only provide defence for Saudi Arabia – it would also give the President the option of recapturing Kuwait.

Perhaps because they were still so stunned that Saddam had broken his promise not to invade, the Saudis hadn't really challenged the American view that they were at risk. In fact, secret intelligence assessments of the danger of Iraqi troops plunging further south were a good deal less alarming than they'd been about the invasion of Kuwait. One defence intelligence analyst told us he was concluding that, while an invasion of the Saudi oilfields couldn't be discounted, it looked 'unlikely'. Air Chief Marshal Sir Patrick Hine, who had now been appointed overall commander of Britain's Gulf forces, judged further Iraqi aggression to be a 'possibility' rather than a 'probability'. Nevertheless, the risk remained and, having been caught out once by Saddam, there was a determination not to get it wrong again. 'It was part of the usual tendency to try to cover one's backside,' according to one Cabinet Office insider.

The Saudis weren't told that. Their traditional hostility towards accepting Western, 'infidel' soldiers on their soil – the home of Islam's two holiest shrines at Mecca and Medina – could only be overcome by stressing the threat to their survival. The Saudis seemed happy enough with Cheney's explanation as it stood. They had only one demand: that it must be made to look as if they had asked for American help. They didn't want to appear to have caved in to American 'imperialist' pressure but the agreed fiction survives in official accounts to this day.

Cheney's phone call was the moment the White House knew that the build-up of American forces could begin. The Defence Secretary wasted no time in asking Bush for permission to order the deployment. 'You got it; go!' he was told. The order was rapidly passed down the chain of command to the first units to be sent: 48 F-15 fighters from Langley in Virginia and the 'ready brigade' of the lightly-armed but highly-mobile 82nd Airborne Division. Thus began Operation Desert Shield, although it wouldn't be made public for another two days.

The speed of the response must have impressed Mrs Thatcher. She sat in the White House for several hours that morning, along with all the President's top advisers. 'In a sense it was an American cabinet meeting,' one of her aides recalls, 'with all the principal players and Mrs T being treated as part of it.' During the meeting, she suggested that Britain would probably send aircraft, and possibly ground forces as well. Charles Powell noticed that she was much more inclined than President Bush to believe that war would ultimately be needed to evict Saddam. At that stage Bush thought the strangulation of Iraq's trade, especially its crucial oil exports, might work. Indeed, even while they were talking, his Secretary of State, James Baker, came in with the news that the UN Security Council had voted for a total trade embargo.

As the press camped impatiently outside, the role of the UN became a key focus for discussion inside. Thatcher stressed that in the UN's charter, Article 51 allowed member states to support others under attack. She'd referred to it during the Falklands campaign and did so again now. She was adamant there was no need to secure any further UN permission for the use of force. And in her view, if an attempt to get UN approval for a military campaign against Iraq failed to get enough votes, any chance of justifying action under Article 51 would be lost. It was a gamble they could not afford to take. James Baker profoundly disagreed. He was convinced they should have the full support of international law behind them. As it turned out, Baker gambled and won and Thatcher was to be proved unduly pessimistic.

There was an unspoken agreement that, in public, sanctions were to be put forward as the primary weapon for liberating Kuwait. But, in private, by the end of that White House session on 6 August, the two principal allies were also agreed that if Saddam did not withdraw his troops, they would have to be expelled by force. The course of events for the next six months had been set – and war was far more likely than the outside world realised.

President Bush is even said to have signed a top-secret intelligence 'finding', authorising the CIA to start recruiting Iraqi dissidents who might overthrow Saddam. For her part, the Prime Minister set off for home in her VC-10, determined to beef-up Britain's response. On the flight, she was thinking about the next day's Cabinet meeting and her intention to commit RAF Tornado interceptors to Saudi Arabia. The British Chief of Defence Staff, Sir David Craig, had already prepared a range of options. Since the greatest risk was an Iraqi air attack paving the way for a ground assault into Saudi Arabia, his advice was to deploy air-defence fighters first, just as the Americans were doing. Indeed, flying on the same route as Thatcher, only a few hours behind her, were the first American fighters bound for the Gulf. Even from these earliest days of the crisis, there was what President Mitterrand called the 'logic of war'.

In Kuwait, there was still the odd flash of resistance but the emirate was now effectively part of Iraq. Kuwaiti flags were banned, as were photographs of the emir and crown prince, and the looting had begun. Houses were stripped of their chandeliers and furniture, the amusement park lost its rides, the car showrooms were plundered and the Central Bank was robbed of $1.5 billion-worth of gold and cash. All of it was carted north, and soon appeared in the bazaar in Baghdad. Even the zoo's animals were shipped out – though the sheep at the National Scientific Institute, which had been carefully bred for eight generations to cope with the Kuwaiti desert, were butchered and served up to the troops. The Kuwaitis themselves were reporting to the outside world that they weren't being treated much better. There were random rapes and shootings. A Kuwaiti doctor who later managed to flee was just one witness to the horror. 'They took my best friend, Bedar, and the next day they dropped his body in the street,' he said. 'They had wrapped his head in a Kuwaiti flag and fired three bullets into his skull.' It was only the beginning.

The hundreds of thousands of Filipino, Bangladeshi and other workers who'd made life in Kuwait possible were allowed to flee via Jordan where they were stranded for weeks in pitiful conditions. Any western-ers caught on the streets were rounded up; thousands of others tried to hide indoors to avoid capture. Soon, together with their compatriots in Iraq, they were to become Saddam's 'human shield' against attack.

It was like standing behind a jet engine at full-blast. The desert heat was at its worst as the first troops from the American 82nd Airborne

ALL NECESSARY MEANS

Division were arriving in Saudi Arabia in early August. They were Washington's 'line in the sand', the superpower tripwire to deter Saddam – and they knew they were vulnerable. It would be weeks before any heavy weapons arrived by sea to support them and air deliveries too were limited. To deploy just 19 Apache helicopters, with their crews and back-up, required no fewer than 24 flights by giant cargo planes. And even when they arrived the forces had to try to orientate themselves with tourist maps that were nearly 20 years old.

Desert Shield had a humble beginning. Lieutenant-General Gus Pagonis, a fast-talking Greek-American logistics genius who would eventually have to keep the 500 000 American troops supplied, started his operation in Saudi Arabia from a hired station wagon. 'We set up our bed in the back and our office on the front seat.' He then managed to move his headquarters to a little flat, where he and his staff worked in the kitchenette and living room, and took turns sleeping in the bedroom. Only later did they move to a proper headquarters building in Dhahran. But as each cargo plane landed, the Americans strengthened their position. Most significantly, Saudi airbases were rapidly filling with US and British warplanes, immediately going on patrol and practising bomb runs.

Under Plan 90-1002, commanders already had a list of 124 potential targets in Iraq, including power stations, missile sites, supply routes and anything to do with Saddam's nuclear, chemical and biological weapons projects. As early as 19 August, not quite three weeks after Saddam's invasion, the chief air planner, 'Buster' Glosson, a silver-haired brigadier-general from America's Deep South, was expanding the original list of targets for actual use. In public, the talk was of 'Desert Shield'; in private, that operation's offensive counterpart, 'Desert Storm', was already its secret shadow. Soon, the list grew to cover some 450 Iraqi military sites – though, as the US Defence Secretary later told the BBC, all talk of 'offence' was kept strictly quiet for fear of provoking Saddam too early.

Britain's Chief of Defence Staff, Sir David Craig, was also worried that the Iraqis might strike before allied forces were ready. At this stage, their superior numbers and their chemical and biological weapons still gave them the edge. Even so, the long-term focus was on driving the Iraqis out of Kuwait rather than just deterring them from attacking Saudi Arabia and, in late August, Air Chief Marshal Sir Patrick Hine flew to Riyadh for his first meeting with General Schwarzkopf to hear of his plans. By then, the RAF had Tornado interceptors, Jaguar fighter-bombers and Nimrod patrol aircraft in the Gulf; more were due, and the possibility of a British tank brigade was being discussed. Hine, tall, soft-spoken and looking very correct in his RAF uniform, was driven down one of Riyadh's palm-lined boulevards and into the Saudi Ministry of Defence and Aviation. He was ushered through the formidable security and into 'the Bear's' make-shift office. Hine got straight to the point: 'How do you see these operations unfolding if we can't persuade Saddam Hussein to withdraw from Kuwait?'

General Schwarzkopf replied that if he was ordered to mount an offensive to liberate Kuwait, he was 'going to insist on two criteria being met'. First, he needed a big enough force to avoid getting 'bogged down in a land battle of attrition with mounting casualties'. As a Vietnam veteran, he was well aware of the potential impact of the 'body-bag' factor on American public opinion. Second, because he would never achieve the classic three-to-one advantage normally required for an attack, he would have to rely on airpower to halve the combat strength of the Iraqi army.

'If those two criteria are met,' he said, 'I reckon I can defeat this guy fairly quickly,' which, at that stage, meant three to four weeks. But that was the ideal scenario, and what no one knew at that stage was that Schwarzkopf's two conditions wouldn't be fulfilled for another five months. In the meantime, there was pressure on him to be ready to fight much sooner.

The commander of one unit, Major-General Royal Moore of the 3rd Marines Air Wing, disclosed to us that he was ordered to draw up a war plan and 'be prepared to execute it very early in September'. He didn't quite manage that. But by 12 September, his superior, Buster Glosson, was able to fly to Washington and tell General Colin Powell that US air power was planned, rehearsed and ready to strike at Iraq. It was an early version of Operation Desert Storm – four months before it eventually happened.

The planning had to be handled with the greatest possible secrecy. The commander of a battalion of Apache helicopters, Lieutenant-Colonel

ALL NECESSARY MEANS

Dick Cody, was given no explanation for an order to attend a special meeting in Dhahran on 25 September. He wasn't even allowed to tell his deputy where he was going. So, instructed to bluff his own staff, he slipped away and followed the directions to a breeze-block building near the control tower at King Fahd Airport. It was the centre for US Special Operations.

The commander, Colonel Jesse Johnson, ushered him in. The planners had identified a pair of Iraqi radar stations which covered the best approach route to Baghdad, Johnson told him. Special Forces had been given the task of destroying them in what would be the first strike of the allied campaign, and they were now wrestling with the options. Johnson went through them. Either commandos would be dropped nearby to blow up the radars, or they would get in close and 'illuminate' the sites with lasers to help bombers make an accurate attack. Alternatively, they'd use Cody's Apache helicopters. Could your team do it? Johnson asked.

Cody forced himself to wait at least a minute before answering, knowing it would be an 'awesome responsibility'. When he replied it was to say he foresaw no problem, given proper intelligence. It was only 25 September and already the first allied blow was being planned.

I n public, the alliance's greatest effort went into enforcing the trade blockade of Iraq. Turkey had agreed to close one of the two pipelines by which Iraq exported some of its oil; Saudi Arabia, now with American protection, shut down the other one. That meant the only possible trade would be by sea or air – and that was terminated too. UN resolutions banned Iraqi cargo flights and allowed allied warships to stop and search any merchant ships heading to or from Iraq. The most effective embargo of modern times was now in place, but opinion varied about how long it would take to achieve its objective – changing Saddam's mind.

It was the most divisive issue of the crisis. In London, some officials in the Foreign Office were arguing that sanctions should be given plenty of time, perhaps as long as a year. Elsewhere in Whitehall, the view was that Iraq was too big and too well organised to be vulnerable to the blockade. By October, Number 10's highly secret Joint Intelligence Committee,

THE NINETEENTH PROVINCE

which draws together all available intelligence for the Prime Minister, reported that though Iraq had 'weak spots', none was important enough to bring Saddam's regime to its knees. It found that the capability of Iraqi aircraft was being eroded quite rapidly, but the country's ability to field a tank army wouldn't be affected for at least five years.

There was another worry as well. As Foreign Office planners churned out dozens of their so-called 'What if?' reports – on the consequences of endless possible scenarios – more and more officials realised that the bigger the coalition became, the shorter would be its likely lifespan. They feared that there was little chance of holding together for very long some 30 countries as diverse as Syria, Senegal, and Argentina. The Foreign Secretary, Douglas Hurd, and his officials gathered frequently in his office for informal debates about the 'What if?' papers and, as they did so, it became clear that unless sanctions suddenly and unexpectedly started to bite, the only other option would be war.

It was a conclusion that President Bush was drawing as well. But there were powerful voices all around him clamouring for sanctions to be given more time. Congressmen and retired military chiefs alike were arguing that the embargo could be made to work – and keep America from drifting towards the nightmare of a Vietnam-in-the-desert. Among the supporters of this view was General Powell who, as chairman of the Joint Chiefs of Staff, was in effect the President's senior military adviser. An expert brought in to help him told us he was struck by the obvious look of strain on Powell's face. 'He's a black man but I swear he looked ashen with the enormity of it all. You couldn't miss it; he wasn't at all the man the public would later see looking so radiant and confident at his briefings on television.'

But whatever Powell thought, Bush was now increasingly convinced that war would be necessary. Indeed, on 10 October, the President was briefed on the latest plans for the liberation of Kuwait. At very short notice, a US Marines major-general, Robert Johnston, had flown out from Riyadh and was now outlining the different phases of bombing that would pave the way for a land campaign. It went down well enough but the strategy for a ground attack struck everyone as hopeless. The planning map showed the US Army plunging straight into Kuwait through the thickest

ALL NECESSARY MEANS

Iraqi defences, while Marines stormed the well-defended beaches. It simply didn't make sense. Dick Cheney asked what – with hindsight – was the obvious question. Couldn't the US forces avoid Saddam's defences by swinging out to the west through Iraq and coming at them from the side? No, said Johnston, the desert there would be too soft and wet for wheeled vehicles. In fact, Special Forces teams, secretly sent in to take soil samples, were soon to prove him wrong. But in any case it was clear that Schwarzkopf's troops in Saudi Arabia were outnumbered and huge reinforcements would be needed.

All through October and November, Saddam was bolstering his defences still further in preparation for what he promised would be 'the Mother of all Battles'. Just inside Kuwait's border with Saudi Arabia, his engineers constructed huge belts of obstacles: sand walls or 'berms' to force tanks to rise up and expose their relatively weak bellies to missile-fire; trenches filled with oil to be set alight in the face of any allied advance; hundreds of miles of barbed wire; and whole swathes of desert peppered with mines. Further back was an army growing by the week. In late October, it reached a total of over 430 000 men and 2000 tanks.

But at least there was no risk now of him attacking Saudi Arabia. The regular infantry and tank units were either stretched out just behind the border or massed in the middle of Kuwait, while the Republican Guard had pulled back almost entirely into southern Iraq, ready to counter-attack. The way his forces were deployed showed that he was willing to take on the United States, the strongest nation on earth, but a country which Saddam believed would never tolerate the '10 000 casualties' he thought he could inflict.

Saddam had incurred the wrath of the world but he always took care to keep his door open to diplomacy. Indeed, he seemed to enjoy all the attention he was getting. In all, 49 politicians or peace campaigners turned up in Baghdad to bring him various peace proposals and initiatives. But the only ones who achieved anything were those who sought freedom for the foreign hostages. With them, Saddam was happy to play along. He calculated that by selectively releasing the citizens of countries which appeared least comfortable in the coalition, like France, Germany and the Soviet Union, he could disrupt the alliance against him. It was just another of his mistakes.

The same day that the former prime minister, Edward Heath, announced in Baghdad that some of the British hostages would be coming home, a meeting was taking place amid great secrecy in Riyadh to lay the plans for war. There were just two men involved: General Schwarzkopf and Sir Patrick Hine, who'd flown out from RAF Strike Command at High Wycombe. It was 21 October and once again they were in the general's office in the Saudi Ministry of Defence and Aviation. Schwarzkopf unfolded the most recent version of the campaign plan, much as Major-General Johnston had done in the White House ten days before. This was the first time that anyone from Britain had seen it.

In the first phase, allied warplanes would try to dominate the skies and to destroy Saddam's most important weapons and installations; in the second, they'd silence the air defence guns and missiles in and near Kuwait; and in the third, they'd attack the Iraqi army and its supplies. Only when the phase three bombing raids had destroyed at least half the army's fighting strength – exactly as Schwarzkopf had outlined to Air Chief Marshal Hine back in August – would phase four begin, the land war.

Hine pressed for more details about that final, crucial phase. It was of particular interest to Britain since the 'Desert Rats' of the 7th Armoured Brigade had now arrived in Saudi Arabia. Hine explained that his own planning team back in the bunker in Buckinghamshire had been quietly devising various options since the beginning of September. They'd come up with three: either a straightforward push up the coast road to Kuwait City; or a double-push, with one column fighting up the coast and the other striking further inland to cut off the highway between Kuwait and Iraq; or a much wider 'left-hook' up through Iraq, aiming at the Republican Guard. Hine told Schwarzkopf that this was the plan he favoured. In language typical of the British military, he suggested that if the allied air

22

forces 'gave them a bit of a pasting from the air, and then we followed through with a powerful armoured thrust up through Iraq, we could polish off the Republican Guard'. The rest of the army would collapse, he said, because most of them were conscripts.

Schwarzkopf agreed. He too thought the 'wide left-hook' was the best choice. But he was worried by the numbers. The latest intelligence estimate gave the Iraqis 90 brigades while the allies at that stage could only rely on 20. Schwarzkopf didn't need reminding that the unpredictable French, for example, hadn't yet decided what role their troops should play. Even if the Iraqi army had been weakened by bombing, Schwarzkopf told Hine, the ratio between the two forces would still be wrong. He said he was going to have to ask for a 'massive reinforcement'.

In fact, he did it the very next day when General Colin Powell arrived to see him. Schwarzkopf said that he wanted to double the number of tanks and troops by bringing in the huge 7th Corps from Germany. He needed to double the number of aircraft carriers from three to six, and the number of warplanes. It was an extraordinary demand. Both generals knew it made perfect military sense – but they also knew that it was political dynamite.

Mid-term elections to Congress were only two weeks away and President Bush wasn't doing well in the opinion polls. Although Schwarzkopf's request was quickly approved, no announcement was made till 8 November, when Bush told the nation he was sending extra deployments to ensure the coalition had 'an adequate offensive military option'. After three months of talking about an 'offensive' campaign behind closed doors, this was the first time he'd mentioned it in public. It caused an uproar.

President Bush was caught. He'd staked everything on liberating Kuwait and time was running out on him. The coalition wouldn't hold together indefinitely, nor could he expect the troops to endure life in the desert until the next cool season. The only answer was to push for a United Nations resolution authorising the use of force. That would spread the responsibility for war and it really would be 'the world', not just Bush, versus Saddam. Already the Secretary of State, James Baker, had shuttled 100 000 miles in the previous ten weeks trying to hold the alliance together. Now it was time to pack his bags again. Getting this through the UN would probably be the toughest test of his career.

Mrs Thatcher had never wanted to seek the UN's permission to fight Iraq. She'd made that plain from the start. The authors have learned of a meeting over supper in the Waldorf Astoria Hotel in New York in late September at which President Bush found himself sitting between her and Baker as they argued it out. There was 'a genuine difference of view' – which, translated from diplomatic language, means it became heated. Thatcher was adamant that if the allies failed in their attempt to get a resolution allowing force, they would then forfeit any right to go to war under the UN's 'self-defence' Article 51. Even if they did get a resolution, she said, it might have so many restrictions it wouldn't make military sense.

Baker argued that, whatever Thatcher thought, UN support for war was essential to win the backing of Congress, and without that there probably couldn't be a campaign at all. The Foreign Office, as it happened, had long thought the same about the Labour Party: that its support would be best secured by planning for war in the name of the UN. But the Foreign Office, rarely influential in shaping her policies, had so far failed to change her mind. Baker went on to challenge the Prime Minister's prediction that he'd never be able to get the required number of votes. He said he was confident he could – and, as it turned out, he did. 'We were unnecessarily cautious,' one of the Prime Minister's officials told us. 'We underestimated Baker's skill in getting the Security Council on board.'

James Baker had spent most of his political life doing deals behind the scenes. But even for him, getting the Soviet Union to support a western-led war was a daunting challenge. He had, though, the advantage of a close relationship with his Soviet counterpart, Eduard Shevardnadze, and together they haggled over the key words of a UN resolution.

Would the phrase 'use of force' be acceptable? Baker asked.

No, it wouldn't, Shevardnadze replied; the memory of Afghanistan was still too fresh in the minds of the Soviet people.

The Secretary of State suggested five other forms of words including:

ALL NECESSARY MEANS

'all necessary means'. Then he backtracked on that phrase because he worried that it might seem too vague. But it was too late. Shevardnadze was now satisfied with 'all necessary means' and he was refusing to budge.

There it stuck and, on 29 November 1990, the foreign ministers of the 15 member states of the United Nations Security Council voted to give the Iraqis till 15 January 1991 to withdraw from Kuwait – and, if they failed to meet that deadline, to authorise countries co-operating with Kuwait 'to use all necessary means' to get them out.

It was an unprecedented moment in United Nations history with the world's most powerful nations, for so long on the brink of war with each other, now approving one against a fellow state. In the aftermath of the Cold War, it was tempting to believe that, at UN Headquarters in New York, the much vaunted 'New World Order' was at last taking shape. The reality, of course, was rather different. The Anglo-American axis had simply found it expedient to obtain United Nations cover for what it wanted to do.

In Whitehall, everyone was agreed a war with Iraq would be difficult but there was a dispute about how tough the enemy would be. The Foreign Office, especially its Middle East experts, argued that Iraqi troops wouldn't have the stomach to fight, while the Ministry of Defence warned that they were battle-hardened after their eight-year war with Iran. The problem was that so much of the intelligence was uncertain, especially when it came to Iraq's most dangerous weapons.

Try as they might, the intelligence services couldn't establish exactly how far Saddam had got in his attempt to develop 'non-conventional' warheads. They knew he had a nuclear programme and guessed that the first warhead was about five years away. They also knew he had biological weapons, including anthrax and botulism, and they'd seen him use chemical agents against the Iranians and the Kurds. Yet there was no answer available to their most urgent question: could he fit any of these frightening germs or agents into the warheads of his Scud missiles? Could he actually carry out his threat to 'incinerate' half of Israel?

THE NINETEENTH PROVINCE

The intelligence seemed contradictory. An eavesdropping satellite picked up an order from Baghdad giving divisional commanders the authority to use chemical weapons, and spy cameras over Kuwait detected decontamination vehicles and a particular type of rocket launcher that's known to fire chemical warheads. On the other hand, satellite photographs of the five main chemical storage sites in Iraq showed a surprising lack of activity, according to one Pentagon source. It didn't add up, and it meant that allied commanders had to assume they'd face chemical weapons – even if in the end they never would.

Another question about Saddam's war machine was worrying the British and Americans: how much of it was underground? Saddam knew well the value of protection. In 1967 he'd seen the Israelis destroy Egypt's air force as it stood parked on open ground, and he was determined not to make the same mistake. So all through the 1980s he invested a huge proportion of Iraq's oil wealth in readying his defences against air attack. Still, it was imperative that allied intelligence should discover any weaknesses.

In fact, an information goldmine lay in their grasp already because so often it was western companies that had designed and built the best Iraqi installations. These firms were now asked to give up their most precious secrets – the specifications that made their products so marketable. 'Whistleblowers', businessmen troubled by their consciences, offered help. In one case, a British construction consultant, who has demanded anonymity, contacted the BBC-2 programme *Newsnight* to provide drawings and details of new 'super-bases' for the Iraqi Air Force. The blueprints showed strengthened hangars of far greater resilience than usually demanded by NATO. Each building had a roof four-feet thick and doors so strong they weighed 40 tons. They looked impregnable, and only by studying the designs, and by interviewing the Belgian and Yugoslav construction teams, could the allied planners devise bombing techniques to defeat them.

British intelligence also interviewed anyone they thought might know anything potentially useful about Iraq, especially if they had recently visited the country. These 'debriefings' lasted for as long as two days. It was laborious work, but made all the more vital by the latest predictions that,

ALL NECESSARY MEANS

in a war with Iraq, the Americans could lose as many as 7000 men, and the British several hundred.

The snow was falling so hard in Washington just before Christmas that the White House helicopter couldn't take off for the regular weekend flight to the presidential retreat at Camp David. The President decided to drive there and invited his guest, John Major, to travel with him in his armour-plated limousine. Major was on his first visit as Prime Minister. He sat with Bush on the vast bench-seat at the back of the car, while the National Security Adviser, Brent Scowcroft, and the Number 10 foreign policy adviser, Charles Powell, perched awkwardly on the jump-seats facing them. The huge car, surrounded by the usual cavalcade of security vehicles and an ambulance, sped off at 80 mph down the freeway towards the hills. Scowcroft and Powell struggled to take notes. It was vital that they did: this was a council of war.

Bush and Major had already been in almost daily touch since Mrs Thatcher's resignation the previous month. By chance, the Americans had installed a secret new hot-line between the Oval Office and Downing Street the previous summer. It had seen constant use ever since. At the press of just one button on a large white console, Major or Powell could get straight through to the desks of the President or Brent Scowcroft for an untappable conversation. Sometimes all four would hold a conference call with the two leaders exchanging views while their advisers listened. It meant there was hardly anything the White House kept from London. Indeed, Scowcroft would often give information to Powell that was considered so sensitive he was only allowed to pass it on to the Prime Minister; not even the War Cabinet could be told. Powell and Scowcroft were already good friends, and Downing Street valued that because in their view Scowcroft spent more time with the President than anyone else in the administration. The relationship between these four men became extraordinarily close – and never closer than on their high-speed drive to Camp David.

This was the moment that the President revealed the date that the campaign would start. As the limousine swept through the Washington suburbs, Bush announced that he'd now firmly decided to take the alliance to war. He said that on a personal level he was 'comfortable' with his decision and he showed no sign of anxiety. He even sat back in his seat and stretched out his legs as he explained the details of the campaign and its timetable. Major already knew the outline of the plan but this was the first time he'd heard that the President wanted to start the air war as soon as the UN deadline had expired.

Major had no objections at all, though Bush probably wouldn't have minded if he had. The two countries had already weathered several disputes during the crisis. They had disagreed over when to abandon their embassies in Kuwait, which the Iraqis were besieging with troops. The last remaining diplomats had been forced to spin out their stocks of food. Britain's ambassador, Michael Weston, and his consul, Larry Banks, had got to work in their vegetable garden, determined to hang on for several more months. Whitehall saw it as a gutsy show of defiance; Washington thought it was irritating. The Americans wanted to pull all the embassy staff out, and in the end they got their way. Another argument between London and Washington was over whether they would need a pretext to go to war. Mrs Thatcher had said that the invasion of Kuwait was 'pretext enough', but for months President Bush hadn't been convinced.

Now though, all that agonising was over, and the discussion in the limousine-summit turned to the risks involved in going to war. They talked of the Pentagon's promise that the bombing would be accurate enough to avoid civilian casualties. Then they mulled over the difficult question of when to tell other leaders the date for the start of Desert Storm. They decided secrecy was paramount, so the others should hear only at the last possible moment. Nothing could show more clearly that this was an Anglo-American campaign. The coalition's membership may now have spanned the globe but these two allies had just made the most important decision of the crisis on their behalf.

Of course to the press, Bush and Major merely repeated their warnings to Saddam to withdraw from Kuwait. 'If he doesn't,' said the Prime Minister, 'he knows what the consequences may be.' In his report for the news bulletins that night, the BBC's Political Editor, John Cole, concluded that the two leaders had 'reached gloomy unanimity' on the need

ALL NECESSARY MEANS

for war. But no one guessed when it would start. Even when they returned to Britain, John Major and Charles Powell were to keep the date to themselves for another week at least.

The hurriedly-arranged talks in Geneva between James Baker and the Iraqi Foreign Minister, Tariq Aziz, had failed. Those who had assumed Saddam would withdraw from Kuwait at the last minute realised that they were wrong. It seemed to make no sense but Iraq was taking on the might of America and her allies. It was estimated that Saddam now had up to 540 000 troops in and around Kuwait, and there was no sign of them withdrawing. On 15 January, the day of the UN deadline, Bush signed a national security directive authorising General Schwarzkopf to begin the campaign the following night at 3a.m. Gulf time, midnight in London. The Defence Secretary, Dick Cheney, got an overnight bag ready but decided to leave it at home in case his driver saw it and realised it meant war.

On 16 January, in Whitehall, Cheney's counterpart, Tom King, signed an executive order to British forces, instructing them to join the hostilities. Like Cheney, King was also worried about giving the game away. Very deliberately he left his office at his normal time. King's order was passed to the Chief of Defence Staff, Sir David Craig, who, in turn, composed his command for war and had it sent to the Joint Forces Headquarters at High Wycombe. As a courier set off to deliver it by hand, Craig called the commander there, Sir Patrick Hine, to warn him it was on its way. Even on a secure line he was cautious, casually referring to the Moor Park golf course in north-west London where both men played – an agreed code for war.

Hine then notified Riyadh, and the British war machine was put into effect. Hine told only his deputy what would happen that night. Then, trying to appear as calm as possible to deceive his 400 staff, he climbed the stairs to ground level and, at his usual time of 8p.m., drove the few miles to his home.

In Riyadh, the British commander, Lieutenant-General Sir Peter de la Billière, issued a message to all British personnel:

THE NINETEENTH PROVINCE

We are poised for war. There will be surprises and setbacks but we have all that we need to do our duty and now it is up to each one of us to do it in the manner that our country would expect.

The first orders to the bomber crews were sent out at roughly the same time. A communications clerk at the RAF base in Bahrain ripped a top-secret message off the teleprinter and sprinted with it across the tarmac, past the sandbags defending the control centre and into the office of the commander, Group Captain David Henderson. It was only a paragraph long but it ordered the bombers to take off at 2.15a.m. local time, 11.15p.m. in London. Henderson told an unsuspecting television interviewer: 'We have a full programme of flying planned for today.' In Riyadh, a British military spokesman went further. He told journalists: 'We are ready.' But none of them took the hint.

The Saudi ambassador to Washington, Prince Bandar, rang King Fahd and ended their conversation with some prearranged code-words: 'Our old friend Suleiman is coming at 3a.m.'

A few American television correspondents in Baghdad received similar tip-offs from their headquarters. Word reached the newsroom at BBC Television centre in London and contingency plans were made to mount an emergency news programme.

In Washington, with a few hours to go, officials were instructed to tell the most important congressmen and the former presidents, including Ronald Reagan and Jimmy Carter.

In Downing Street, Charles Powell was also ringing round those he thought should know – Edward Heath, even as a former prime minister, was not included after so angering the government with his visit to Baghdad. As John Major sat upstairs in his flat watching television, Powell made his calls. Such had been the secrecy that only now did John Wakeham, who as Energy Secretary was a member of the War Cabinet, hear that hostilities were imminent. Likewise, Mrs Thatcher, whose role had proved so significant in the first four months of the crisis. From the woman who'd suspected all along that a war with Saddam would be inevitable came a characteristic response to Powell's phone call: 'Jolly good, about time too.'

Chapter 2
THUNDER & LIGHTNING

'Now you must be the thunder and lightning of Desert Storm'

General H. Norman Schwarzkopf's message to the troops, 17 January 1991.

Jamal, citizen of Baghdad, 18 January 1991.

'There was nothing left of the building or anyone working in it. It was as if some huge fire-breathing monster had come and sucked the life out of it.'

One by one the giant American bombers and tankers lumbered into the night sky over the Indian Ocean and headed north-west. The crews had rehearsed, sweated and fretted in the isolation of the tiny island of Diego Garcia since early August. Their deployment there had been one of the fastest yet most secret responses to Saddam's invasion. Now, one day after the United Nations deadline expired, they were summoned to a briefing. The commanding officer had told pilot Bill Kewley that he wouldn't discuss anything over the telephone. But Kewley had guessed that, at last, after five months of waiting, it was to be war. As he began what was to be a 13-hour flight, he tuned his radio to the BBC World Service. Hearing the talk of final diplomatic efforts and chances for peace, he smiled to himself. It was about 10p.m. in the Gulf, 7p.m. London time, on 16 January. Already, the first stream of allied bombers was on its way to Iraq and only a tight circle of people knew.

Certainly the Iraqis manning the early-warning radar sites that night didn't. Their screens showed only the routine pattern of allied flights which had been repeated time and time again since the previous summer. They could see the radar blips of the American AWACS control planes along the Saudi border and the fighters circling them. What the Iraqis would not detect over the next few hours was that just beyond the range of their radar another, far more menacing, formation of flights would rapidly grow. Hundreds of allied bombers would take to the air and then wait to get their final top-ups of fuel from airborne tankers before turning north. The clouds of Desert Storm were massing unseen.

It was now 12.30a.m. in the Gulf on 17 January, 9.30p.m. in London. At a base in the mountainous south of Saudi Arabia, Major Blake Bourland ran through his final checks in the strangest of allied aircraft: an F-117A Stealth fighter-bomber. Its ungainly triangular shape, like a spacecraft from a science fiction film, was supposed to help it slip through Iraqi radar. The technology was advanced but untested, and even though American air force commanders couldn't be sure it would work, they had assigned the Stealths to about one-third of all that night's targets. Bourland and nine colleagues took off, knowing they would drop the first allied bombs. He remembers it as his worst moment, gripped by an 'incredible fear of the unknown'.

Half an hour later, at 1a.m. Gulf time, a remote American Special Forces base, further north at Al-Jawf, reverberated to the roar of massed rotor-blades. Major Bob Leonik was at the controls of one of a pair of enormous blackened MH-53J Pave Low helicopters as he took off with four of the US Army's Apache helicopter gunships. At 1.06a.m., an identical team followed. The Pave Lows, crammed with state-of-the-art navigation equipment, were leading the Apaches, which were laden with missiles. They were heading towards the two Iraqi radar sites which had been identified in September as crucial targets. Computer calculations had shown that if they could be destroyed, a radar-free air-route to Baghdad would be created. It was the opening mission of the campaign and the Apache commander, Lieutenant-Colonel Dick Cody, recalled the promise he'd made four months earlier to the Special Forces that his team wouldn't let them down. 'I'll never forget that feeling of awesome responsibility: it was the first night and the first mission.'

ALL NECESSARY MEANS

At 1.30a.m., 10.30p.m. in London, the first Royal Air Force planes took off to join the allied air armada. At their base in Dhahran, Saudi Arabia, Wing Commander Jerry Witts and his team had spent the evening checking and re-checking every detail of the plan. Nervously, they'd walked across the tarmac to their Tornado bombers. Such was the tension, they'd found themselves in their cockpits far too early and 'sat there in strained silence waiting for the minutes to tick by to take-off time'. Suddenly it came, the planes were airborne and Witts found the sky full of aircraft. The radio channels of the AWACS control planes, which were co-ordinating the operation, were 'nearly jammed with mission after mission checking in'. With immaculate precision, the plan was unfolding.

At exactly the same time that Witts and his colleagues were taking off, there was an explosive rumble from beneath the decks of the USS *Bunker Hill* in the Persian Gulf: the first Tomahawk cruise missile was being launched. Once clear of the ship, the bright flame of its rocket motor died away as the missile's main engine took over, driving this high-technology successor to Hitler's Doodlebugs towards Baghdad. Its on-board computer had pre-stored images of what the ground below should look like along the journey; soon a camera in the Tomahawk's belly would check that it was on the right route.

As the missile began its flight, with some 90 minutes to go before 'H-hour' at 3a.m. Gulf time, the atmosphere in the War Room, 70 feet underground in the Saudi Ministry of Defence in Riyadh, was electric. Officers were watching the three huge video screens which displayed thousands of tiny dots of light representing each allied plane and missile – now converging on Iraq. The aim was to overwhelm Saddam's defences and 'knock out his eyes', according to Stealth pilot Major Rod Schroeder. Since there was no turning back, General Schwarzkopf asked his staff to break away from their desks and maps to join the chaplain in 'a little prayer for the protection of our troops'. Schwarzkopf had a few words himself. 'This is it. Remember, everything you do is going to affect the lives of our troops.' To the surprise of some of the War Room staff, he played a tape of the Lee Greenwood song 'God Bless the USA'. A few senior officers were close to tears. It was 'a very emotional moment', according to Brigadier-General Richard 'Butch' Neal.

THUNDER AND LIGHTNING

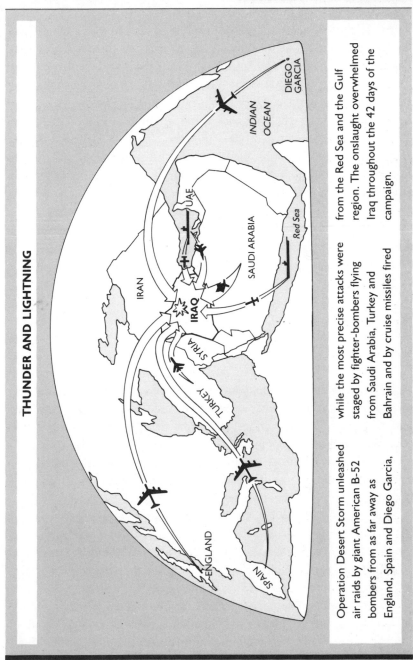

Operation Desert Storm unleashed air raids by giant American B-52 bombers from as far away as England, Spain and Diego Garcia, while the most precise attacks were staged by fighter-bombers flying from Saudi Arabia, Turkey and Bahrain and by cruise missiles fired from the Red Sea and the Gulf region. The onslaught overwhelmed Iraq throughout the 42 days of the campaign.

ALL NECESSARY MEANS

As H-hour approached, Neal later wrote in his diary: 'Watching CNN, my stomach is in knots.' Britain's Gulf commander, Lieutenant-General Sir Peter de la Billière, was feeling apprehensive about the likely allied casualties but thought that 'everything that could be done had been done and either we'd got it right or we'd got it wrong'. The man with most responsibility that night, Brigadier-General 'Buster' Glosson, the architect of this immense and intricate air campaign, was just as tense. He could only sit and watch his plan take effect. He had plotted the routes and split-second timings for the hundreds of bombers, and for the fighters, tankers and electronic warfare planes that would support them. There were so many aircraft involved, all flying on different but often overlapping paths, that a computer had been brought in to check that none of them would collide. By this stage, Glosson could do nothing except think that 'for every oversight or mistake, somebody dies now'.

The first allied forces crossed into Iraq at 2a.m., 11p.m. in Britain. The Special Forces helicopters leading the Apache gunships slipped low over the border. They swept through dry river wadis and skirted past bedouin camps. Suddenly they saw rifle and missile fire coming their way. They'd been heard – but none of them was hit and for some inexplicable reason the alarm wasn't raised. They continued on their way, with Major Bob Leonik still leading. His night-vision goggles were his best guide even though it was like 'looking through a toilet-tube roll with a green shade on it'. However difficult it was, he knew the allied plan depended on him getting the Apaches to the right positions in Iraq's featureless desert so that they could launch their attacks.

At about the same time, the RAF base at Bahrain echoed to the scream of Tornado engines. It was another batch of British warplanes preparing to take off and join the others already airborne from Dhahran. The chocks holding the planes in place were pulled away and then the jets, each laden with a pair of enormous JP233 coffin-shaped bombs, eased their way towards the runway. In one of the many ironies of the war, they were setting off from a base originally established by the British, to attack another base designed by British engineers – with British-built bombs. Each

JP233 would scatter hundreds of tiny bomblets and mines over Tallil air base in south-east Iraq, in the hope of grounding the Iraqi Air Force for at least a day.

Although a mass take-off at night had become routine in Bahrain by now, even those on the base who hadn't been told that the campaign was under way suddenly realised that something unusual was happening. The cooks left their kitchen tent, and the ground crews came out of their hangars and workshops to line the taxi-way. The base commander, David Henderson, noticed these 'little clumps of people watching' and felt a lump in his throat. Someone called out to him, 'what's going on?' As the Tornados reached the start of their take-off run, he replied: 'They're going to war.' At 2.15a.m., 11.15p.m. back home, a blaze of afterburners lifted them over the palm trees and off towards Iraq. Even now, the rest of the world didn't know.

'**Y**ou'd think if they knew we were coming they'd turn the lights down or something,' whispered the navigator of one of the Apaches to his pilot. 'They don't know we're here,' came the reply.

It was about 2.30a.m., and one of the Apache teams had arrived near one of the radar sites a little too early. They endured an agonising wait, 65 miles inside Iraq, and tried to busy themselves with preparations for their attack. The Special Forces' Pave Low helicopters had marked an agreed point with bundles of 20 'chem-sticks', luminous plastic tubes, by which the Apaches could adjust their navigational equipment. At this stage, the helicopters were some 10 miles from the radar installations.

At 2.36a.m., they approached. With their night-vision systems, they could now see the radar dishes, along with the electrical generators, the support buildings and even the Iraqis' cars and vans. Suddenly, they saw the Iraqis running. Lieutenant-Colonel Dick Cody thought they'd either been heard or detected by the Iraqi radar, despite their attempts to avoid it. Not that it mattered: the attack was about to begin anyway and the Iraqis still had no conception of who or what was out there in the dark.

The Apache crews had agreed to break radio silence only 10 seconds

ALL NECESSARY MEANS

before the planned time of attack. 'Party in 10', was the signal for one team, 'Joy in 10' was the similarly tasteless message for the other.

At exactly 2.38a.m., 22 minutes before 'H-hour', the Apaches fired the first shots in the allied campaign. Cody saw 'one big light-show' as each helicopter launched a barrage of Hellfire missiles, each one homing in on the reflected light of their laser-guidance systems. First they hit the generators, then the communications trucks, and finally the radars themselves. Once the missiles were fired, the Apaches moved in closer and fired smaller rockets, and then closer still to 'finish off' with cannon fire, at 11 rounds a second from each barrel.

The Iraqis were terrified. They ran in panic seeking shelter as building after building erupted in flame around them. They were shot down by the waves of gunfire – from an enemy they could not even see.

Cody watched some die as missiles hit the vans they were clambering into: 'By the time they sorted out what was happening, they were dying in place.'

Within four and a half minutes the radar stations were wrecked and all the Iraqis presumed dead. Each Apache team leader radioed an immediate report to the Special Forces Pave Lows. 'Oklahoma Alpha Alpha', they said. 'Oklahoma' was their codename, the first 'Alpha' meant the enemy had been totally destroyed, and the second that there had been no losses. In turn, the Special Forces commander, Major Bob Leonik, then transmitted a single-word message back to the War Room in Riyadh. 'California', he said, to report total success.

'Thank God,' said Schwarzkopf. The opening move had worked; so far so good. For one of the Apache pilots it was 'exactly like a video game'. For the Iraqis though it had been a massacre. The war had begun as it was to end, with computer-assisted slaughter from the skies.

In a matter of minutes, more than 100 bombers were taking advantage of the gap ripped in Saddam's defences, racing down the new 'radar-black corridor' towards the heart of Iraq. As Cody and his colleagues turned south for home, they gazed at the huge stream of warplanes passing above them the other way. It was a 'good sight and very exciting', said Cody. 'I was also very relieved and proud that we'd done so well.' Leonik was less restrained: 'I felt like I was on the 50-yard line of a football game, yelling Go, Go, Go!' as the jets roared overhead. It was 2.45a.m., 11.45p.m. London time, and the most powerful air force ever assembled was about to attack.

Baghdad's skyline was alight with explosions and the whole city was shaking. Key buildings were taking direct hits from the Stealth fighters and then the Tomahawk cruise missiles, which had now arrived at their targets. Anti-aircraft crews fired repeatedly, but hopelessly, into the air. The flashes of tracer fire and the exhaust plumes of the SAMs (surface-to-air missiles) spewed without direction into the dark. The Stealths were invisible, laser-guiding bombs to the weakest spots of their targets from high above the city. One bomb was steered in through the middle of the roof of the Iraqi Air Force headquarters. Other specially-designed bombs were deliberately set to detonate just above the main power stations so that they could scatter thousands of metallic threads to cause short-circuits. Ministries and military installations were being picked off, first by one wave of Stealth fighters, then by Tomahawk cruise missiles, and then by another wave of Stealths.

Major Rod Schroeder was in that second wave and, as he approached Baghdad, he saw 'a bunch of small lights coming up all over the town' and initially thought it looked like the moment at a rock concert when 'the whole crowd turns on their cigarette lighters'. In fact, it was the anti-aircraft guns starting up again.

Despite the danger, Schroeder found the sight almost beautiful as he circled the city in the orange sky. 'It was like being in a surrealistic dream, looking at it knowing that you have to go into it and yet you're detached from it at the same time, thinking "my goodness, isn't that a wonderful sight?"'

Minutes later, he turned and approached his target. Everything worked 'as advertised'. He released his bomb, kept the cross-hairs of his laser sight aimed on the roof of the building and watched as the weapon fell through five of its floors. He could then see the 'heat and the smoke coming out of all four sides of the building; it was a spectacular sight'.

Radar installations around Baghdad were being jammed or bombed

ALL NECESSARY MEANS

or duped. Some screens turned white with 'snow', or started strobing uncontrollably as the full force of American electronic warfare planes was directed their way. Radar operators brave enough to increase the power of their beams, to try to break through the jamming signal, found themselves easy prey to allied radar-homing missiles. Others carefully tracked what they thought were allied aircraft only to discover that the blips were from mini-gliders acting as decoys.

All of this meant that Iraq was rapidly becoming unable to receive any warning of the attacks let alone direct its fighters to meet them. 'Schwarzkopf basically dismantled Iraq's electromagnetic spectrum,' as one general was to put it later. The plan to overwhelm Iraq was working – but allied commanders couldn't be sure.

In the War Room, all Schwarzkopf and his commanders could do was watch the waves of dots moving across the video screens. None of them knew if a plan that was flawless on paper would be flawless in action, especially since the intelligence indications were that some Iraqi installations were twice as heavily defended as any in the Soviet Union. The allied air commander, Lieutenant-General Chuck Horner, admitted he was feeling uncertain. He of all people was even wondering if the fabled Stealth fighters would work: 'Theoretically it worked but we've never really been shot at.'

Ironically, despite the sophistication of allied intelligence-gathering, Horner's first tangible evidence of the plan's success came from television. 'The first time I knew we were really hitting the targets was when, up in my office, CNN was on the television. I sent one of the guys up there and I had a hotline from my position to there, and I said "What do you see on CNN?". He said, "Bernard Shaw is reporting that the bombs are falling on Baghdad." So, we felt a kind of enthusiasm then.

'Then, at nine minutes past the hour, we were supposed to take down the communications centre. At exactly nine minutes, as the second hand went through nine minutes, he said "Bernard Shaw just went off the air." So we had direct feedback that we were accomplishing our missions because his transmission was being powered through that centre.'

Horner told us that throughout the campaign he would use the reports of CNN correspondent Peter Arnett to gauge the effectiveness of his air-strikes. Warfare-by-television had been born: the bombs had been guided to their targets by pilots watching the tiny screens in their cockpits – and now their impact was being judged by television too. Hours later, Major Rod Schroeder and the other Stealth pilots who had attacked Baghdad, would rush from their planes to the nearest television to watch CNN's footage of their bombing. 'We'd huddle around and jab each other and say, "Hey, that's my target", or "Wow, look at that one go".'

John Major was watching the same pictures in Downing Street. So too, in the White House, was President Bush. He instructed his spokesman, Marlin Fitzwater, to confirm what the rest of the world was coming to learn, that the war was under way. In what was to be one of his briefest appearances, Fitzwater confirmed that Operation Desert Shield had become Operation Desert Storm and declared: 'The liberation of Kuwait has begun.'

The reporters in Baghdad were only describing one part of the operation. The rest of Iraq was under attack as well. Captain Bill Flood was navigating one of the US Air Force B-52s which had taken off from Diego Garcia six hours earlier. He identified the sprawling oil storage site in southern Iraq that was to be the target for his aircraft and the two others with him. They were flying at low level and so far they were undetected. But one of the three bombers arrived over the site a few seconds too early. If it had released its bombs they would have 'fragged' or caught the other planes. It was ordered to pull away and make another circuit. By the time it was back in position, the other bombers had dropped their weapons.

Flood watched the huge explosions 'light up the sky in a great flash' but then saw the anti-aircraft guns firing in response – just as the last bomber was passing overhead. There was so much tracer in the air that the bomber's night-sights were blinded. It was fortunate to escape. As it rejoined the others, the crews once more tuned in to the BBC. By now the secret was out and 'we heard the panic reports on the air'.

Not far away, in this first hour of the campaign, 12 of the RAF Tornados, eight from Bahrain and four from Dhahran, were approaching Tallil air base. It was known to be well-defended and vast – twice the size of London's Heathrow Airport.

Wing Commander Jerry Witts remembers the sensation of hurtling towards it:

> It all seems very unreal, creaming along at 500 knots through the thick velvet darkness. The Head-Up Display tells me we're 180 feet above the desert but it could just as well be 18 000 feet because I can't see a thing ahead. Thank goodness it's flat, at least we think it is! Perhaps I should have put the night-vision goggles on after all? Too late now.
>
> We recite the litany of checks just as we've done a thousand times before. But never like this. This time it's for real and ahead, in only 30 seconds, lies an Iraqi airfield. Twenty seconds, fifteen, five, committing, there they go. The aircraft vibrates rapidly as our JP233s dispense their loads. There's a pulsing glow from beneath the aircraft, then suddenly two massive thumps as the empty canisters are jettisoned. Simultaneously, alarms sound, the autopilot drops out, we lurch sharply upwards and my heart rate increases to about 400 a second as I fight to get back down.

The Iraqis, though probably more frightened, still managed to organise retaliation – a massive barrage of anti-aircraft fire, which looked at first to Witts and his colleagues like flashing lights.

> The flashing lights become white stair-rods arcing over and around us. Away to the right the sky erupts in orange flames, quickly followed by a curtain of incandescent white light as more and more AAA barrages fire into the darkness. We rush onward. Check the rest of my formation in. All there, thankfully. Time seems to stand still and the brown line that marks the international border creeps so slowly down the moving map display. I suppress the irrational desire to laugh as we

ANATOMY OF AN AIR ATTACK

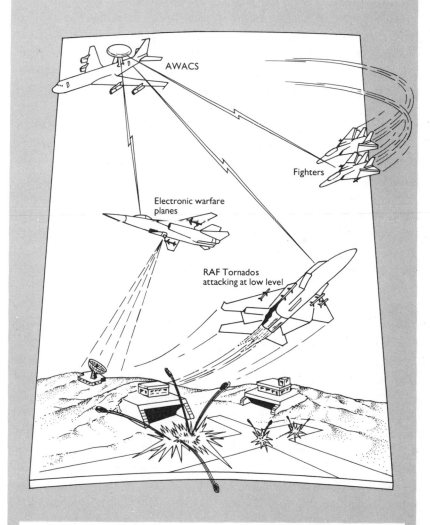

Up to 50 aircraft would be involved in each major air raid. Up above the RAF's Tornados, American fighters would provide cover, electronic warfare planes would jam Iraqi radar, and AWACS control planes would co-ordinate the operation.

pass over a printed notice on the map: WARNING, flight in Iraq outside controlled airspace is STRICTLY PROHIBITED. Then, just as suddenly, we're over the line. We're safe, we're alive!

Witts and his colleagues were through the most formidable defences the Iraqis were to offer, what became known as the 'walls of lead'. The tracer rounds – the only ones that were visible – represented just a tenth of what was being shot into the sky. 'What looked like a wall of fire,' according to Chuck Horner, 'was in fact ten times worse.' To one British crew, it looked like a set of 'roman candles, shooting out orange and red balls, coming towards the airplane and just going up ahead of you in a great mass of fire'.

Back in Bahrain, the base commander, David Henderson, was nervously waiting in the Operations Room for news of the first British mission. One after the other, each pilot checked in. Henderson was delighted and noticed that the radio operator couldn't help smiling too.

Only one hour into the onslaught, American pilots were transfixed by the sight of Baghdad below them. Lieutenant-Colonel Don Klein couldn't count the number of explosions, so many bombs and cruise missiles were falling. 'There were things going off all over the place. If you saw any footage from World War Two, that's exactly what it looks like.'

According to Captain Steve Tate, 'flames rising up from the city left some neighbourhoods lit up like a huge Christmas tree. The entire city was just sparkling at us.'

For the Iraqis down below, there was no beauty that night, just blind terror. They didn't know the bombing was meant to be selective. One man, Jamal, who lived near the telecommunications tower, thought the world was ending:

The windows shattered and we were thrown out of bed by this hot blast of air. My wife started praying to God. The room was filled with thick black smoke and heat and the whole sky seemed to be on fire. A few minutes later it started all over again, and we could hear bangs and explosions and gunfire and breaking glass everywhere around us and further away. We were terrified and we lay on the floor of our bedroom all night just waiting for it to end.

If the Iraqis were to put up any serious defence, the only hope lay with their air force. For the allies, this was the great unknown. Not only was it vast, with some 800 aircraft, but it could boast two of the most effective modern jets available. It had an estimated 40 of the Soviets' MiG-29s, which had impressed the crowds at the Farnborough Air Show with an agility that outclassed anything in the Royal Air Force. It also had 100 French-built Mirage F-1s, one of which had attacked and crippled the USS *Stark* in the Gulf less than four years earlier.

The allied commanders were certainly braced for an enormous dogfight. One of those glued to his video monitor was Major-General Royal Moore, in charge of a US Marines air wing. At 5a.m. he was studying the picture relayed from one of the AWACS airborne radar planes controlling allied flights. 'I watched as the F-15s started their first wave and I saw 25 Iraqi airplanes up there and I said: "OK, here's the start of the great air war." Well, they just turned and ran and that's the last we saw of them for 70 hours.'

Some Iraqi pilots did resist and were promptly shot down. A few pursued America's electronic warfare planes and fired missiles at them. Though unarmed, the Americans simply dived and then accelerated so vigorously that they got away. The Iraqis were quickly finding out that all the odds were stacked against them. Two of their MiG-29s tried an attack that could never succeed. They raced to meet an allied bomber force.

One of the American crews, Major Dave Wells and Captain Jeff Latas in an F-15E, recalled how they were flying in strength, in a 'package' of 22 warplanes, including advanced fighters and electronic warfare aircraft. They were in a loose formation that stretched over 80 miles of airspace, and they were spoiling for a fight. It was still dark, and the Iraqi Air Force had rarely trained at night. The Americans were flying at low level, and the Iraqis hadn't had much practice at that either. Nevertheless, they didn't give up; they tried to fight, but it ended in disaster.

ALL NECESSARY MEANS

One of the MiG pilots launched a missile – which flashed straight at the other MiG. It hit the plane and sent it crashing down, presumably killing the pilot inside. The Americans, who had yet to fire a shot, could only watch in astonishment. But there was more to come: the MiG which had opened fire got into trouble, misjudging its height above the ground. It crashed and exploded.

The Americans were left feeling sorry for their enemy. 'I don't think they knew what was going on,' said Wells. 'They can't have understood the scope of what was happening; in other words, that Desert Storm was kicking off.'

Almost from this very first night, the Iraqis surrendered control of the skies. The air commander, General Horner, was able to conclude that though initially 'they tried to shoot us down, when it was nose-to-nose and fighter against fighter, we just overwhelmed them'. Someone in the US Air Force was more mocking. He quickly designed a car bumper sticker, which read: 'Honk, if you've seen Jesus – or the Iraqi Air Force'.

Henderson and the rest of the senior RAF staff in Bahrain had gathered again in the Operations Room to hear the second wave of Tornado crews report back. The first wave had returned safely from Tallil and now, at about 7.30a.m., the next four Tornados should have bombed another airbase near Iraq's second city, Basra, and been heading home. The lead crew duly called in, then the second and the third – but from the fourth there was only a chilling silence. Henderson knew who was missing: Flight Lieutenants Adrian 'John' Nicholl and John Peters. Their colleagues in Bahrain feared the worst, but later it transpired that, although they'd been shot down, Nicholl and Peters had survived and their battered faces would soon be paraded on Iraqi television. (After the war they would be returned home safely.) It was the first British loss of the war – on a night when the allies suffered far fewer casualties than they ever dared hope for.

So as dawn broke over the Gulf, there was palpable relief in the allied camp. Nearly all the aircraft were heading home. Some pilots were crying. At the British headquarters in Riyadh, the chief of staff, Ian

MacFadyen, quoted Shakespeare's *Henry V* on the eve of the Battle of Agincourt: 'And gentlemen in England, now a-bed, shall think themselves accursed they were not here.'

Commanders couldn't believe their losses had been so light. 'God, can this be true?' wondered Brigadier-General Neal. 'We have not lost a lot of kids.' He'd been watching on CNN the barrage of anti-aircraft fire over Baghdad and had said to himself: 'How can anything fly through that?' Suddenly there was euphoria. Voices around the planning-tables were getting louder, jokes were being cracked and there was a good deal of back-slapping.

Chuck Horner, their boss, felt that he had to introduce a note of caution. He didn't want to dampen spirits, just to put things in perspective. He told his staff: 'We must be careful because this is just the beginning of a very long and hard task.' Horner was only half right: the air campaign would be long but, for the allies at least, it wouldn't be as hard as they feared.

A calm, determined President Bush, in a night-time television address to the nation, said that the operation was going according to plan. 'Kuwait will once again be free,' he said, 'we will not fail.'

The Pentagon reinforced the President's confidence, reporting that 80 per cent of pilots had reached their targets, dropped their weapons and returned. That didn't mean 80 per cent of the targets attacked had been successfully destroyed but, in the excitement, not many noticed.

Video footage released in Riyadh seemed to confirm the first wave of success. Blurred black-and-white images showed the mesmerising accuracy of the laser-guided bombs as they flew in through ventilation shafts and doorways. One Stealth commander even said: 'You pick precisely which target you want, the men's room or the ladies' room.' The clips had been carefully selected, of course, so that no one would see the bombs that missed, or the people they killed. The public perception was one of immediate allied superiority. Stock markets around the world warmed to it. The war would surely would be over soon – and without the horrific allied casualties that Saddam had threatened.

ALL NECESSARY MEANS

Yet, behind the scenes, military commanders knew the air campaign was scheduled to last at least a month. John Major hinted at it, warning Parliament that there was a 'great deal more yet to be done before we can be certain how the course of this conflict will run'. He knew the allied air forces had to destroy countless command centres, aircraft shelters, supply-lines, and chemical weapons storage sites, some of which were the size of central Paris. Then they had to knock out at least half the Iraqi tank force, all before they could even think of recapturing Kuwait without large loss of life. As they kept stressing, Iraq had the fourth largest military machine in the world.

There was another good reason to prepare the public for a long haul. The huge American 7th Corps, which was to be the backbone of the allied offensive, was still moving from Germany and General Schwarzkopf knew it wouldn't be ready before the middle of February. Ministers and senior commanders weren't as confident as they appeared that the campaign would work. Its success hinged on so many different, unpredictable ingredients.

Sir Patrick Hine, the joint commander of British forces, feared a long campaign would lead some in the coalition to think that the bombing was more about smashing Iraq into oblivion than about liberating Kuwait. He'd discussed the problem with Schwarzkopf and they decided they'd have to 'ride it out'. Their worry was that too long a bombing campaign would be opposed by many at the United Nations – and force President Bush to shorten the air war by ordering the ground offensive to start before Schwarzkopf was ready.

Tom King, the British Defence Secretary, shared their fears. In an interview with us after the war, he admitted that he hadn't been sure whether 'there would be the political and public will to sustain week after week of bombing, or whether the accuracy of the attacks would convince world opinion that we were not out to kill Iraqi civilians'. Most worrying of all to King was the danger posed by Iraq's forces themselves. He wondered whether the Iraqis would strike the allied ports and disrupt the arrival of the American reinforcements, who were so central to the whole strategy. As he studied the highly-classified planning maps that covered one entire wall of his office on the sixth floor of the Ministry of Defence,

King knew all these factors would affect the timing of the operation – and that was critical. The war had to be over by the time both Ramadan and the terrible Gulf heat began in March. It all depended on the air campaign, and on how it was conducted.

■ ■o the soldiers waiting in the desert and watching the warplanes leave vapour trails above them, the first night seemed a good start. They knew that the more bombing there was, the less they would have to fight. Lieutenant-Colonel Rory Clayton, the commander of a British artillery regiment, thought that since, for the moment, he couldn't contribute to the war effort, he may as well mark the occasion of the beginning of the campaign. In a throwback to grander Army days, he decided to give a dinner in his desert camp for 10 friends and colleagues. After agreeing a suitable menu with his cook and sending out the invitations, Clayton despatched his driver to the nearest hotel, the Holiday Inn at Jubayl, to buy three cases of the best non-alcoholic champagne. That night, on 17 January, the Desert Rats dined in style.

A s their meal began, three giant B-52s were taking off from their base in Spain. They flew the length of the Mediterranean, crossed Turkey and then, in the middle of its most mountainous stretch of border with Iraq, they dipped into hostile territory. It was just past midnight and, with the Iraqi Air Force showing so little resistance, steadily larger numbers of allied bombers were being sent against the military installations judged by allied intelligence to be Saddam's most precious: his nuclear research centres, the chemical and biological weapons plants and the arms factories that gave him the power to dominate his neighbours.

The lead B-52 pilot, Captain Mark Medvec, had been watching the first night of the war on CNN with his colleagues when they'd been told that they were soon to be part of it. Now, as Medvec crossed the border into Iraq, he immediately brought his huge aircraft down as low as he dared between the mountains to avoid Iraqi radar. On a moonless and cloudy night, the three enormous planes were swooping through the val-

ALL NECESSARY MEANS

leys, passing just 200 feet above the villages, swerving violently to keep their wingtips away from the cliffs that loomed up at them.

The night was so dark that Medvec could discern only the vaguest of images on his infra-red camera. The only way he could see the outside world was by radar and, with that as his guide, he wrestled with the controls for the 40 long minutes it took to pass through the canyons and reach the flat, more open land around the target – a missile factory, near Mosul.

Captain Medvec's B-52 plane dropped its bombs first, with the other two aircraft close behind. Some 60 tons of explosive fell onto the plant. 'The effect was like a small nuclear explosion, setting off several other explosions; it was quite a show,' said Medvec. But he and the rest of the aircrews were far too busy and too frightened to be entertained. They had to try to return the way they'd come, but this time the Iraqi anti-aircraft units would be fully alert, and waiting. It was not much comfort that the electronic warfare aircraft accompanying the bombers were busy jamming nearby radars; they couldn't stop the gunfire.

Captain Medvec chose to stay low and zig-zag his plane as vigorously as possible to confuse the gunners on the ground just below him:

Coming in we just worried about hitting the mountains. Coming out we worried about hitting the mountains *and* avoiding the very heavy ground fire. At one point we were in a real jagged part of the mountain range when they must have had anything between 50 and 100 anti-aircraft guns shooting at us, and it was really a challenge weaving past them and the rocks. We had a couple of extremely close calls, with one burst that flew right off our nose, maybe 15 feet away.

Somehow, none of the three planes was hit. They decided to keep low and then, in what was already an exhausting mission, they passed over a highway teeming with Iraqi soldiers. One managed to launch a SAM missile. Captain Medvec saw the flash of light. 'I called out to our electronic warfare officer to launch flares, and sure enough the flares suckered the missile. It was very spooky; time kind of slowed for us but we were so busy not hitting the ground that the adrenalin took care of the fear.' It was a further six hours before they were back in Spain.

Another B-52 crew would never shake off the fear they felt on that first night. Several times they were pursued by SAM missiles. The pilot, Captain Scott Ladner, would hear his electronic warfare officer shout, 'we have missile searching!' The rest of the crew would carry on with their work while waiting, agonised, for his next report. 'We have missile lock-on!' he would call out. That meant the next few seconds would decide their fate. 'It was an extremely tense time for us, thinking we could be taking a hit. Luckily the Iraqis weren't very accurate.' They did manage to hit two of the B-52s, but only minor damage was done. The airmen flew in trepidation but the campaign was going their way.

T he campaign lasted about ten days longer than planned. The huge raids of the first night were to be followed up day-in, day-out for another five and a half weeks in all. Many of Iraq's most important military installations were much larger than allied planners had realised, and they were taking longer than expected to destroy. The planners had allowed only one week for these 'strategic' targets in what was called phase one of the campaign but they were so big and so numerous they had to remain under attack till the war ended.

The weather wasn't helping either. It was the worst known in the Gulf for at least 30 years. There was twice the average amount of cloud, and storm fronts that would normally have been expected to pass through the area twice a week were rolling through every day. Despite the Pentagon's two special weather satellites over the Gulf, pilots frequently had to return to base without dropping their bombs. The cloud cover was even thwarting some of the much-vaunted high technology. The laser beams used to guide bombs were weakened by cloud and, anyway, they were no help if the crew operating them couldn't see their targets.

But it was Saddam's answer to the bombing that did most to slow the campaign. Because of his Scud attacks on Israel and Saudi Arabia, allied commanders were forced to divert three times more aircraft than they'd planned in the effort to destroy his missiles and launchers. It sparked off some heated arguments in the Riyadh air planning room, nicknamed the 'Black Hole'. The team preparing raids on the Scuds suddenly started calling on aircraft already assigned to other missions – and disrupted the work of their colleagues planning the rest of each day's sorties.

Since, in the first 48 hours, everyone was going without sleep, tempers were getting short. Chuck Horner had already warned his staff that 'war is chaos and we've got to learn how to manage chaos'. He'd deliberately only allowed plans to be drawn up for the first three days of operations because he wanted the campaign to be as flexible as possible. He didn't want a 'seven- or eight-day script'. Now he had to use the flexibility he'd created and reorganise. The Scud team, Horner decided, would be allocated a set number of warplanes and tankers every day. That meant the rest of the campaign would have to take a back-seat but at least it could continue without interruption. Tempers soon cooled.

None of the allied air crews paid a higher price than those in the RAF Tornados. One official in the Pentagon told us they were 'ruthlessly brave' in performing missions from which the US Air Force shied away. 'They really scared them with their low-level stuff.' The RAF were consistently flying at much lower altitudes than any other air force – and their losses were proportionately much greater. After the first five days, five Tornados had gone down. The planes only made up four per cent of the allied force, yet they were suffering over a quarter of the losses. Questions about whether to continue their operations were soon being raised in Riyadh. In fact, the chief allied air planner, Brigadier-General Buster Glosson, was worried the British casualties were starting to look glaringly out of proportion:

> I was not naive enough to think that percentage-wise, every time we lost a Brit I wanted to make sure we lost a Saudi or an American. I knew that wasn't going to happen. However, I didn't want it to get out of kilter either, I didn't want all of a sudden the Brits to be the only ones paying a price for this war.

In fact, Glosson had originally planned that the RAF should only attack Iraqi airfields for the first three days of the campaign anyway. The best of Iraq's warplanes operated out of seven of the bases and the Tornado/JP233 combination was the best way of making sure they didn't get off the ground. 'Nothing else could have done the mission near as well as they did.' Glosson knew there would be a price: his computer model of the campaign had showed him how many Tornados might be lost.

But the losses may have come more quickly than he'd expected. In the first two nights of bombing, three Tornados had gone down, two of them to gun or missile fire and the third probably because it crashed into the desert at low level. It was this last loss that forced Glosson to think again. He decided to tell Air Vice Marshal Bill Wratten, the RAF's Gulf commander, that he would halt the attacks 'as quickly as I can'. Glosson declared, 'I can't really conceive doing this for more than about one more day.' The RAF were already considering changing tactics and switching their bombers to higher altitudes. 'They were in the process of not going in low because I wasn't going to let them go in low anyway.' But for years low-level attacks have been the foundation of Britain's doctrine for fighting war in the air and Chuck Horner felt that the RAF were 'locked into it' by their training and their equipment.

It was Bill Wratten's view that the RAF were suffering from bad luck – and he kept telling himself that 'bad luck doesn't last forever'. On the third day, the Tornado crews tried a new tactic. Half of them would lob 1000-lb bombs set to 'air-burst' over the heads of the Iraqi gunners, while the rest would slip in to drop the JP233 bomblets. It was a bold plan, but it failed. The anti-aircraft gunfire was just as intense. Glosson talked to Wratten again and they agreed that there was little point in carrying on, with attacks which forced crews to fly smack into Iraqi 'triple-A'. Glosson decided the risk was 'too high for the pay-off'.

From the sixth day of the campaign, the RAF's planes abandoned low-level bombing. That brought its own problems. The Tornados weren't geared to operate from higher altitudes. The software for their on-board computers had to be revised and the number of bombs carried was cut from eight to five to help the planes fly higher and faster. They even tried dive-bombing in an attempt to achieve more accuracy. None of this helped very much and, in one attack on an airfield, the bombs apparently fell outside its perimeter fence.

ALL NECESSARY MEANS

It was only when laser-targeting devices were rushed to the Gulf that the RAF's accuracy improved. Two were carried on Tornados, the rest on Buccaneers, which flew with other Tornados to 'illuminate' targets for them. They were immediately ordered to join in the attack on 300 aircraft shelters which were protecting the best of Iraq's Air Force – or what was left of it. American bombers had already started doing this and one by one the shelters were being destroyed. The Iraqis tried hard to deceive allied aircraft by painting large circles on them to make it look as if they'd already been hit. It was then that commanders in Riyadh realised to their horror that they hadn't kept a record of which shelters really had been attacked. So, as Wratten was to reveal later, they had to begin all over again.

It was complicated work, often needing two bombs to destroy each shelter, as well as a steady hand and steady nerves. The laser beam had to be kept pointed at exactly the right spot as the bombs guided themselves towards it. Crews found it so absorbing that one pilot, Flight Lieutenant Rupert Clark, failed to heed warnings of a SAM missile launch. Radio frequencies were busy with messages from the AWACS control planes, and from colleagues in accompanying aircraft, and the missile alarm wasn't noticed until too late. 'The first one got us as we were trying to evade, and then the second one also hit. The whole cockpit was shattered. The instruments were gone, as were both engines. We tried to glide for a minute or two but the controls froze up and then I ejected.' Clark's navigator was killed but the missions had to continue. 'Precision' bombing had never been more important.

At first they were scared but gradually the people of a tiny village outside Baghdad got used to it: the regular appearance of a cruise missile flying down their dusty main street. Every day at 3.30p.m. for four days running, the missile would pass their houses, make a left turn and then slam into the side of a factory at the end of the road. The first day eight people inside were killed; later the factory was abandoned. Ibrahim was one of the many who turned out to watch. He'd fled from Baghdad to avoid the bombing, only to find himself in the thick of it:

On the first day everyone hid when they saw the missile coming and we prayed to Allah that we'd be safe. On the second day, people were still afraid but they could see that the missile was taking exactly the same course. On the third day, many people were waiting on the street to watch it go by and on the last day, the people were all outside taking photographs and laughing. When there was nothing left of the factory, and the missile didn't come on the fifth day, people actually felt disappointed.

This was precision bombing at its most bizarre. Most of it worked. The shattered aircraft shelters at Tallil airbase in southern Iraq are testament to that. We were the first journalists to see how each of the huge concrete hangars had been holed in its roof with brutal force and the heavy reinforced doors torn away like paper. The aircraft inside were wrecked, with rubble and unexploded bombs littered around them. Other MiGs that had been towed off the base to a road near by, and hidden rather feebly under camouflage netting, had also been picked off – all within sight of the massive pyramid, or 'ziggurat' of Ur, the ancient capital of the Euphrates valley civilisation until 2000BC. Saddam had rebuilt the pyramid as a monument to his own 'civilisation' 4000 years on, only to have some of his best weapons destroyed around it. The pretension and the reality of his rule lay side by side.

Saddam's only hope now rested not with his own military machine but in exploiting mistakes made by the allies. One was an RAF attack on a bridge in the town of Al Fallūjah, which went disastrously wrong when the laser-guidance system failed and a bomb fell into the market area, possibly killing as many as 50 people. The injured were still being pulled from the rubble 48 hours later. Other bombs went astray in Baghdad and Basra, demolishing homes, leaving vast craters by the roadside.

But the most controversial and tragic raid was also one of the most accurate. At 4a.m. on 13 February, two Stealths dropped bombs on a bunker in the prosperous Amiriya district of Baghdad, one weapon slipping through a ventilation shaft, another demolishing the entrance. To allied planners, it was the routine demolition of yet another of Saddam's 25 command bunkers. According to Buster Glosson, American

ALL NECESSARY MEANS

and British intelligence believed that ten of those bunkers had been specially hardened and, of these, five were likely to be used by Saddam or his key staff. The bunker at Amiriya fell into that category. Glosson's information was that the bunker housed the Iraqi president's personal security force, 'the people who were actually keeping him in power and protecting him'. What intelligence did not tell him was that it was packed with hundreds of civilians. More than 300 were incinerated or suffocated. Among the dead were at least 100 children.

Within four hours of the attack, word reached the western journalists working in Baghdad. Until now, the Iraqi Information Ministry 'minders' had been organising visits to see the bomb damage. This morning was different: the reporters were free to rush down to Amiriya on their own. BBC TV's correspondent Jeremy Bowen was among them. He arrived while the bunker was still burning. There was a crowd outside clamouring to find out if their families had been killed. A lorry was being loaded with human remains charred beyond recognition.

The entrance-way to the bunker's upper level was blocked by rescue workers and rubble so Bowen and his cameraman ran to another entrance, a ramp that led straight down to a lower floor. It was knee-deep in water. With no minders there, they looked into virtually every room. They saw a first-aid post, a security room from which the outside doors were controlled, a kitchen – but nothing military at all. On this floor, which the Pentagon was later to say had been used by Iraqi commanders, they saw no trace of any charts torn from walls or abandoned uniforms. They wondered if there was yet another floor below and then thought that if there was, the water through which they were wading would surely have flowed down to it. If the army had been in the bunker at all that night, they had pulled out with remarkable efficiency in just four hours. It seemed improbable. The rescue operation looked too chaotic and, according to Bowen, the Iraqi authorities weren't even organising a serious attempt to exploit the tragedy for propaganda.

Up above, there was carnage. Television crews filmed more than could ever be shown to family audiences: twisted bed-frames and children's chairs, wobbling lumps of flesh, severed torsos. But the pictures of covered bodies, of fathers screaming for their children, of relatives howling in mourning at the loss of entire families, were broadcast around the world. One man lost his family of 12; another was able to identify the bodies of his wife and daughter only by their bracelets. By mid-morning, it was all being screened on CNN.

The hotline rang in Buster Glosson's room while he was in the shower and an aide told him: 'There appears to be a problem with one of the targets we struck last night. A lot of civilians may have gotten killed.' He switched on CNN and saw the aftermath for himself. He felt there wasn't much he could do about it – and simply stepped back into the shower.

Allied commanders knew the survival of the coalition depended on the accuracy of their bombing and on their choice of targets. Schwarzkopf was reported to be 'concerned, perplexed and generally damned upset'. Chuck Horner knew this kind of mistake couldn't be allowed to happen again, chiefly – in his view – because of 'the impact it would have in the world's press'.

As it was, the lines between Washington and Riyadh were soon buzzing. The US Defence Secretary, Dick Cheney, told his commanders 'he wasn't pleased', but, at the same time, he said that he understood: 'that's the price of doing business'. He stood by the explanation coming out of Riyadh: that their intelligence showed the bunker had been transmitting military signals and was, therefore, a 'legitimate military target'. But the first presentation of this line was a public relations disaster. Brigadier-General Butch Neal, the American spokesman in Riyadh, appalled many officials, especially in Whitehall, by declaring that he was 'comfortable' with the intelligence advice that the bunker had been a military target.

Nevertheless, British officials supported Riyadh's account. Sir Patrick Hine, the joint commander of British forces, was shown the intelligence by Schwarzkopf and is adamant that it proved the bunker had been used by military personnel for the previous 36 to 48 hours. He believes the Iraqis delayed telling the western media for eight hours to allow the military time to remove their equipment and to flood the lower level – an account that is flatly contradicted by correspondents on the scene.

At the Stealth base in Saudi Arabia, the news that so many civilians had been in the bunker was greeted with shock. The two pilots who carried out the attack cannot be identified but, on their behalf, their colleagues still feel outrage. 'Why in God's name would you put any civilians in any military facility?' Major Rod Schroeder said. 'We were amazed there was even one civilian in the building.'

The pilots believe that they were lured into attacking the bunker by an Iraqi leadership desperate to discredit the coalition. The theory runs that a small army unit, based temporarily in the bunker, could have transmitted enough false radio traffic to be noticed by American spy satellites and attract a raid. Lieutenant-Colonel Barry Horn, the commander of one of the two Stealth squadrons, blamed Saddam for what he said was the 'unforgivable act' of putting civilians in the bunker. Horn says that he was briefed in detail on the intelligence: 'We were convinced it was a command and control bunker actively employed by the military.'

But one senior Pentagon official was later quoted as admitting that there'd been a mistake because the intelligence was out of date and hadn't been verified by agents on the ground. It's possible that the information may have been right at one stage, but, by the time it had been processed and the raid planned and then carried out, the use of the bunker had changed. It is the most plausible explanation but it has not, to date, been confirmed.

As long as the Pentagon refuses to produce any of its intelligence evidence, the tragedy will remain unexplained and embarrassing – a stain on an allied bombing campaign which otherwise caused remarkably few civilian casualties. In the event, it didn't significantly damage the coalition or disrupt the war. But it left air commanders like Bill Wratten furious with the media for 'putting us in the witness-box'.

Schwarzkopf explained it in terms of an old cowboy film. 'The guys in the black hats, the bad guys, they can do anything they want to. The guys in the white hats have to play by a certain set of rules. And that's what we have here.' He meant that the guidelines imposed on him by the allied leadership not only called for the bombing to be accurate, with as little danger as possible to civilians – it also had to be 'legal' and morally justifiable as well. A war fought in the name of the United Nations had to respect its opinion.

The difficulty was getting everyone to agree on what that meant. According to sources who asked not to be identified, British planners had long worried that raids on Saddam's biological weapons centres would release the germs and spread epidemic among innocent Iraqi civilians. They thought that the explosions would fail to burn off all the toxins, with lethal results. Only after experts had 'argued it all through' were they convinced these attacks would be safe and, in the end, biological weapons sites were only attacked on days when there was no wind.

British officials had also been pressing Washington for months to make sure that there was no possibility of any damage to the Shia shrines in Karbala and Najaf. The officials knew there was an important chemical weapons centre near by and they feared that, if the shrines were hit by mistake, the repercussions could be devastating. They thought neighbouring Iran might even be forced to abandon its neutrality. It took 'a lengthy exchange' to persuade the Americans to alter their plans.

Most of London's concerns over targeting policy were conveyed to American commanders by General de la Billière in Riyadh. He enjoyed extraordinarily good access to Schwarzkopf – unmatched by any other coalition general. Every day he was the only non-American invited to join Schwarzkopf's 7p.m. planning conference, 'the nineteen-hundred', where he would sit alongside the commanders of America's air force, army, navy and marines contingents even though Britain's contribution was smaller than any one of them. De la Billière knew that 'the Americans could have done the whole thing themselves' and even believed that, if they had, 'it would have been a damn sight easier for them'.

But, politically, Britain's support was critical. It meant that de la Billière had Schwarzkopf's ear, and would linger after the meetings to raise sensitive issues privately. At one stage, he was asked to convey London's concern that American planners had not studied properly the side-effects of bombing Iraq's nuclear installations. The fear, according to de la Billière, was that the American attitude might be: 'Don't worry, it'll work, old boy, on the day.' It led to a long technical debate about the potential dangers of contaminating Iraq and neighbouring countries. In the end, London was satisfied that the attacks would be safe 'as far as science could predict'.

ALL NECESSARY MEANS

Some potential targets were dropped altogether – on legal grounds. A lawyer, Harry Heinztleman, was on permanent call in the Black Hole, the air operations planning room, to check that all allied bombing was within international law. Heinztleman approved most of the bombing list but he ruled against attacking dams because the ensuing floods would endanger civilians living downstream. On the other hand, he did not object to the bombing of locks, which were surrounded by uninhabited salt marshes.

Another question attracted a degree of attention out of all proportion to its importance: should the allies attack a statue of Saddam in Baghdad and the giant replicas of his hands holding two enormous swords? Both had been on the original target list but, several weeks into the war, neither had yet been hit – though reporters had seen them lit up by the flashes of bombs going off near by. Buster Glosson decided to delete the swords monument from his list, only because it was beside a war memorial and he didn't want the Iraqis 'to be able to get any propaganda mileage out of it'. But he had left his options open on the statue, and came to consider it again very late in the conflict. 'I was sitting and thinking about the message we were trying to send the Iraqi people, that this is the wrong leadership.' They were already attacking the Ba'ath party headquarters, and Glosson remembered the statue. He asked his advisers whether it was near the party building.

'It's over near a park,' he was told.

'Well, is it near a lot of civilians?' Glosson asked.

'No, it's sitting there by itself.'

'Well, I think I'll take that down,' Glosson decided. Then he checked with Harry Heinztleman, who told him that since 'arts and antiquities' cannot be attacked under international law, the statue should be spared 'no matter how ugly it was'. Glosson felt that he ought to ask his Commander in Chief as well.

'Ironic you should mention that,' said Schwarzkopf. 'Someone back in Washington asked, were we going to take down the statue?'

'Sir, I had the lawyers look into it, and they're telling me that I can't really do it, and they've showed me chapter and verse.' Schwarzkopf agreed that the statue should be left alone. According to Glosson, reports that President Bush had vetoed this particular mission were 'bullshit'.

Another decision triggered a much more heated argument – which until now has remained secret. For several days, Stealth fighter-bombers had been attacking the six bridges in central Baghdad that cross the river Tigris. Not only did the bridges connect the two halves of the city, but they also carried the fibre-optic cables by which Baghdad was communicating with western and southern Iraq – in particular with the Scud units operating against Israel, and with the Iraqi army in Kuwait. Since Iraq's microwave transmitters were already bombed and its radio signals were being intercepted by allied intelligence, the fibre-optic landlines were Saddam's best link. For the air planners, they became a priority target.

Suddenly, though, Glosson was told that London and Washington wanted the attacks halted. He was given no reason. But he suspected that ministers in Whitehall and officials at the White House had seen television footage of children playing near the three damaged bridges and had felt the image was wrong. Glosson had a vision of them saying 'oh my goodness, here's brutality for no reason'. But Bill Wratten of the RAF told him that 'knocking out the bridges in downtown Baghdad was not a popular thought in London', while, at the same time, Schwarzkopf let him know that Washington also disapproved. It was the first time there'd been any political intervention during the campaign and Glosson angrily objected.

> I resisted it to the maximum extent I could. I repeatedly went back to General Schwarzkopf and said, 'militarily, this is just not the right thing to do'. But I was told: 'No, they're off the target-list until further notice.'

Glosson was disappointed. He had deliberately ordered the attacks to take place at 4a.m. to avoid hitting civilian traffic. In his view, halting the raids would put more allied lives at risk. If the cables couldn't be bombed they would have to be severed some other way. That could only mean sending in Special Forces, including the SAS. If the air campaign was to succeed, Saddam had to be denied access to those cables. He had to be prevented from any attempt to control his army – and, most crucially, his missiles.

Chapter 3
SADDAM'S STRATEGY

'There is not a single chance for any retreat. Let everybody understand that this is going to become the mother of all battles.'

Iraq's Revolutionary Command Council, 21 September 1990.

General H. Norman Schwarzkopf, on Saddam, 27 February 1991.

'He is neither a strategist, nor is he schooled in the operational arts, nor is he a tactician, nor is he a general, nor is he a soldier. Other than that, he's a great military man.'

At first the three orange streaks that shot through the night sky looked like falling stars. From the cockpit of his plane, First Lieutenant Terry Abel was watching them intently before he suddenly worked out what they were: Scuds, hurtling through the air at 3000 mph on their way to Saudi Arabia. There were three altogether, and Abel had the most extraordinary view of them; not from below, like everybody else, but from above. He was in a KC-10 re-fuelling tanker, 15 000 feet up, just south of Riyadh.

On the tarmac of the airport below, Captain Scott Hackney and his crew were about to take off in their RC-135 spy-plane when their worst fear was realised. Over the radio came a warning: 'Scuds are inbound'. Hackney's plane was loaded with over 100 000 lb of fuel and the smallest piece of shrapnel, let alone an explosion near by, would have ignited it immediately. 'We all wanted to get out of the aircraft,' said Hackney. 'We had about 15 to 20 seconds, so we were running away as fast as we could.' As he was racing for a bunker in the dark, Hackney looked over his shoulder and saw the Scuds, huge 'beams of gold' across the sky.

He was still running when he heard a deafening double boom from just 100 yards away. The now-famous Patriot anti-missile missiles were launching. 'They made a tremendous noise and there were a lot of scared people around.' By bizarre coincidence, as Hackney and his colleagues watched the missiles climb to meet their targets, Hackney's wife Fran, a US Air Force nurse, who happened to be posted to the same base, was desperately trying to put on her chemical protection gear in her unlit tent near by. 'She only had her pants half-on when the Patriots went off. In her fright, she pulled a muscle trying to get the damn things on.'

In his tanker up above, Abel watched as five bright white streams of light rose from the ground – the Patriots soaring to intercept the trio of Iraqi missiles in what looked like an 'extravagant fireworks display'. For Abel, it was a beautiful, if frightening, sight which he would never forget. It was certainly a triumph of technology, a high-speed interception in the dark, that was repeated again and again during the war and, each time, acclaimed around the world.

Underground, in allied headquarters, Brigadier-General Butch Neal would be the first to hear the Scud alarms. The alerts were relayed directly to the War Room from spy satellites. As the officer in charge of the headquarters at night, he would regularly hear the warning scream out from a tannoy: 'We have Scud launch! we have Scud launch! Area at risk is Riyadh!' Neal was in charge of the War Room for all but one of the Scud attacks on Saudi Arabia, and he knew the routine well. Part of it involved waking General Schwarzkopf, whose small bedroom was just down the corridor. Schwarzkopf always wanted to be told. He understood only too well how Saddam was using his Scuds to try to change the course of the war.

He knew that by terrorising Saudi civilians and, most importantly, by provoking Israel into the fray, Saddam hoped to undermine the coalition ranged against him. The Scuds themselves, old and inaccurate, were militarily insignificant but, politically, they could be devastating. Schwarzkopf understood their power over public opinion and he worked to combat it through the media. Early in the war, he invited the BBC to his headquarters for an interview, in which he ridiculed the Scud threat.

ALL NECESSARY MEANS

Frankly, I would be more afraid of standing out in a lightning storm in southern Georgia than I would be standing down in the streets of Riyadh, when the Scuds are coming down. If it's going to hit you, it's going to hit you.

But the reality was that the Scuds were terrifying to civilians within their range, no matter what Schwarzkopf said.

For a general like Schwarzkopf, trained to fight a conventional enemy, this was to be a war of many surprises. Saddam had his own agenda and his own objectives. As a man who portrayed himself as a leader of the Arab world, as the new Saladin who would defeat the infidels, Saddam wasn't playing so much to win, as to lose in a way that would discredit and humble his enemies. He had seen Nasser lead Egypt into defeat against the West in the 1950s, only to emerge as an Arab hero for attempting to stand up to the colonial powers. He believed that he could achieve a similar surge in his prestige if only his forces could inflict some damage on the allies. In that Saddam judged that the coalition had two weak links: first, public opinion in the event of heavy allied casualties and, second, a country that was not even part of the alliance – Israel.

Iraq's answer to the opening of the allied air campaign came within 24 hours, when the first Scuds were launched at Tel Aviv. The world waited for Israel's response. Ministers and commanders anxiously asked themselves if Jerusalem would retaliate and so force key Arab members of the coalition to withdraw.

Initially, the signs did not look good. A dozen Israeli warplanes were scrambled and there was acute tension in London and Washington. Charles Powell had just got home from Downing Street in the early hours of the morning, and had changed into a pullover and a pair of jeans, when the phone rang. He was given the news that the first Scud had just been launched towards Israel. It was vital for London to co-ordinate an immediate response with Washington. He leapt back into his car and, on the short drive from South Kensington to Number Ten, cursed the fact that his journey was taking longer than the Scud's had to Tel Aviv.

The casually-dressed Powell was embarrassed to see the TV cameras, still outside Number Ten, film him as he walked through the front door. Inside, Powell set to work. He rang Bush's National Security Adviser, Brent Scowcroft, in the White House. It was agreed that both governments should urge the Israelis to show restraint. So worried was Downing Street that two messages were sent to the Israeli Prime Minister, Yitzhak Shamir. But Powell knew that only the Americans could stop Israel from falling into Saddam's trap.

It wasn't long before the Israeli Defence Minister, Moshe Arens, was on the secure hotline, codenamed 'Hammer Rick', to his counterpart, Dick Cheney. Arens said that his generals were planning to seek out and destroy Iraq's mobile missile-launchers, and the mission might last several days. It would involve a large force of aircraft, helicopters and commandos, initially attacking Scud targets at the H2 and H3 airbases in western Iraq. Cheney was horrified. The coalition might just have been able to survive a limited Israeli retaliation – perhaps a salvo of its Jericho 2 missiles being fired at Iraq. But what Arens was talking about was a sustained offensive in the air and on the ground.

Fortunately for the Bush administration, it held most of the cards. Arens needed the American IFF 'friend or foe' identification codes which would prevent Israeli aircraft being mistakenly shot down by the allies in the congested skies over Iraq. The request was refused. Arens then asked if the allies could suspend their missions over the Scud launch-zone, to give the Israeli Air Force a free run? Again, the answer was no.

What Arens did not know then – and what has only emerged in the research for this book – was that if his warplanes had been sent to Iraq without Washington's approval, nothing would have been put in their way. In the air operations room in Riyadh, Lieutenant-General Chuck Horner had privately decided that, should the Israelis choose to attack, he would simply pull all the allied aircraft out. He knew his AWACS early-warning planes would spot the Israeli jets taking off and would then track their flight-paths. Horner guessed that they would fly over Jordan, violating its airspace and provoking a token response. He believed the Jordanians would have had a few of their fighters shot down and then

ALL NECESSARY MEANS

given up. Once the Israeli planes reached Iraq they would have had the skies to themselves. Horner told us:

> All we'd have done when we saw them coming is pull our forces out and let them do whatever they wanted. In some ways, they had a legitimate right to attack someone who was attacking them ... I was prepared to pull my force out anywhere I had to.

So, the Israelis needn't have worried about identification codes after all.

What most worried Horner was that the Israelis might choose to get to Iraq not through Jordan, but via Saudi Arabia. That would have complicated his plans enormously. He thought the Saudis, whose planes were integrated into allied operations, would probably have tried to defend their airspace against the 'Zionist enemy'. Horner, in charge of all allied flights, would then have found himself in an impossible position. 'We'd have had political decisions as to whether to shoot or not to shoot, and that would have been difficult.'

In any case, Horner didn't think the Israeli Air Force would have done as good a job as his own pilots. He believed their technology didn't match that of the F-15Es and Stealths operating in western Iraq at that time, though he knew Israeli Air Force generals would 'bristle' to hear him say that. Their view was that Israeli pilots had more combat experience, and had even trained for the very mission of hunting down Iraq's missiles. They also thought that their pilots, motivated by the threat to their own country, would be prepared to fly lower and take greater risks – especially if they were assisted by Israeli commandos deployed on the ground.

For so long sensing themselves besieged, the Israelis had made a tradition of retaliation, driven by the instinct of self-preservation. They had also come to depend on their strength alone for protection. But this time, it was different. To respond would play into Saddam's hands. It would force the Arab members of the coalition, unusually sharing the same enemy as Israel, to review their positions.

For the first time in the history of the Jewish state, logic demanded restraint. Not only would it allow the allies to continue their bombardment of her most powerful adversary in the Middle East; it would also leave the West indebted to Israel. The policy of restraint stuck – but not without a good deal of effort by the allies.

Soon after the first attacks, President Bush rang the Israeli Prime Minister, Yitzhak Shamir, offering him Patriot missile batteries. Before the war, Shamir had stubbornly rejected a similar offer. Although Israel's own missile defence system, the Arrow, would not be ready until 1995, the plan until then was to tackle the missile threat with pre-emptive air strikes. Saddam's Scuds showed up the weakness of that strategy. Now Shamir relented and American Patriot teams were allowed into Israel.

The Patriot seemed like a saviour. At last, Tel Aviv and Haifa, the cities most regularly under attack, had some defence. But research has shown that the Patriots may have had little more than psychological value – and may even have done more harm than good.

Dr Theodore Postol of the Massachusetts Institute of Technology studied the Scud attacks in detail and produced a startling conclusion: that after the Patriots arrived, the number of homes damaged increased three times, while the number of injuries rose by almost half. The explanation, according to Postol, was that in hitting a Scud, a Patriot merely broke up the Iraqi missile more thoroughly, scattering debris over a much wider area than if it had been left untouched. Worse, with the Patriot disintegrating as well, the amount of shrapnel in the air was actually increased. Sometimes, the Patriots also chased the wrong bit of the Scud, whose warhead would separate from the main body of the missile before landing.

At the time, none of this seemed to matter: the diplomatic objective was being achieved. Just as the Scuds were being used by Saddam to tempt the Israelis into the war, so the Patriot was being used by George Bush to keep them out of it. It was doing its job.

Nobody knew how long the threat would last. Schwarzkopf had rashly promised King Fahd that Iraq only had two to three dozen mobile Scud launchers and, in an early televised briefing, he claimed that 16 had already been destroyed. In Downing Street, officials watched his performance and were incredulous. They thought he was being wildly optimistic; certainly the figures they'd been getting from Saudi Arabia were in 'a different ball-park' and they said to themselves that Schwarzkopf was 'way off mark'.

It later emerged that, in fact, Saddam had at least 150 launchers. Before the war, he'd been manufacturing crude but adequate systems, which the spy satellites had failed to detect. At the end of the campaign, Schwarzkopf blamed the advice he'd been given by his experts. 'We went into this war with intelligence estimates which I have since come to believe were grossly inaccurate.'

Saudi Arabia was the target for about half the total of 81 Scuds that were fired. Here, the Patriots proved more effective than in Israel because they had much smaller, more closely-defined areas to defend: military bases and key districts rather than whole cities. There were also more of them. That was because the previous July, Schwarzkopf had endured an inordinately long briefing on the Patriot system from his army commander, Lieutenant-General John Yeosock. It convinced him though, and made a critical difference.

Such was the success in Saudi Arabia of the Patriot 'Scudbuster', that people began to get blasé about the risks. The Saudi commander, Prince Khaled bin Sultan, only put on a gas mask once. It was when he and General Schwarzkopf were giving King Fahd a briefing in his palace. The sirens warning of a Scud attack were sounded but the King carried on talking.

'Please, Your Majesty,' said Khaled, 'you've got to go down to the basement.' The King did so, and Khaled felt obliged to reach for his mask.

On another occasion when Riyadh was under attack, Schwarzkopf didn't even bother to get out of the shower. His right-hand man, Chuck Horner, was equally phlegmatic. While everyone else in his 'Current Ops' room would clamber into their chemical warfare suits and put on their gas masks, Horner wouldn't bother. It wasn't that he had no faith in the equipment, it was just that some of the local workmen in the air force building had no protective gear at all.

'I didn't want panic,' he explained later. 'I didn't want them to feel they'd been left to die.'

Horner also failed to take the immunisation shots because, curiously, there weren't enough to go around. He thought he should show leadership by making a personal sacrifice, though he wasn't entirely comfortable with his decision. 'I felt kind of goosey about it. I thought I was stupid personally, but there are some things you must do. I thought I was dumb as dirt!'

It wasn't only the generals who were guilty of adopting a cavalier attitude towards the Scuds. The journalists – among them one of the authors – soon no longer ran to the basement shelter when the air-raid sirens wailed. Instead, they sprinted up to the roof of their hotel, the Hyatt Regency, just across the road from the War Room, to watch the 'Scudbusting show'. One night they saw an entire, 30-foot Scud fuselage land intact in Riyadh city centre. By the time film crews arrived, American and Saudi troops were nervously guarding the battered missile in a side-street, as if they'd captured a rare but dangerous animal which they weren't quite sure how to handle. It was still smouldering and although the fumes were pungent, it had been declared 'chemical free'.

Close up, the Scud looked antiquated and rather Heath Robinson, with the most rudimentary wiring. Nothing exemplified the war's technology gap more than the difference between this decrepit piece of piping and the computer-guided Patriot. They were more than a generation apart.

The Scud was a weapon that was much feared before the war, and much laughed at during it. 'Scud' was NATO's codename for what Moscow had originally called the SS-1 missile, first seen in 1957, a descendant of the Nazis' V2 rocket. Ironically, the next generation of German rocket scientists then helped Iraq to develop several bastardised versions with longer ranges. They achieved this by stretching the original missile body and by reducing the war-load to carry more fuel. The result was the 'al-Hussein' missile, which could travel double the usual distance, some 400 miles, and the 'al-Abbas', with a maximum range of 550 miles. But the longer the reach, the lighter had to be the warhead and some only carried the same amount of explosive as a standard bomb.

On 25 February that was enough. One of the last missiles the Iraqis fired fell by chance on a barracks in Dhahran and killed 28 American troops. The high-technology which had served the allies so well had suffered a rare, though disastrous, failure. The nearby Patriot crews of Alpha and Bravo batteries were on duty as normal that night – but knew there was a problem. Bravo battery's radar had been shut down for maintenance work. No one was too worried because, in theory, Alpha battery was capable of covering Bravo's sector of air-space as well as its own.

Four hours later, that assumption was put to the test when the Iraqis launched a Scud at Dhahran. Patriot batteries further north detected it and thought Alpha battery could cope. It couldn't. Deep in the Patriot system's sophisticated computer system, something went wrong. One calculation among thousands was incorrect – the Scud never showed up on the screen. It was similar to a failure that had occurred five days earlier in Israel, and new, corrected software had been rushed out to Saudi Arabia. It had arrived the day before but wasn't to be delivered to the Patriot batteries until the day after.

Alpha battery may also have been in use for too long. It had been at work for 100 hours when the normal stretch would be 14 hours. In addition, this was a freak Scud: its altitude, speed and angle of approach made it difficult to detect and it was the only one of the war not to break up before hitting the ground. Since Alpha battery didn't see it, no Patriot was fired to stop it and in the converted warehouse just outside Dhahran 25 men and three women were killed, another 97 injured. They had just arrived in Saudi Arabia and believed that, as the war reached its climax, there was only a slim chance of them seeing action, let alone dying.

The troops were part of the huge logistics team run by Lieutenant-General Gus Pagonis, who was heartbroken. The soldiers had come from near his home town of Charleroi in Pennsylvania. Pagonis described it as 'the worst moment of the war'. Central Command's press officers announced that the troops at Al Khobar had died because the Scud had broken up during its flight; they hardly mentioned the Patriots. The truth, as it later turned out after an investigation, was precisely the opposite: the Scud was unique because it had stayed intact. It had worked, while the Patriot had not. Until then the American 'anti-missile missile' had been hailed as the great success story of the war, along with other miracles of modern technology like Stealth and smart bombs. But suddenly, the wonder weapon looked a little less wonderful.

The American commanders in Riyadh were fond of saying that the only surprise about Saddam's strategy was that there were no surprises. It wasn't quite true. Some of the moves made by the Iraqi president wrong-footed the allies. When he ordered the best of his air force to flee to Iran, it caused consternation in the Black Hole planning room. Although, the man in charge there, Brigadier-General Buster Glosson, had correctly predicted the planes would be evacuated, he had banked on them flying to Jordan. That's where they'd been sent in 1973, during the war against Israel, and in 1980, in the early days of the war against Iran. Jordan, once again, seemed the most likely location since King Hussein was one of Saddam's very few sympathisers in the region. But on 26 January, American AWACS radar operators could hardly believe their eyes: the blips on the screen showed a large number of Iraqi aircraft flying to Iran, the country they'd been fighting until only three years earlier. Among the first to join the exodus were twenty transport planes. They were followed by the best of Saddam's fighters and bombers: the highly capable Soviet MiG-29s, Su-24s and French Mirage F-1s. Two Ilyushin-76 early-warning aircraft also fled.

Buster Glosson wanted to stop them getting away. He was happy enough for the planes to be out of the war, but no one could guarantee that they wouldn't attack the allies from Iran. It was unlikely, but conceivable, and the commanders in Riyadh, desperate to avoid allied casualties, preferred to leave nothing to chance. Glosson's problem was that because he'd assumed the Iraqis would go to Jordan instead, none of his planes was in a position to intercept them. The F-15s weren't close enough and for a moment Glosson conceded defeat. 'There's not much I can do about this,' he admitted. Saddam's jets could take off from bases around Baghdad and, flying at low level for just 68 miles, would reach Iran. One Iraqi, interviewed later, saw the jet crews sitting in their cockpits for hours on the ground, waiting until they were certain the sky was clear of allied aircraft. Then they would make their dash to Iran.

ALL NECESSARY MEANS

Glosson's team in the Black Hole came up with several ideas. One planner suggested running a special patrol of allied planes all the way from Saudi Arabia, over eastern Iraq and up to Turkey. They could refuel there, and then patrol the border on the way back as well. The trouble was that the operation would need a constant cycle of 32 fighters, in eight batches of four. It was impractical, Glosson reluctantly decided.

Finally, he devised his own solution. He called in the three wing-commanders in charge of F-15C fighters, which are equipped with exceptionally sophisticated radar. Glosson wanted to use them in a special 'Combat Air Patrol', or CAP. There was nothing unusual in that but when Glosson spelt out where he wanted them to do it – over Baghdad – the wing-commanders were astonished. That was exactly where Iraqi anti-aircraft fire and SAM missiles were at their most dangerous.

'We're going to do what?' gasped the three wing-commanders.

'We're going to CAP over Baghdad,' Glosson repeated, firmly.

It would involve four planes, with their pilots flying gruelling missions up to nine hours long. Glosson knew it would wear everyone out, but he pressed ahead with the idea, and after a week he had succeeded in stemming the flow. Now, not a single Iraqi plane was trying to escape. 'Well, I guess there's a chance that maybe they're not going to do this any more,' he said confidently.

But the patrols had been grinding down his pilots, who were flying their nine hours, then returning to base to snatch some food and some sleep, before taking off again for another nine hours. 'I'd better give them a break,' Glosson told his staff. 'We'll stop it tomorrow.' It was a mistake because 23 Iraqi planes immediately took advantage of the break in the patrolling and fled east. The following day another 19 flew to Iran. Glosson had no choice but to order his exhausted pilots back into the air to resume their patrols between Baghdad and the border. He didn't dare let them stop until the end of the war: 'I wasn't going to give Saddam a second chance to prove he could still take a few aeroplanes off.'

Glosson's superior, Chuck Horner, was pleased that the F-15Cs had shot down as many Iraqis as they had, given that it was such a short run to the border. Two even managed to down four Iraqis on one mission. But Central Command was still puzzled by what was going on. Major-General

Royal Moore of the US Marines came up with one theory. Saddam, he decided, was getting his youngest, least experienced airmen to fly out his best planes. Moore was struck by the terrible panic of the Iraqi pilots, 'landing on roads, running out of gas, having to be led into airfields. The shoot-downs that occurred, they just didn't move at all. These guys just flew along like they were saturated with what they were doing, and couldn't look outside.' Moore was convinced Saddam wanted to hold on to his more experienced men. 'They were saving the older pilots for whenever the great air war was going to take place.'

But other generals in Riyadh thought that at least some of the aircraft might have been flown by defectors. One explanation was that they were fleeing after an unsuccessful coup attempt against Saddam that ended with the execution of the air force commander. At first, that was the view of Lieutenant-General Horner. But when the planes flew out for a second day running, he changed his mind. 'If those are defectors,' he told his colleagues, 'every pilot in the Iraqi Air Force would be chained to the bedpost.'

The escape of these planes puzzled many Iraqis. Even after the war, a 28-year-old helicopter pilot, who'd been trained at a private flying school in Cumbria, was still trying to work out what had happened at his airbase in Basra:

Some fighter pilots came to the base. After two days they went away as mysteriously as they came, and we later heard they had gone to Iran. It wasn't until after the ceasefire that I saw one of them again – he came back through the base on his way to Baghdad. He said they'd been instructed to go to Iran and dump their planes. This pilot was adamant that he'd been told to do it and said he hadn't wanted to.

As for Chuck Horner, he was well aware that many 'naysayers', as he called them, were warning that Saddam could attack the allies from Iran. The allied navies were particularly worried that their warships, especially the American aircraft carriers, could become targets for Iraqi planes approaching from an unexpected direction. But Horner was absolutely

72

certain that wouldn't happen. 'I never believed that. Iran would never allow that. The price for them would have been too high.'

Certainly, Iran's President, Hashemi Rafsanjani, improved his credentials with the West by refusing to release the aircraft. At the same time, he kept them as valuable bargaining-chips in his quest for reparations from Saddam over the Iran–Iraq war. It's been suggested that when the two countries signed an agreement the previous November to end the conflict between them, there was also a secret protocol, in which Rafsanjani said he would let Iraqi planes seek sanctuary in his country. But if that protocol went on to promise that the aircraft could take off again whenever they wanted, Saddam Hussein was double-crossed. Publicly, the Iranians said they had only about twenty of the aircraft; the allies said the real figure was 137. Saddam had succeeded in saving the best of his air force, but getting it back would prove much more difficult.

Only once did the Iraqis mount an air attack on allied territory. Predictably, it ended in disaster. It happened shortly after a report appeared saying that Iraq's parliament, meeting secretly in a Baghdad bunker, had decided the air force should carry out suicide raids on aircraft carriers in the Gulf. According to American generals, the Iraqi plan was 'a good one'. They would confuse allied radar by sending one group of planes towards Iran and, at exactly the same time, send some Mirage F-1 fighter-bombers south to Saudi Arabia, one of them carrying an Exocet missile. Their mission was to attack one of the allied ships in the Gulf and, had they succeeded, it would have been, in the words of one American commander, 'a political statement' from which Saddam would have no doubt sought to get maximum mileage.

But in practice, the plan failed. A sharp-eyed naval officer on one of the AWACS early-warning aircraft managed to spot the Mirages, as they headed south at high speed and low altitude. If this was a suicide mission, it finished not in martyrdom, but in humiliation. Two of the Mirages were shot down by one Saudi pilot, Captain Ayed al-Shamrani, who had been on patrol with the allies that day. He was proclaimed a Top Gun hero by his own country's press and the international media. Later, a story was leaked from the Pentagon that he had been 'given' the two kills by the AWACS controller, who allegedly 'waved off' Canadian and American fighters already queueing up to shoot down the unfortunate Iraqis. The suggestion was that the Americans had engineered a clever political ploy, boosting the morale of their Saudi hosts, improving their image, and enhancing their contribution to the air campaign.

It sounded quite plausible but allied air commanders claim the explanation wasn't true. They say the AWACS controller, on discovering that the American Navy planes which were on patrol in the area were not immediately available, called in Captain al-Shamrani, who was on back-up patrol with another Saudi F-15. Commanders insist that the Saudis were not given preferential treatment. They would be one week later though, when once again Saddam tried to launch a counter-attack – this time, on the ground.

I t was when the Iraqi troops were given chicken to eat that they knew they would soon be ordered onto the offensive. Until then, they had been living on bread, water and tinned milk. They were being fattened up for the great battle of Khafji. There could hardly have been an easier target: a seaside town just a few miles inside Saudi Arabia, which had been evacuated because it was within range of Iraqi artillery. Its only inhabitants were a few Saudi and Qatari troops, and a friendly bunch of a dozen Kuwaiti soldiers, who had built themselves an extraordinary bunker in the middle of the town. Behind their sandbags, they had an international telephone line which they once used to call Kuwaiti oil executives in London. The soldiers were reporting on the progress of the oil slick along the coast, and describing its consistency so that experts could calculate its type and from which terminal it might have come. But just as Kuwaiti troops saw no point in putting up a fight when their country was invaded, so they judged it useless to resist on the moonlit night of 29 January when Iraqi tanks rolled forward into Khafji. Following the example set by their emir on 2 August, the Kuwaitis jumped into their private cars, which were parked next to the bunker, and fled for their lives.

The first the outside world knew of the 'invasion' was the next day

ALL NECESSARY MEANS

when an Egyptian journalist telephoned the town's Beach Hotel only to hear two Iraqi soldiers answer her call. 'We believe in Arabism and Saddam Hussein,' they said defiantly. 'See you in Jerusalem!' To the acute embarrassment of the allies, they had to admit that Khafji had been occupied. It was one of a series of probing attacks along a 50-mile stretch of the border. It looked as if this was either a determined effort to gather desperately-needed intelligence about allied troop deployments, or a bid to provoke the allies into a ground war before they were ready.

More likely, it was an attempt by Saddam to show the world that he could fight. For the past fortnight, the allies had set the pace; now, by claiming the advances into Saudi Arabia as a military triumph for Islam over the corruption of the West, Saddam was making the headlines. As one intelligence analyst put it, 'he's after an honourable bloodying'. It was a view shared by Lieutenant-General Sir Peter de la Billière. He had always feared that Saddam would try to inflict casualties on a scale comparable to the losses in the Falklands War on the British landing ships, *Sir Galahad* and *Sir Tristan*, to 'enhance his position in the Arab world'.

Now Khafji would show that some of Saddam's troops were prepared to take on the coalition. Although these were conscript soldiers, not from the Republican Guard, they were to surprise – and embarrass – the allies with their tenacity. Most of their incursions, to the west, had been at anonymous map co-ordinates, but Khafji was more than a strip of desert. Empty or not, it was a Saudi Arabian town under Iraqi control. It made a mockery of the original reason for the deployment of allied forces to Saudi Arabia, to defend its soil under Operation Desert Shield.

General Schwarzkopf inaccurately dismissed Khafji as a 'village' and insisted that the attack was 'about as significant as a mosquito on an elephant'. But inevitably Saddam played it for all it was worth. An enthusiastic Iraqi soldier told Mother of Battles Radio how the allied troops had 'fled like women and like shepherds wandering aimlessly in the desert'. Saddam's newspapers reported how the 'battlements of atheism' had been stormed. His sympathisers in Jordan and Israel's occupied territories lapped it up. Khafji had become synonymous with Arab heroism; for the allies, this was not how the script for the ground war was supposed to start.

Undoubtedly, they had been careless. Khafji was within easy reach of Iraq's frontline troops yet Schwarzkopf's planners had left it poorly defended and temptingly vulnerable. They had failed to consider its potential propaganda value, leaving it to the protection of a few inexperienced soldiers. Now Schwarzkopf had to act quickly to stop Saddam exploiting his 'victory' but he couldn't simply send in his own troops. This was Saudi soil which had been violated, and the Saudis had to be the ones who would 'liberate' it. In the words of Brigadier-General Buster Glosson, 'there had to be some political statements made there'.

US Marines around Khafji kept their distance, with platoon commander Captain John Borth admitting, 'we've been pretty much ordered to stay away from the town'. But the Saudis made pretty heavy weather of it; their battle to eject the Iraqis took about 36 hours and they lost 18 men to the enemy's 30. Curiously, a British military spokesman announced that, in fact, 300 Iraqis had died but later claimed it was just a typing error: a nought had been added by mistake. It was an unlikely explanation because only the previous day Downing Street sources had put the Iraqi death toll at 'several hundred'. Some suggested that was a more credible figure but that the Saudis felt uncomfortable confirming they had killed so many brother Arabs.

To those who criticised the Saudi performance in Khafji, Schwarzkopf pointed out that they hadn't fought a 'major war in 1400 years', and certainly their leader, Prince Khaled bin Sultan, seemed to be less than an inspiration in command. He was trained at Sandhurst, but he never shone as a strategist and his enemies put his high rank down to the fact that he's the King's nephew. Still, Prince Khaled tried to keep in shape during the war; he took all his physical fitness equipment to allied headquarters in Riyadh, to offset the effects of the enormous appetite which he shared with Schwarzkopf; 'when we get nervous we both eat, and we both love to eat'. To ease the tension he would watch a comedy video every night. After Khafji, the portly general was obviously relieved and swaggered into the Hyatt Regency Hotel to brief reporters on his victory. The truth was that he had relied almost entirely on American artillery and air power.

At one stage, while Prince Khaled had been just outside the town try-

ALL NECESSARY MEANS

ing to win it back, he was frightened the Iraqis might advance, cut off him and his troops from their support, and 'annihilate' them. An alarmed Prince Khaled got on the line to Riyadh, calling up the air operations room. First he spoke to his own air force commander, who then handed the phone to his American counterpart, Chuck Horner.

'I'm worried,' said Khaled, anxious for reassurance that American air power would back him up. Horner calmed him down. 'We'll keep them off you,' he promised.

The two men discussed logistical details. Then Horner laughed and said: 'Khaled, I want you to keep one thing in mind.'

'What's that?'

'You're in a bunker in Khafji, and I'm here in Riyadh. It's easy for me to be calm!'

In the end the Iraqis paid dearly for their adventure. Because they were on the move, they became easy prey for American warplanes. In one of the more tasteless analogies of the war, Lieutenant-Colonel Dick White said that it was like turning on the lights in the kitchen at night when 'the cockroaches start scurrying'. As Iraqi forces manoeuvred on their side of the border, whole columns of armour were destroyed by A-10 tankbusters, firing up to 70 shells a second. Intercepted Iraqi communications were reporting a substantial number of dead, injured and missing. Iraq's formidable 3rd corps had suffered badly. Brigadier-General Butch Neal couldn't help wondering: 'What did they have to show for it?' Nothing, he concluded, but he'd misunderstood the nature of Saddam's strategy.

America is angry' said George Bush when captured pilots were paraded on Iraqi television, speaking like zombies and denouncing the war. Saddam must have thought that, like the sight of body bags, the images of captured airmen would turn western opinion against the war. Yet again he was wrong; the pictures only served to strengthen international resolve. Everyone assumed that the airmen's cuts and bruises were the work of sadistic Iraqi torturers. Lieutenant Jeffrey Zaun, for example, had been 'slapped around', yet most of his wounds were in fact 'flail injuries', caused by ejecting from his plane at 500 miles per hour. Then, when he realised he was going to be put in front of a television camera, he beat himself up in the hope that would stop the Iraqis using him for their propaganda show. 'I hit myself in the nose and in the face as hard as I could stand it, when I knew they were taking me to the TV station.' It didn't deter the Iraqis, but when he found out they wanted to film him again, Zaun hit himself even harder. 'I beat my right eye until I couldn't see out of it. I tried to break my nose.'

In his forced confession, the lieutenant said that his country had wrongfully attacked 'the peaceful people of Iraq'. But his time in Iraq had given him a slightly different perspective on the war, as he later disclosed to his local newspaper back home in Nevada: 'I don't ever want to kill anybody again. This country didn't get to see the cost of the war; I did. They didn't see Iraqi mothers getting killed.'

Many of the captured pilots didn't have to make it look like they'd been physically abused – they had. After Flight Lieutenant Rupert Clark of the RAF was shot down, he was caught by armed Iraqi farmers and taken to the airfield he'd just been trying to bomb. Later he was interrogated and tortured. When the war was over, he described his ordeal.

I was whipped, probably with a whip made of electric heavy-duty cable. These beatings averaged about 30 lashes over my legs, my feet, my lower body, my hands. I was lying on the ground and this bastard would just come up and start thrashing me.

The interrogators seemed to take care not to hurt Clark above the shoulders, in case they wanted to put him on TV as well. Even so, one of his fingers and a leg were broken. 'I probably resembled a steak which someone had been beating with a hammer for 24 hours.'

Another Flight Lieutenant, David Waddington, drifted in and out of consciousness during his interrogations. But the technical questions he was asked about his RAF Tornado were naive and ill-informed, and Waddington managed to provide answers to the Iraqis which they could have found in newspaper and magazine articles anyway.

ALL NECESSARY MEANS

For the pilots still in the air, there was a new hazard – the choking black smoke that was turning noon into night, and reducing the sun to a faint glow through the swirling soot. Saddam had carried out his threat to torch the oil wells of Kuwait. It was an act of spite like that of a spoilt child who can't have what he wants, an act of utter pointlessness. Like looting the car showrooms and palaces in Kuwait City, it was delinquent vandalism, which was neither good propaganda nor significantly disruptive to Schwarzkopf's war plan. Flying through the dense black clouds, Lieutenant Mark Davies had to turn off the light in the cockpit of his Lynx helicopter just so that he could see his instrument panel: 'It was like going into a cave – darker and darker the further we went, until it turned black.' An American pilot had another analogy: 'It's what I imagined hell would look like.'

It was back in August, only a few days after the Iraqis invaded, that they had started laying anti-personnel mines around the oil wells and planning how best to blow them up. With oilfields the size of Kuwait's, it was no easy task but they went about it with patient determination. After some experiments, they decided to use Soviet-made plastic explosives, which were packed against the wellheads, with a detonating wire leading out to a bunker a safe distance away in the sand dunes.

Allied commanders could only look at the satellite photographs and despair; there was nothing they could do to stop the sabotage. But they did have some success in foiling Saddam's first strike of 'eco-terrorism'. In the last week of January, he had ordered oil to be spilled into the waters of the Gulf from the Sea Island Terminal, with disastrous effects. Schwarzkopf asked Buster Glosson if there was any way to stop it. Glosson said that he could drop a 2000-lb bomb and 'blow away' the pumping facility. 'I don't know anything about oil,' he admitted, 'but it seems to me that would have to stop the flow.'

Oil experts were consulted and agreed that the plan would work, but first Washington and London had to approve. To Glosson's immense frustration, it took them two days to give the go-ahead. 'We sat there and waited.' As the minutes and hours ticked by, more oil gushed out, threatening the fragile ecology of the Gulf. Glosson accepted that it had to be a political decision because the target was in Kuwait and there was an outside chance bombing could simply make the oil spill worse. Even so he was disheartened by the delay because he knew the mission could be accomplished quickly and the oil stopped. 'From the time they said "do it", we shut it down in three hours.'

Still, the world feared the worst from Saddam. The greatest danger was that he would make use of his chemical arsenal: in the summer after the war, it emerged that Saddam had no fewer than 46 000 chemical weapons, including bombs, rockets, grenades, artillery shells, and – most significantly perhaps – missile warheads. Quite why he had never used this vast stockpile against the allies may never be known. Perhaps he took to heart the threats that such an attack would provoke a coalition response even more devastating than that which had already been unleashed on Iraq.

Yet, while Saddam's Scuds may have failed and his air force vanished, some allied commanders still talked of the possibility of an 'Air Tet', a massive Iraqi air strike reminiscent of the Viet Cong's devastating Tet Offensive against American forces in Vietnam. Before the war, the fear had been that Saddam would make good his threats to unleash a wave of international terrorism against the West. It didn't happen. In many ways, Saddam failed to live up to expectations. In all the rhetoric, 'the Butcher of Baghdad' had been portrayed as a much more formidable enemy than he proved in practice.

He did, however, manage to hold on to power and for a man afflicted with megalomania, nothing could have been more important than that. He survived. Of course, the allies always insisted that he personally was not a target – but if he'd been killed, it would have been a 'right bonus', in the words of Sir Patrick Hine, Britain's Joint Forces Commander. The allies were hoping that they might catch him in one of his bunkers. But Hine and the other commanders were constantly frustrated: 'We just didn't know where he was. He's just very adept at looking after himself. He moves around constantly, and his programme is kept on a very tight hold.' Only once, it seems, did the allies come close to succeeding. It happened when Saddam was being driven from Basra back to Baghdad. Both

ALL NECESSARY MEANS

ends of his convoy were bombed and several of his security guards were killed. But Saddam himself was in one of the middle vehicles and escaped uninjured.

'That's the only instance I knew of that we might have got close,' Brigadier General Butch Neal said, a little ruefully.

Saddam was an almost impossible target. He had doubles who looked almost exactly like him and acted as decoys; he would also hide in residential areas which he knew the allies would avoid. As long as the unpredictable Saddam remained in power, the allied campaign would have to continue – and with weapons both seen and unseen.

Chapter 4
THE INVISIBLE WAR

'I'll tell you who destroyed the Scuds; it was the British SAS. They were fabulous.'

John Major, British Prime Minister, May 1991.

General H. Norman Schwarzkopf, on allied Special Forces, 27 February 1991.

'We put them deep into enemy territory . . . they let us know what was going on out there. They were our eyes.'

He had a swarthy complexion and looked like he'd probably been born in India or Pakistan. Every day he would wander into one of the most-closely guarded rooms in Riyadh, the air operations centre, and then, a few hours later, drift away again. The strange thing was that no one appeared to know his name, not even the most senior American generals he was working with. But it didn't seem to matter and he had no problems breezing through the elaborate security because everybody there knew he had a vital role to play. They all thought he was 'a neat guy, really a good guy'. It was just that they weren't sure exactly what to call him.

He was an officer in the British Special Air Service and his job was to direct the teams operating deep behind enemy lines, co-ordinating their movements with allied warplanes. Lieutenant-General Chuck Horner considered it 'an extreme pleasure working with him'. He usually turned up at four or five o'clock in the afternoon and stayed until eight or nine at night. It was during the hours of darkness that most of the Scuds were attacked, and before sunset the 'neat guy' from the SAS would

ALL NECESSARY MEANS

come in to discuss that night's missions.

His regiment is as famous for its secrecy as for its courage, and the public's first tantalising hint about its role in the Gulf came from the Prime Minister's off-the-cuff remark – made at a private dinner, and subsequently leaked. Throughout the war, John Major had been given his own personal briefings on SAS operations. While most details of Desert Storm were shared with the whole War Cabinet, the activities of the Special Forces were considered too sensitive to be reported to anyone but the Prime Minister. Even when the Gulf honours were later announced, the awards to 52 men from Britain's Special Forces Group – the SAS, the SBS and other related units – were only explained in four terse paragraphs in the *London Gazette*.

In his report, as overall British commander, Air Chief Marshal Sir Patrick Hine described their contribution to the allied campaign as out of all proportion to their numbers. What Hine did not reveal in his account was that the first SAS teams were inserted into Iraq as early as 2 September 1990, exactly one month after Saddam's invasion of Kuwait. On that same day, the Iraqi authorities announced a limit on the length of time foreign journalists could stay; the men from the SAS would remain as long as they chose. Two teams had been flown in at night by helicopter and set themselves up 20 kilometres south of Baghdad. They probably sheltered in 'safe houses' and lived as Iraqis. The undercover soldiers had been selected for their fluency in Arabic, and for their physical appearances. The ideal, we were told, was 'not too tall – in fact a bit short and stocky; the last thing you want is to be noticeable'.

One of their tasks was to establish the precise locations of potential targets and to relay the co-ordinates back to allied headquarters in Riyadh. On the secret planning maps, each target would be marked with a symbol – a triangle, square, hexagon or circle – indicating the strength of the intelligence about it. According to the system, targets marked by circles were the ones about which the allies had the most solid information – usually confirmed by SAS men on the ground. 'The nicest symbol to have is a circle,' it was explained to us. 'The circle is the most positive, and if you have a circle there, pilots have a nice, warm, comfortable feeling of certainty.' According to one source, by 17 January, allied planning maps were marked with 'dozens of circles' around Baghdad and Basra.

The SAS also wanted a role in the war itself. The stumbling block was General Schwarzkopf's hostility to Special Forces. In the United States, although they are held in high esteem by the public, they are derided as 'the snake-eaters' by the rest of the army. Disasters like Jimmy Carter's abortive attempt to rescue the American hostages from Iran in 1980 had done nothing to improve their reputation. 'They can't make up their minds whether they love us or hate us; whether they're afraid of us or want to work with us,' said a former Green Beret, Major Andy Messing, who was in Saudi Arabia during the war.

But the SAS had an advantage over their American colleagues. Britain's commander in the Gulf, Lieutenant-General Sir Peter de la Billière, was one of their own, an SAS veteran, both in the field and in command, in Oman, Malaya, Aden and the Falklands. His exploits and daring had made him Britain's most decorated soldier. Now he became his old regiment's lobbyist in the War Room. If Schwarzkopf's early career was every bit the straightforward infantryman, de la Billière's was every bit the secretive commando.

'The fact that everybody knew I had a Special Forces background lent weight to any argument that I presented in their favour,' Sir Peter told us, in rare public remarks about the SAS. He hadn't wanted to win them a leading role in Desert Storm just out of a sense of nostalgia. 'Special Forces are a very useful club in the bag but I'm not into finding them jobs just for the sake of it. I am perhaps more likely to find them a job than other people because I know from a great deal of experience what their capabilities are and what they can do.'

Even so, Schwarzkopf still took some persuading that they were suitable for this war. 'He had a reputation for having reservations about the employment of Special Forces,' recalled de la Billière, who never established why Schwarzkopf felt so uneasy about them. Nor did Sir Patrick Hine, who had also noticed that Schwarzkopf's experience of American Special Forces 'had not been an entirely happy one'. Not surprisingly, when it came to considering what Britain could offer in this field, Schwarzkopf was 'a bit suspicious', according to Hine. But on the other hand, as de la Billière discovered, 'he didn't know the British Special

Forces at all – he'd never had anything to do with them'. Unlike the Americans, they were starting with a clean sheet.

Schwarzkopf allowed British commanders to give him a full, detailed briefing on SAS training and capabilities. He wanted to be sure that they could make a useful contribution, de la Billière explained to us.

> He and I were 100 per cent in agreement that there was no question of zapping off Special Forces so they could have a 'good war' – and then finishing up with a load of casualties from some mission that was quite useless. What was necessary was to convince Schwarzkopf that British Special Forces had a worthwhile role and they weren't just going off to have a fight, for no better reason than battle honours.

Schwarzkopf was worried about having to mount a large-scale rescue operation if the SAS ran into problems. His experience in Vietnam had shown him the heavy strain put on conventional forces by special operations going wrong. Hine recalls that he 'didn't want to find himself in the middle of a land war having to divert a division or two to get the SAS out of trouble'. Hine and others had assured him that, 'that's not the way we operate, they can look after themselves'.

According to Hine, 'once he'd had all that explained, and had his questions answered, he was happy enough to use them'. Schwarzkopf agreed to make the SAS an integral part of Desert Storm. He was 'prepared to cut them into the pack'.

It meant that the first teams despatched to Iraq to hunt for Scuds were British, not American. Brigadier-General Buster Glosson, the chief allied air planner, thought that this was because the SAS were the first to 'work up a concept' for tracking and destroying the missiles. But it still needed de la Billière and Hine to push the idea, and Schwarzkopf to accept it. In fact, one of Schwarzkopf's qualities was that he regarded the coalition as a single unit; he would take the best that was on offer whatever country was involved, and, in this case, he thought it was Britain. His own 'snake-eaters', though, couldn't help feeling overlooked.

If Schwarzkopf thought he'd taken a gamble, it didn't take long for him to realise it had paid off. Hine has disclosed to us that by 26 January – only nine days into the war – no more Scuds were fired from the sector of western Iraq assigned to the SAS, a tract of land covering hundreds of square miles. 'They were spending most of their time on Scuds,' said Hine, 'because by the time they were inserted, the Scud was a major concern.' It was at this early stage of the campaign that allied commanders were under the greatest pressure to keep Israel out of the war. But Hine told us that the SAS also found time for different missions: 'They would take on other targets on the basis of opportunity.' Those targets included command centres, radar installations and surface-to-air missile sites.

The Gulf crisis was taking the Special Air Service full circle, back to the Middle East where it had been founded half a century earlier in the Second World War by an enterprising young officer, David Stirling. His Long Range Desert Group carried out secret attacks on German airfields in North Africa. His successors had become renowned for their dramatic ending of the Iranian embassy siege in London, for helping to recapture the Falkland Islands, and for their covert operations in Northern Ireland. Now the SAS was undertaking what would be its biggest operation by British Special Forces since 1945. They were enduring climatic extremes, from fog to sandstorms, from desert heat to freezing cold. The missions were long and arduous; some patrols had to operate in Iraqi territory for well over a month. Not all of them came out alive.

The SAS had a variety of means for entering enemy territory. Most spectacular, according to some insiders, were their motorised hang-gliders, which could either be dropped out of the back of a Hercules aircraft or could simply take off from northern Saudi Arabia. With a range of about 150 kilometres, 'they were just the stuff for reconnaissance around the border'. Secret armies across the world have been working on this skill: the Soviets are said to have perfected it with a hang-glider that can be packed away into a bag, which a commando can carry in one hand, with the motor in the other.

But the SAS usually slipped behind Iraqi lines by helicopter. They travelled in Chinooks, painted in desert camouflage and armed with Gatling guns of the kind used in Vietnam. 'The great thing about the

ALL NECESSARY MEANS

Chinook,' we were told, 'is that you can fill it with all the kit in the world and you still won't overload it.' The Chinooks often flew into Iraq in pairs, guided by the more sophisticated American Pave Lows, whose night-vision and radar systems allow them to fly just 20 feet above the ground, even on moonless nights. The Chinook wasn't completely indestructible – during the war, one was shot at while on the ground during an SAS mission behind enemy lines. However, before the Iraqis could capture the crew, the Chinook was repaired and flown out.

Once in Iraq, the priority was to hide. The SAS teams would dig themselves a 'scrape', a small hole in the ground from which to wait and watch. Before long it would be so well covered with camouflage and sand that not even the most observant Iraqi could spot it; the only possible clue was a minute periscope poking up through the sand. That 'scrape' had to become home to the SAS, for days at a time if necessary.

Their transport became known as 'Dinkies and Pinkies'. The Dinkies were dune buggies which had been flown in by the Chinooks. Although these are only fitted with a standard 1900 cc Volkswagen engine, they reached speeds of 60 miles an hour during operations in Iraq. Silencers meant that there was only a faint spluttering sound as they darted across the desert and because they are much smaller than the buggies used by American Special Forces, they were easier to hide. They were also light enough to be pushed out of a rut or a sand dune if they got stuck.

The Pinkies were open-topped Land Rovers, also known as 'Pink Panthers' because of their matt pink camouflage. Like the dune buggies, they bristled with grenade-launchers and machine guns. These were weapons for defence not attack – for getting out of trouble, not into it. Once, a Pink Panther was driving north through Iraq when it passed an enemy vehicle heading in the opposite direction. Nervously, the SAS men waved, hoping they'd be taken for Iraqi soldiers. Because they were so deep inside enemy territory, it worked – the Iraqis simply waved back.

SAS orders were to concentrate on Scud launchers because allied pilots were finding them infuriatingly hard to track down, let alone destroy. 'You might say, "why couldn't we put aircraft overhead and monitor every vehicle that went down the road?" ' said Buster Glosson. 'We could, but then sometimes at night we couldn't tell if it was a fuel tanker or a Scud missile on an 18-wheeler going down the highway.'

According to Sir Patrick Hine, it took as little as 30 or 40 minutes for the Iraqis to rush a launcher out of its hiding place, raise the missile on its hydraulic arms, pump it full of fuel and despatch it to Israel. Not much later, it could be concealed once more – easily done in western Iraq which, as Schwarzkopf pointed out, is the size of Massachusetts, Vermont and New Hampshire put together.

But the SAS had one advantage: they knew the launch vehicles could only be driven on or near roads. That's where many of them spent their war, waiting and watching in their four-man teams, peering out through periscopes or from behind whatever cover they could find. Usually, they would pass information to the AWACS control aircraft, telling them the exact co-ordinates of a Scud convoy with the help of hand-held Global Positioning System (GPS) navigational aids. Sometimes the commandos tuned into the same radio frequencies as the warplanes above them so they could speak directly to pilots, and to guide them in for the kill.

The air crews' missions now became far more straightforward, especially when SAS men, crouched less than a mile from a Scud launcher, aimed their hand-held laser designators at the target. That would fire a laser beam which would be reflected upwards in the shape of a cone or 'basket' into which the pilots could then drop their smart bombs. American F-15E commanders like Lieutenant-Colonel Steven Turner attributed as many as a third of the Scuds destroyed by his planes to the SAS. 'They are the true unsung heroes of the war. It was effective to have someone who was able to provide that needle-in-the-haystack information.'

Back in Riyadh, Buster Glosson marvelled at how SAS men would sometimes launch flares over the Scuds and tell the pilots: 'hit the flare!' He knew that meant the commandos were uncomfortably close. Occasionally, they got even closer. If no planes were available or the cloud cover was too thick, the SAS would ambush Scud convoys themselves. According to one source familiar with their operations, 'they hit the front and the back vehicles first, jamming anything in between'. Usu-

ALL NECESSARY MEANS

ally there would be up to a dozen vehicles in the convoy, including the launcher itself, a fuel tanker, and vehicles to carry the warhead, technical support staff, as well as meteorological and communications equipment. Surprise and speed in the SAS attack would be of the essence, we were told. 'Shock action is the secret. Your move has to be sufficiently hard and fierce to paralyse them.' Even with small-arms fire, holing fuel-tanks and rupturing control wires, the SAS found that they could put the Scuds out of action. Seizing the initiative was the key, even if that meant acting without authority from headquarters. 'Sometimes there wasn't time to get the aerial out and call mother.'

In Riyadh there were sighs of relief that the SAS were making rapid progress in their 'counter-Scud campaign' because, while the politicians were demanding results, Glosson had to admit that his aircraft had been 'searching in the blind'. It was only when the SAS were sent in that he could relax a little; 'sanity', he decided, was prevailing at last. Yet Glosson was also worried that the SAS were too exposed, and he felt that occasionally the regiment paid 'an unacceptable price' for its success.

According to the official Ministry of Defence record, SAS troops 'had to close with the enemy and there were many individual acts of outstanding bravery'. The SAS had at least two ferocious fire-fights with Iraqi troops. One SAS man was badly injured in the legs and, although his colleagues tried to carry him out of enemy territory, he insisted that they should leave him behind for their own sakes. Reluctantly, they agreed and a day later he was discovered by an Iraqi patrol and taken prisoner; along with several other Special Forces troops, he was handed back to Britain after the ceasefire, his face hidden from cameramen by a blanket.

Others weren't so lucky. The regiment lost four of its members in all. Twenty-six-year-old Corporal David Denbury died in a shoot-out with Iraqi troops in the last few days of the war. Mystery surrounds the death of the three other men, Sergeant Vince Phillips, who was 36, and Corporals Steven Lane, 27, and Robert Consiglio, 24. A source at the Ministry of Defence told us that they had suffered from hypothermia, among other conditions. This was hinted at in the official Gulf Honours account, which spoke of the SAS having to endure night-time temperatures so cold that 'diesel fuel froze'.

Some of the relatives of the three men who died found it difficult to accept that explanation. After all, the SAS are trained to survive in Arctic conditions. But it seems likely that Phillips, Lane and Consiglio had run out of rations – and possibly lost the use of their radio as well – as they tried to escape across the border into Syria after a successful attack on a Scud convoy. They'd had to march through mountains and even swim across the river Euphrates. 'Things go wrong,' said one Ministry of Defence insider. 'They could end up wet and cold and with no food, living off what they were carrying on their back.'

Others close to the regiment have told us the SAS made two mistakes during Desert Storm. First, some of them went with the wrong equipment and, as a result, 'they had a really miserable war'. Despite their experience in the Middle East, they hadn't expected the sort of weather described in the official history as the worst in the area for three decades. 'They went equipped for a desert war,' we were told. 'They really were not prepared for the mud and the rain; they had expected it to be hot and dry.'

The second mistake seems to have been over-confidence. It is suggested that because the SAS found that, at first, they were able to roam around Iraq with remarkable freedom, they started taking their safety for granted, and that's when they got caught. One source says that because the British Special Forces have less back-up than their American counterparts, they do not always have an easy escape from trouble: 'The Yanks are always very well-resourced, but the Brits are run on a shoestring – they don't have as many helicopters to help.'

The chief allied air planner, Buster Glosson, thought some of the SAS's tasks could be done from the air instead. Ten days into the war he put an extraordinary proposal to Schwarzkopf to take the pressure off the Special Forces hunting the Scuds. He disclosed to us that his plan was to shut down completely the main highway that runs west from Baghdad to the zone of western Iraq from which the Scuds were being launched. It became known as 'Scud alley'. The mobile Scud-launchers were being hidden during the day in the giant culverts under the highway, ready to be pulled out at night to be fired against Israel. Glosson wanted to sow mines on the highway to stop all traffic and then bomb every single culvert, whether it had a Scud in it or not. He guessed it would take three days of high-intensity bombing. Much to his disappointment, the suggestion was turned down flat by Schwarzkopf – because it would divert too many resources from the rest of the air campaign.

As it was, the Americans did attack the road repeatedly anyway, more to harass the military traffic and to prevent the movement of fuel trucks than to close the road altogether. Civilian lorry drivers found their vehicles being mistaken for Scud-launchers and sometimes they were targets in their own right because the allies wanted to stop fuel getting in from Amman.

One Iraqi driver, Ahmed, was travelling with his brother. 'It was night and we knew the route was dangerous,' he recalled. 'My brother Ali had done the trip twice before and had asked for my help this night.' They were heading to Baghdad in a four-truck convoy from Jordan, with a Red Cross sign painted on the roof of the lead vehicle in case they were spotted. 'Suddenly there was a great white flash and my lorry spun off the road. I hit my head and the truck crashed. The front two trucks had been hit. They were blazing – actually melting in the road.' It was one of several attacks that caused outrage in Jordan and condemnation at the United Nations. But the raids continued: Glosson believed 'Scud alley' was a priority target, particularly since the Special Forces teams on the ground needed all the help they could get.

One of their most perilous missions was on the same highway – and Glosson believes it need never have been mounted. They were ordered to try to cut the fibre-optic cables which Saddam was using to communicate with his Scud teams in western Iraq. Originally the cables had been attacked from the air. Glosson had identified that they were most vulnerable where they were carried across the river Tigris on bridges in Baghdad. After politicians in Washington and London stopped the attacks because of the risks they posed to civilians, the SAS had to be despatched to finish what the bombers had begun. They had to do it virtually by hand. One source told us that the SAS, wherever they found manholes leading to the cables, would open them and drop in timed explosives. In Glosson's opinion, this was 'unnecessary exposure' for the SAS and it troubled him deeply. He couldn't understand why British commandos were being

THE INVISIBLE WAR

imperilled, when the guiding philosophy was supposedly to minimise allied casualties.

America's secret warriors joined the Scud-hunt later. Although Schwarzkopf had already sent in the SAS, he only agreed to use his own Special Forces in the search for mobile missile-launchers after he was told to. The instruction came from the chairman of the US Joint Chiefs, General Colin Powell, and Dick Cheney, the Defence Secretary. They had been impressed by a briefing from the head of Special Operations Command, General Carl Stiner, who showed them how, like the British, his commandos could help find the Scuds. By the end of the war, there would be a small army of American Special Forces in the Gulf: one estimate put its strength at 9000.

One of their most important missions came right at the end of the war. A combined team of American and British Special Forces discovered a large batch of Scuds, ready to be fired in a final barrage against Israel. There were 29 in all, mounted on their launchers in western Iraq. If they had been fired together, they could have overwhelmed Israel's Patriot defences, and perhaps even forced Jerusalem to abandon its policy of patient restraint. The American commando who spotted the Scuds immediately called in A-10 Thunderbolts to attack them and, after six hours of relentless air strikes, they had all been destroyed. Schwarzkopf didn't hide his relief; 'thanks for keeping Israel out of the war', he told the Special Forces involved. There was gratitude too from Dick Cheney, the American Defence Secretary, when he met the man who had first seen the Scuds. 'Oh, you're from the Scudbusters,' said Cheney. 'You kept Israel out of the war.'

Like the SAS though, American Special Forces teams also ran into serious trouble. Just before the ground war, three sergeants who had dug themselves a hideaway were suddenly discovered, not by Iraqi troops but by a young girl who lifted the lid of their 'scrape' and screamed. The Green Berets were tempted to kill her, but they couldn't bring themselves to do it and she ran away to fetch her father. He summoned Iraqi infantrymen near by and, within minutes, the Americans were surrounded by scores of enemy soldiers. But, by radio, they had managed to call up a helicopter, which arrived in time to fire on the Iraqis with its machine-guns. Against all the odds, the Green Berets were rescued.

The same thing nearly happened again when a bedouin tribesman noticed a radio antenna sticking up through the sand and decided he'd like to take it. He promptly found himself looking down several gun barrels. It's not known if he was killed or taken prisoner. The bedouin had stumbled on a six-man team of reconnaissance scouts from the 24th Mechanised Infantry Division. There were 13 of these units operating up to 300 miles inside Iraq. They would also hide in the desert in scrapes covered with chicken wire and camouflage, and monitored the enemy on missions that usually lasted for five days. There was a communications specialist with each of these 'Long Range Surveillance Detachments', who sent and received electronic messages, but was never allowed to write anything down; everything had to be commited to memory in case the team was 'compromised' or 'came into hot contact'.

At least two American Special Forces helicopters were hit by gun and missile fire while on missions inside Iraq. Ground crew who'd worked at an airbase in Turkey told us that they saw the helicopters returning riddled with holes, despite their armour-plating. One had a gap about six inches wide torn in its tail and had only just limped back across the border. Its crew were later seen watching CNN in the airbase's TV tent – still laden with their weapons.

In one of the most remarkable admissions of the extent of secret activity behind enemy lines, one American officer described Iraq and Kuwait as a 'Special Forces theme park'. They carried out no fewer than 43 different types of missions. Among the most difficult were search and rescue operations for aircrew who'd been shot down. If they ejected safely, their calls for help would be heard by the AWACS control planes on station near by. Captain Bill Flood, the navigator of a B-52 bomber, was returning to his base in Diego Garcia when he heard the pilot of one crashed plane screaming for assistance. 'It was really something to hear him calling out. His navigator had been hurt pretty bad and the pilot was desperately talking to the AWACS to get help.' He never found out what happened to them. In all, at least eight airmen were saved.

Some attempted rescues did not go according to plan. When Colonel David Eberly and Lieutenant-Colonel Tom Griffith were shot down while Scud-hunting in their F-15E over north-west Iraq, close to the Syrian border, they parachuted into the desert and immediately activated their rescue beacons. Yet it was almost three days before an operation to help them could be launched. First, the Americans had to go through diplomatic channels to get clearance for two Special Operations helicopters to take off from Turkey. Then they needed permission from Syria for a refuelling plane to fly through its airspace. Finally, the rescue teams couldn't locate the two men, and it later emerged they were 10 miles from where it was reported that they'd been shot down. Commandos on the ground were searching for them fruitlessly; it was 'totally frustrating,' according to one officer, and by the time the helicopters finally found the spot where Eberly and Griffith had been waiting, they'd been captured by the Iraqis.

There are few natural hiding places in the desert and, according to Brigadier-General Buster Glosson, 'if you haven't started a rescue mission within 30 to 45 minutes of a crew coming down, in many cases you're a day late and a dollar short'.

But Captain Paul Johnson led a more successful mission to rescue the pilot of a Navy F-14, Lieutenant Devon Jones. Jones only had to wait about eight hours before a Pave Low helicopter with its quietened rotor blades hovered down to him. Two A-10 Thunderbolt attack planes circled above in protection when, for a moment, it looked like everything might go wrong. Two Iraqi army trucks were closing in, trying to get to Jones before the Americans. No chances were taken; the lorries were destroyed. Just in time, the relieved pilot had been plucked to safety and Captain Johnson was elated. 'It was a rather indescribable feeling to know that he was now on the helicopter, and we were coming out of enemy territory – that we were about to pull this off.'

Inevitably, myths about the exploits of Special Forces have already taken hold. One report said that they flew into Kuwait and snatched an Iraqi SAM missile so that experts could devise ways of defeating it. Cen-

ALL NECESSARY MEANS

tral Command's head of Special Operations, Colonel Jesse Johnson, laughed at that one: 'I thought it was a good story but it's not true.' When half a dozen helicopters were seen flying into Saudi Arabia, it was first reported as a mass defection from Iraq, and later claimed to have been American aircraft disguised in Iraqi colours bringing commandos back from a secret mission. According to Chuck Horner, neither story is accurate; indeed there was probably no flight of helicopters at all. He believes that what happened was a classic case of Chinese whispers, or 'circular reporting'. Different border posts and reconnaissance units thought they saw or heard helicopters and their information became exaggerated as it was reported up the chain of command.

Sometimes, though, fact was stranger than fiction. On 21 February, the Central Command reported that seven American soldiers had died when their helicopter crashed during a medical evacuation. It was only part of the story. In fact, the helicopter involved was a Special Operations Black Hawk, which had flown into Iraq to rescue commandos whose dune-buggy had overturned. On the way home, the chopper had run into a fierce sandstorm, killing everyone on board.

But the worst single loss suffered by American Special Forces came when an AC-130, a gunship nicknamed 'Puff the Magic Dragon' because of its terrifying firepower, was shot down over Kuwait on 31 January. The AC-130s are converted Hercules transport planes, adapted to carry a huge array of guns, but still as slow as the original version. Even with allied air superiority, the planes depended on the cover of the night. One of them had been firing almost continuously through the hours of darkness. As dawn approached, 'Puff the Magic Dragon' was suddenly vulnerable, but its crew, who were busy supporting Marines on the ground, made the mistake of refusing to head home. An AWACS controller tried to alert them: 'Hey, the sun's coming up. It's going to get light.' But a preoccupied answer came back from the gunship: 'I can't believe I got so many targets here I'm hitting.' Amid its orgy of destruction, the plane became a victim too, downed by Iraqi gunners with all 14 crewmen killed. Their colleagues mourned the loss with tasteless T-shirts printed in their memory: '14 gunship crew members touched the hand of God and became true Ghostriders.'

THE INVISIBLE WAR

The allies relied on psychology as well as firepower. Even before the
war began, American 'psychological operations' teams were trying
to persuade the Iraqi army to give up. One British commander learned in
early January that as many as 20 000 propaganda leaflets had already
been dropped on the Iraqi lines. In all, by the end of Desert Storm, the
Americans had scattered 29 million. They didn't always get their 'psy-
ops' quite right though. One of their propaganda letters bore the insignia
of the US 7th Corps, which resembles the Star of David, Israel's national
symbol. Iraqi conscripts thought it was 'Zionist indoctrination'. Other
leaflets were more successful, especially those that used comic-strip pictures to communicate with illiterate enemy soldiers. There was a cartoon
of an elderly Iraqi couple worrying about the fate of their son. The mother
imagines her little boy bandaged up after being horribly injured in battle
with the allies and there's a caption in Arabic which reads: 'Oh my son,
when will you return?' Another sketch shows Saudi Arabia's King Fahd
with a bubble coming from him which has three different Arab soldiers
holding hands in unity. Saddam Hussein's bubble, by contrast, contains a
tank, a Kuwaiti flag and a couple of dead troops.

The leaflets were packed into a special M-129 fibreglass bomb and
dropped in a blizzard of paper. Titled 'Safe Conduct Cards', the leaflets
instructed the troops on the procedure for surrendering. Take the magazine from your gun, it said, and put the weapon over your left shoulder
with both arms raised above the head. Then approach the allies slowly. If
you're in a group, one soldier should walk ahead with the 'Safe Conduct
Card' held above him. 'If you do this, you will not die,' the Iraqis were
assured, and on the other side of the leaflet was a visual inducement to
surrender: a picture of three prisoners-of-war sitting down to a meal of
fruit. It was put together like an advertising campaign. US Army psychol-
ogists worked with artists, linguists and specialists on Iraq to dream up
the most effective ideas. They even carried out their own kind of market
research, with psy-ops experts interviewing prisoners of war to find out
which of the leaflets had had the most impact.

Some techniques were far from subtle. One leaflet told the Iraqis that
if they didn't give themselves up, 'we're going to drop on you the largest
conventional weapon in the world'. The next day, hapless conscripts

found the Americans true to their word as a BLU-82 'Daisy Cutter', with a massive high explosive payload of 12 600lb, dropped near by. The bomb creates a mushroom cloud frighteningly like that of a nuclear explosion. Indeed when a startled soldier from the SAS saw one go off in Kuwait, he shouted down his radio, 'the f---ers have dropped the big one; they've nuked Kuwait!'

Later, as ground troops went into areas which had been bombed with Daisy Cutters, they found every Iraqi within a three-mile radius was dead. British soldiers arrived soon after the explosion at a wadi in Kuwait which had been hit by a BLU-82. At the first Iraqi line of defence near by, they found no enemy troops; but at the second, there were many Iraqis and all of them dead, lying in their foxholes. Despite the carnage they brought, 8th Special Operations Squadron liked to put an inscription on their Daisy Cutters: 'The mother of all bombs, for the mother of all wars'. They dropped 11 in all.

The most thunderous attack was on Faylakah island just off Kuwait – a tiny patch of land, but bristling with radar and anti-aircraft guns. Three Daisy Cutters were dropped on it within three seconds. Their main use though was to blast a corridor through Iraq's minefields and defensive berms. That's why Central Command's head of Special Operations, Colonel Jesse Johnson, had recommended the BLU-82s to Schwarzkopf. Unexpectedly, their psychological impact brought a breakthrough in the mine-clearance operation. After one Daisy Cutter drop, an Iraqi battalion commander gave himself up, crossing into allied lines with his intelligence officer who handed over detailed maps and plans of all the minefields in his area.

The Iraqis were also being bombarded by propaganda on radio. The Fourth Psychological Operations Group from Fort Bragg in North Carolina set up a station called the 'Voice of the Gulf'. It featured interviews with Iraqi PoWs on how well they were being treated, and tried to intimidate others into giving up by broadcasting details of the next units to be bombed. For those parts of Iraq and Kuwait where reception was poor, an airforce EC-130E plane flew over to relay the broadcasts. In turn, the Iraqis put out their own propaganda of course. Most notable was 'Baghdad Betty', an Iraqi woman commentator who tried to undermine American morale by describing the alleged infidelity of the troops' wives back home. Unfortunately, she and her producers weren't quite as expert as the men from Fort Bragg. Baghdad Betty made a disastrous blunder when, in telling the troops that their wives were sleeping with screen idols like Kevin Costner, Tom Cruise and Tom Selleck, she also listed the cartoon character, Bart Simpson. She had mistaken him for a sex symbol. Her credibility was in ruins.

The Iraqis were taking on an almost invisible enemy because they had virtually no means of gathering intelligence. The allies, by contrast, were awash with it. The problem was assessing its value and making proper use of it. The Baghdad bunker disaster had shown that information wasn't always accurate and there were other serious mistakes, like the calculation of the number of Saddam's mobile Scud-launchers. But some intelligence was astonishingly specific. Once, the allies got word of a top-level meeting of the Iraqi 3rd Corps commanders in Kuwait. They discovered not only in which building it was due to happen, but the exact time. Aerial reconnaissance showed that, at the appointed hour, dozens of vehicles were parked at the supposedly secret location. It was immediately bombed and many of the generals inside presumably killed.

Some allied commanders complained about what came to be called 'intelligence overload'. When Brigadier-General Butch Neal was running the Riyadh War Room at night, he got impatient with the young 'intel' officers who would rush in with a 'hot' piece of news. Neal parodied them: 'Oh God, the world's ending; Saddam's coming down, he's going to attack with 80 trillion tanks; we've got to do all of this, all of that. We've got to stop all this.' Neal had to try to distinguish between fact and fantasy. He learned to become more sceptical but he also knew there was a danger of treating warnings too lightly: 'After a while, the "cry wolf" syndrome would set in, where you'd just say "he's lying" and it *would* be for real.'

It wasn't surprising the 'intel' men were so frenetic – they had more sources of information available to them than in any previous war, including at least 40 satellites. US Air Force Chief of Staff General Merrill

ALL NECESSARY MEANS

McPeak could justifiably claim that this was 'the first war of the space age', a war in which his side had a monopoly on all the weapons. American intelligence were particularly proud of their six 'Keyhole' satellites, which some experts claim can take pictures of a car's registration number from hundreds of miles overhead. As it turned out though, thick cloud cover meant that, for days at a time, Keyhole couldn't see anything at all. Another satellite, called Lacrosse, which worked by radar rather than photography, could see through bad weather and even in the dark but failed to produce images that were clear enough for detailed analysis. Allied spacecraft listened as well as watched. From 22 000 miles above the earth, Vortex, and the more powerful Magnum, monitored the most important communications channels. Analysts back in America would try to decipher the messages and judge the importance of each command centre by the volume of signals traffic it generated.

Ironically, some experts believe America's satellites were more useful before the war than during it. They produced the pictures of Iraqi troops massed on the Saudi border that convinced King Fahd he should 'invite' US troops onto his territory. They enabled President Bush to call Saddam a liar when he said his army was withdrawing and it wasn't. And they were invaluable in planning the air campaign, helping to create maps of Iraqi terrain which could be fed into the computers of cruise missiles.

Once hostilities had begun though, Lacrosse and the Keyholes were less productive because events moved too fast for them. They would only pass over Iraq periodically, and were unlikely to spot Scud-launchers on the move. Despite their eyes and ears in space, the allies had very little chance of getting advance warning of a Scud attack. Instead, they relied on two Defence Support Programme (DSP) satellites, whose usual job is to alert the West to a Soviet inter-continental ballistic missile (ICBM) attack, to detect that Scuds had been launched. In the Gulf, they raised the alarm when their infra-red sensors spotted the intense heat given off from the Scud exhausts. According to one report, in the early days of the war it took seven minutes to transmit the alert to a ground station in Australia and then on to America and Israel.

The system was later short-circuited so that the satellite signal went straight to Riyadh, Israel and the Patriot batteries. That could be done in only two minutes – giving precious extra time in which to warn people to take to the air-raid shelters. There were plenty of false alarms because other intelligence sources were sometimes mistaken about Scud launches and the DSP operators didn't want to risk being caught out either. Dr John Pike, a space scientist, said:

> Better to duck first and ask questions later. If everybody else was setting off false alarms, there was no reason for DSP to be the exception to the rule. The negative consequences of a wrong warning about Scuds are a lot less than a wrong warning about World War Three.

But in this war, like no other before, satellites were used not only by the shadowy 'intel' experts, but also by ordinary foot soldiers on the ground. There was a fleet of 15 navigational satellites or Navstars, which achieved, at the push of a button, something armies have sought for centuries: an immediate read-out of exactly where they are. It was a godsend in a desert with few landmarks. The receiver unit is only the size of a cigar box but by switching on this high-tech compass, a soldier could quickly find out his exact longitude, latitude and altitude. Navstar receivers were to be used for aiming artillery fire, marking mines in the Gulf, locating pilots who'd been shot down and helping the commanders of tanks to know where they were supposed to meet up with their refuelling trucks.

Later, even burial detachments depended on these hand-held gadgets to record where they had dug mass graves for the Iraqi dead. The Pentagon ordered thousands of the receivers to be shipped out to the Gulf but they were so popular that some of the troops who didn't have them wrote directly to the manufacturers, enclosing a credit card number and asking for one to be sent as soon as possible. It was later pointed out that because Navstar is a commercial rather than a military system, it could even have been used by the Iraqis.

Between the satellites in space and the Special Forces on the ground there was another level of spying: by high-technology aircraft operating over Iraq in secret. Among them were RC-135s, dark, windowless old Boeing 707s converted to carry out surveillance. Since early August, from their base in Riyadh, they had maintained 24-hour cover over Iraq, not only decoding the enemy's messages but also plotting their sources and calculating their co-ordinates for raids once war began. The crews spent up to 20 hours at a time in the air but one mission specialist, in a rare interview, told us it was worth it. According to Captain Scott Hackney: 'If you look at the targets of the first few days, you can see for yourself how our hours of surveillance paid off.' Hackney was ordered not to disclose any operational information but he was allowed to claim: 'We had a pretty big hand in putting a "Kick Me" sign on Saddam's back.'

One of his tasks was to track down the locations of any Iraqi air-defence units trying to combat the allied raids. Hackney wasn't allowed to describe this operation except in the most general terms: 'We couldn't win the war with electrons but many aircrews are alive now because of what we did with them. Our time in the air paid off in lives saved, time saved and it enabled our commanders to fight a "smarter" campaign.'

But one spy plane didn't even need a pilot – the tiny UAV or 'unmanned air vehicle', which was remote-controlled and buzzed around like a little model aircraft. Iraqi troops might have thought it looked more like a vulture because its morbid job was to fly behind enemy lines and judge the accuracy of artillery and battleship gunfire. The UAV had a video camera to relay pictures back to the allies, who could adjust their aim accordingly. These tiny aircraft had never been tried in battle before, but like Tomahawk and Stealth, they came of age in Desert Storm. Their obvious advantage was that if they got shot down, the Americans simply launched another one; they didn't have to mount any search and rescue mission, and they didn't have to inform any relatives.

The only country which could challenge the American intelligence monopoly was the Soviet Union. Although President Gorbachev had formally endorsed the allied action, there was constant fear that Soviet generals – acting on their own initiative – might help their old client-state Iraq. Certainly, Soviet satellite surveillance of the Gulf region intensified

MOSCOW'S SECRET VIEW

KOSMOS 2108
19-28 Jan 1991

23-28 · 22 · 21 · 20 · 19

TURKEY

SYRIA

IRAQ

IRAN

KUWAIT

Persian Gulf

Red Sea

SAUDI ARABIA

TURKEY

SYRIA

IRAQ

IRAN

SAUDI ARABIA · KUWAIT

Persian Gulf

Red Sea

27-28 · 26 · 25 · 24 · 23 · 22

KOSMOS 2124
22-28 Feb 1991

The Kremlin ordered intense satellite surveillance of the Kuwait Theatre of Operations at key stages of the conflict. Some American commanders feared that the intelligence would be passed straight to Saddam by hard-line Soviet generals keen to support their former ally. Other western officials now believe that the pictures were used to persuade him, in the end, to order his forces to withdraw.

dramatically when the air campaign started and, once again, with the launch of the allied ground offensive. The Kosmos 2108 satellite was manoeuvred towards Kuwait between 19 and 21 January, and then maintained in a fixed orbit, passing over the Saudi-Kuwaiti border and southern Iraq every day for a week. Later, in February, another satellite, Kosmos 2124, took over, taking high-resolution pictures of the troop deployments – both Iraqi and allied.

Many in the Pentagon believed the details would be passed straight to Saddam. But there is another possible explanation: that the satellites' movements were timed to produce the very latest information with which to convince the Iraqis that they should withdraw from Kuwait. Kosmos 2124, for example, would have been in an ideal position to come up with pictures for the last-ditch shuttle diplomacy of President Gorbachev's special envoy, Yevgeni Primakov, and the Iraqi Foreign Minister, Tariq Aziz, in mid-February. It is conceivable that these images helped to persuade Saddam eventually to pull out his troops – albeit too late.

But if the Kremlin was using all its power to persuade Saddam to withdraw, some in the Soviet military were doing the opposite. Throughout the war, and after it, there were persistent rumours of Russian being heard on the Iraqi military radio networks. Schwarzkopf's deputy in Saudi Arabia, Lieutenant-General Calvin Waller, has been quoted as saying that he believes Soviet advisers did continue to work for Baghdad, with possibly devastating consequences. 'If they were helping with air defence, I'm sure their advice helped to down some of our aircraft.'

Although Moscow insisted that all its personnel had left Iraq by 9 January, many allied commanders remained sceptical. According to Waller: 'We asked that the advisers not be there, but from a Central Command point of view we did not pursue that to the nth degree because we had other things to worry about. We let the Joint Chiefs of Staff and the State Department worry about that.'

A senior British diplomat in Moscow told us that he is inclined to believe there may well have been an innocent explanation. 'The Russians, when they teach you, do it all in Russian. You spend a year learning Russian and then all the instructions are in Russian. I can imagine Iraqis

I The United Nations Security Council authorises the use of 'all necessary means' to liberate Kuwait. (*Left to right*) Soviet Foreign Minister Eduard Shevardnadze, Britain's Douglas Hurd, UN Secretary General Javier Perez de Cuellar and the American Secretary of State, James Baker.

2 Saddam Hussein with his soldiers in Kuwait. He believed they could hide underground and then 'rise up' to defeat the allies.

3 President Bush meets his troops in Saudi Arabia on Thanksgiving Day. Sending them into war would be the greatest gamble of his presidency.

4 Selling it to the Saudis. (*Left to right*) Allied Commander-in-Chief General Norman Schwarzkopf, Chairman of the Joint Chiefs of Staff, General Colin Powell, US Defence Secretary Dick Cheney and the Saudi Defence Minister, Sultan Ibn Abd-al-Aziz.

5 Iraqi anti-aircraft gunners light up the night sky over Baghdad, but to little effect.

6 A view through the periscope as a Tomahawk cruise missile is launched from a US Navy submarine in the Gulf.

7 The American F-117A Stealth fighter-bomber, which was designed to evade radar detection, carried out many of the most devastating attacks on Iraq.

8 The allied air force chief, Lieutenant-General Chuck Horner, shows reporters a Stealth pilot's video of a raid on a Scud storage bunker.

9 The White House, 17 January 1991: Operation Desert Storm has started, but the telephone diplomacy goes on; President Bush and his National Security Adviser, Brent Scowcroft, make use of their hot line to Downing Street.

10 RAF Tornado fighters on patrol. Initially, the bomber version of the plane was used in low-level flying raids. After a few days, however, these raids had to be abandoned because of unacceptable losses.

11 Allied bombing of Iraqi bridges resulted in some of the only 'political interference' of the war from Washington and London.

12 The raid that went tragically wrong. Allied intelligence, which said Baghdad's Amiriya bunker was military not civilian, was probably out of date.

13 Co-author Ben Brown reporting to camera beside the wreckage of a Scud missile which landed in Riyadh a week into the war.

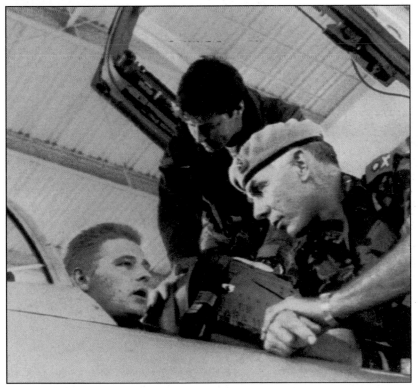

14 The British commander in the Gulf, Lieutenant-General Sir Peter de la Billière, talks to a Tornado pilot. A veteran of the SAS, de la Billière helped persuade Schwarzkopf to use them in Iraq.

15 A unique photograph showing a pilot being rescued by helicopter in the desert. Flight Lieutenant Devon Jones, on the left, had been shot down over Iraq and now runs towards an American Special Forces soldier.

16 A heavily-armed American Special Forces buggy, spotted during the liberation of Kuwait City. Britain's SAS used similar vehicles behind Iraqi lines.

17 Desert Rats on parade. These are men from the Royal Regiment of Fusiliers, which was to lose nine soldiers in a 'friendly-fire' attack by American jets – the worst single British loss in Desert Storm.

18 The Second World War battleship *Wisconsin* opens fire on Iraqi positions in Kuwait with a barrage from the allies' oldest but biggest guns.

19 A look-out on HMS *Brazen* scans the waters of the Gulf for mines. The whole issue of mine-clearance led to bitter arguments between the Royal Navy and the US Marines.

20 In the early hours of 17 January the first shots of the campaign were fired by American Apache helicopter gunships like these.

21 An Iraqi tank is showered with the debris of an exploding bunker as the US 82nd Airborne Division sweeps towards the Euphrates Valley. 'We never stood a chance,' said one Iraqi deserter.

22 The 'mother of all surrenders': clutching anything white – and a copy of the Koran – these Iraqis gave themselves up on the second day of the ground war.

23 The Mutla Ridge, where part of Iraq's occupation army was annihilated as it fled from Kuwait City. One American general told us it was 'an execution'.

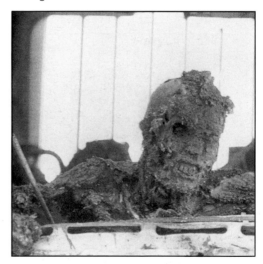

24 The charred remains of an Iraqi soldier. The allies refused to give 'body counts', and pictures of the dead were rare, but 100 000 Iraqi soldiers probably died.

25 Prime Minister John Major is presented with a captured Russian-made Iraqi rifle.

26 Misery for the Kurdish people who were encouraged to rise up only to find that Saddam's army was still strong enough to crush their revolt and force them to flee.

27 Jubilation in liberated Kuwait while in Iraq the suffering continued. The use of 'all necessary means' had only driven back Saddam, not unseated him permanently.

talking in Russian to each other if it's something technical; that's how they've been taught.' Instead, it is probable that the Soviet Union provided more help to the Americans than to the Iraqis by handing over classified information about the weapons systems they had sold to Iraq. The Red Army's then commander, General Mikhail Moiseyev, was personally involved in giving data to the US embassy in Moscow. No doubt rather reluctant, he insisted, perhaps a little disingenuously, that the CIA already has 'as much information as I do'.

The allies were also helped by the people they were trying to liberate. The Kuwaiti Resistance, although militarily weak, provided useful intelligence. After the war, Abu Fahd, the codename for one of their leaders, took us to his mansion in a particularly pretty suburb of Kuwait City, which was one of the 25 safe houses from which he directed espionage operations against the occupation army. But this was not the rugged resistance movement of Second-World-War France; instead of guns and grenades, Abu Fahd took on the enemy with word processors, fax machines and satellite telephones. Computer floppy disks stored the information his spy networks ferreted out, and the details were passed by fax or phone to allied headquarters in Riyadh. Abu Fahd even called up President Bush, and proudly showed us the White House phone number in his address book. If the Iraqis came, there were clever hiding places for the communications equipment. A hole had been dug underneath an animal pen, and when it was covered with a wooden board and soil on top, it was impossible to see. A baby's cot in an upstairs bedroom even had a secret compartment.

Resistance leaders would telephone Saudi commanders in Riyadh because it was easier speaking in Arabic than English. If the message was especially urgent, sometimes the phone would be handed to one of the American generals there, but they always double-checked any 'feeds' they got from Kuwait because nothing would have been easier for the Iraqis than to pose as resistance agents and to call up with false information. After all, it was only a voice at the end of a phone, so every lead had to be corroborated by another source. The other problem was that Kuwaiti

ALL NECESSARY MEANS

Resistance members were not, on the whole, trained soldiers. That meant that their reports about Iraqi deployments often had to be taken with a pinch of salt, and certainly Brigadier-General Butch Neal took nothing at face value. 'You just questioned whether they had the military expertise. It's like the uninitiated looking at a tank and saying, "Oh! that looks like an artillery piece!"'

The Iraqis, too, had their spies in Saudi Arabia. At the beginning of January, the War Room staff in Riyadh were put on a higher state of alert and they were no longer allowed to wander around the city when off duty. The feeling was that enemy agents would not necessarily be Iraqi citizens, but either Islamic fundamentalists, who saw this as a war against their faith by the infidel, or mercenaries who were simply in the pay of Baghdad. But the Iraqis could never even hope to match the mass of intelligence information produced every minute of every hour by America and her allies. Saddam Hussein's army was being beaten with technology it didn't understand, in the hands of an enemy it often never saw.

Chapter 5
TO KILL AN ARMY

'First we're going to cut it off. Then we're going to kill it.'

General Colin Powell, chairman of the US Joint Chiefs of Staff, on the Iraqi army, 23 January, 1991.

Iraqi deserter, March 1991.

'It was like 32 hungry men with knives pouncing on a sheep. We never had a chance.'

When the first allied planes came overhead, Mohammed and the rest of his crew fired their anti-aircraft gun wildly into the air. They could hear the jets above them but they couldn't see a thing. To help their aim, they loaded their weapon with tracer rounds. But as soon as they fired, they gave away their position and the allied pilots shot straight back. 'The difference,' according to Mohammed, 'was that they were on target.' The two guns near his were hit and the officer in charge of the battery was killed. Mohammed and his two companions covered their gun with blankets and ran to hide. To them, Kuwait wasn't worth dying for. This was the state of Saddam's army as it faced the allied onslaught in what was only the first week of the war.

Whenever officers turned up to check on Mohammed and his friends, they'd quickly uncover the gun and pretend to be re-loading it. But after a few days, the officers didn't bother any more. Their troops had hardly any food or water. They couldn't sleep because the noise of the bombing kept them awake all night. Soon, they heard rumours of people deserting or

ALL NECESSARY MEANS

giving themselves up. Since nobody seemed to know what they were supposed to do, they decided to go home. The ground war was still a month away.

Mohammed and the other two soldiers gathered together what they had – some biscuits, some water and tins of tomato paste – and started to walk and hitch lifts across the desert back to Baghdad. They were to see many others doing the same. Some of the soldiers who'd come from units near the southern city of Basra were in bad shape. 'Many were deaf from the bombing and there were dozens with burns and appalling injuries. We saw many dead and dying. Some of them had been injured as they fled across the minefields.' Mohammed joined the desultory efforts to bury the dead but soon gave up. There were simply too many. 'Eventually we just took their shoes and food,' he remembers. They reached a village but found its inhabitants were all in shock from the bombing and could hardly help themselves, let alone the soldiers.

Mohammed finally arrived in Baghdad about four weeks later. By that time, the allies had bombed the crowded bunker at Amiriya and his uncle and a cousin had been killed inside. He arrived at his parents' house to find it draped with black mourning banners. 'The house was full of people who'd come to pay their respects and I had to hide in a hut in the garden in case anyone saw me. I thought I would be shot for desertion.' He stayed in the hut till his mother read that an amnesty had been declared for deserters. Only then could he tell his story – one shared by as many as 100 000 others. The fact was that, unknown to the allies, Saddam's army in Kuwait was melting uncontrollably into the desert. The allies didn't realise how far they had already achieved their aim of shattering the morale of the Iraqi troops. General Powell's strategy of encirclement was working well. Not only was Iraq cut off from outside help, its army was gradually being cut off from its own supplies and, in the morbid military jargon, it was also being 'softened up' like no other force in history.

Within a week or so of the start of the campaign, the first 'linecrossers' appeared. These were soldiers who'd found their way through the minefields, past the Republican Guard patrols that were trying to stop them, and across the border into Saudi Arabia. They told their interrogators of the appalling conditions brought about by the endless bombing. Many arrived so hungry they even ate the packets of sugar and salt that came with the American Meals-Ready-to-Eat, or MREs. Allied troops watched them swallow chewing-gum whole. The Iraqis said they were ravenous because they'd been getting only one meal a day of rice or beans. Others were infested with lice and because they'd had no change of uniform they had also suffered from chafing, which turned into open sores. They painted a picture of utter misery and disenchantment.

Later, American soldiers found the diary of an Iraqi platoon leader covering 15 to 28 January. At one stage his platoon had run out of water. 'But God's kindness hasn't left us alone,' the Iraqi wrote, 'because it started raining heavily and we collected adequate supplies which we used to drink, cook and wash.' Then on 23 January, he noted that an air strike came close while the next day 15 American aircraft attacked them throughout the morning, one bomb landing close to his bunker. 'Thank God, nobody was hit,' he wrote. The final entry was dated 28 January: 'Thank God, nobody was injured, even though bombing in our area was very heavy.' After that line the diary is blank. Presumably, in the next raid, the Iraqi officer was killed.

But until the ground war, the allies could only rely on the testimony of deserters. Anxious to please their new hosts, many of them would exaggerate the extent of their knowledge of Iraqi plans. Others would recycle rumours. And, most significantly, nearly all defectors came from the worst-supplied, worst-treated units on the front-line. Their claim that morale there was low seemed perfectly plausible – but, on the other hand, no one could tell whether the same went for the much better, and more formidable, units further back.

Surprisingly, the traditional Iraqi system under which troops bribe their officers to let them go on leave continued, even when the war had started. The soldiers took full advantage of it, and left in their thousands. They never came back. The exodus was almost expected and tolerated, so widespread was the collapse of morale. One soldier, Latif, who'd been posted to the headquarters of an infantry division in Kuwait, said that within the first week of bombing everyone was talking openly about desertion. After all, their situation looked hopeless: the unit's medical tent had taken a direct hit and many of Latif's friends had been killed.

ALL NECESSARY MEANS

Only the senior officers had bunkers that offered any realistic chance of protection. The rest had to cope in inadequate dug-outs, covered only with corrugated iron and sandbags. They became determined to leave, but it wouldn't be easy. They'd all heard that the gaps in the minefields to their south were being patrolled, and in any case they had little idea where exactly they were in Kuwait.

Quickly though, a strange bout of glasnost seized the Iraqi army. According to Latif, even the officials from Saddam's Ba'ath party, who were with each army unit to deter rebellion, joined the discussions about why they were in Kuwait and whether they should leave.

> The young officers were telling everyone they didn't want to fight. This kind of openness had never happened in our war with Iran. But the bombing came again and again. I even saw the high-ranking officers ordering the anti-aircraft teams not to shoot in case they saw us and bombed us more.

Latif, who had trained as an English teacher, said that, with their camp under attack every day for a week, all they could do was try to survive. There was no question of being able to retaliate. With extraordinary understatement, he concluded: 'It was not beneficial to stay, so we went home.'

The Ba'ath party representatives seemed to have lost all faith in Saddam's adventure and they made no attempt to stop Latif and his colleagues from escaping. The commanding officer even told his men that rather than leave with them, he'd decided it would be better to wait and be captured by the allies. No amount of high-technology or Special Forces operations could detect the true extent of this collapse in morale. In fact, as far as allied intelligence could tell, the Iraqis still had 600 000 soldiers in or near Kuwait. It was one of the great misjudgements of the war. Analysts had heard of a few deserters trickling back into Iraq – but they never guessed that a flood was under way.

he bomb attacks were unrelenting. The American air staff knew that in Iraq's war with Iran both armies had regularly paused between battles and for holidays, and Chuck Horner had no intention of being so gentlemanly.

'We're not going to give you the pause,' he would say, 'we're ugly Americans and we're going to go for your throat.'

That meant the allied bombing of the army's supply routes continued round-the-clock. The bridges were obvious targets. Of the 36 spanning the Tigris and Euphrates rivers along the highways between Baghdad and the south, 33 had been attacked by the end of January. General Schwarzkopf claimed in a news conference that Iraqi military traffic had been cut by 90 per cent. But he wasn't giving his enemy enough credit. Within hours of a bridge being hit, they were either building a pontoon replacement or bulldozing the rubble into a makeshift causeway.

The allies hit one bridge while an army truck was crossing it, killing about 50 soldiers and flinging their bodies into the river. Hurriedly, the Iraqis built a pontoon bridge beside the wreckage only to see it bombed just as quickly by the allies. Still the Iraqis weren't deterred and constructed another pontoon, which did survive, though the bodies of the soldiers remained in the mud below. British intelligence took account of these Iraqi efforts and, rather more cautiously than Schwarzkopf, they estimated that the flow of traffic had only been halved. Western reporters found this claim more credible, since as late as February they were still able to drive south to Basra on a highway clogged with heavy military traffic. On the way, they listened to Schwarzkopf on the BBC World Service claiming the roads were virtually closed. One journalist who made the journey was the BBC TV correspondent, Jeremy Bowen. 'Where the bridges had been bombed,' he said, 'they'd usually filled that stretch of the river with rubble and everyone was able to cross it – even in cars like our little Honda.'

Still, makeshift repairs were not enough to save Iraq's occupation army from the bombing. The B-52s were sweeping in from Spain, from RAF Fairford in Gloucestershire and from Diego Garcia with 20-ton loads of bombs. RAF Jaguar pilots were reporting spectacular explosions from ammunition dumps. The conscript units were bombarded regularly but the allies' main focus was the Republican Guard. Each of its eight divisions would be attacked for several days in turn. The problem for Central Command was deciding which units to target – and that was the cause of arguments in the War Room almost every day. The US Army, which was to swing through Iraq, wanted the Republican Guard near Basra to be dealt the severest blow. The US Marines and the Arab armies, who were to charge straight into Kuwait, pressed for more attacks along their line of advance.

At the daily planning meetings in the Black Hole, the air force chief, Chuck Horner, became increasingly irritated with army commanders who 'always wanted to pick the airplanes', and impose their views on exactly how the Iraqis should be bombed. He didn't like it: 'that wasn't their business'. In the end, it was left to Schwarzkopf to act as an umpire to try to ensure that each commander 'received fair treatment'. They all wanted their share of the B-52s. More sophisticated planes were probably destroying a larger number of tanks by picking them off one by one, but there was nothing as psychologically devastating for the Iraqis on the ground as the thunderous raids by B-52s. The desert would shake for miles around. Allied troops felt the vibrations from their side of the border. Even Royal Navy frogmen searching for mines in the Gulf could feel the sea-bed quake. But, up above, the B-52 crews were immune to the carnage they were causing. 'We were removed from it all,' said one pilot, Captain John Scott Ladner, 'and it was just mechanical'. The bomber crews merely had to fly to a given set of coordinates and then try to identify the Iraqi positions with their cameras or radar.

The Republican Guard divisions were the easiest to spot – even from 30 000 feet. They usually arranged themselves in a large circle made up of six camps which stood out clearly against the desert, no matter how well the troops had dug themselves in. They looked 'like little molehills', according to one B-52 pilot, Captain Mark Medvec. He found it 'easy to see them' and to attack was equally simple. According to Medvec, the B-52s dropped their bombs in a huge 'box' pattern about half-a-mile long. 'We'd normally just lay that box right over the top of the circle. If we had more than one aircraft, then we could overlap different areas of the encampment. We could see the lights as the bombs detonated.' The fighters escorting them would dive down to watch from a lower level and radio back with messages of praise: 'that was real neat-looking', or 'you did a good job, we really enjoyed it'. For the Iraqis, it meant a nightmare of destruction, numbing noise, sleeplessness, injury and death.

The B-52s weren't all that they had to worry about; helicopter gunships were also hunting them out. The Apaches roamed around Iraqi positions like hornets, taking advantage of their night-vision equipment to launch surprise attacks. In the televised briefings, it was part of what the allied spokesmen clinically referred to as 'preparing the battlefield'. A pair of Apaches once attacked a series of bunkers so accurately that the 500 Iraqis who surrendered allowed themselves to be herded back over the border: even helicopters were now taking prisoners.

The Apaches would set off with their Hellfire missiles inscribed with abusive messages for Saddam – one pilot writing his with coloured chalk sent by his mother – and then quietly hover towards their prey. 'We caught them with their shorts down. They were in their sleeping bags,' boasted Captain Jess Farrington, after a particularly devastating raid on an artillery unit in mid-February. The Iraqis were confused and disorganised and 'were running around like a bunch of goobers; they didn't know which way to turn'.

For some pilots, there was no question of any ethical dilemma about the death and injury they had inflicted. Their power was intoxicating and Captain Stewart Hamilton admitted it in three short, disturbing sentences: 'The air smells good. The cold feels good. It's great to be alive.' There were others though who began to feel uncomfortable. 'It's almost a form of cheating,' said Staff Sergeant Michael Osborne. 'There's just no place for them to hide.'

Still, their orders were to carry on. To allied commanders, the approaching ground war was still fraught with uncertainty.

President Bush admitted that it was beginning to frustrate him and General Schwarzkopf was obviously annoyed. It was early February, the ground campaign was due to start in about a fortnight, and the allies were in dispute over Battle Damage Assessment or 'BDA'. Every analyst seemed to have a different estimate of the damage done to the Iraqi army. While Schwarzkopf's own staff were announcing to the media that at least 35–40 per cent of Iraq's tanks and artillery had been destroyed, French and British military officials put the figure at less than 30 per cent. In Washington, the CIA had another opinion entirely: they put it at only 10–15 per cent. As Schwarzkopf was later to tell Congress, if he'd relied on that most cautious assessment, 'we'd still be sitting over there waiting'. There was a joke doing the rounds in Riyadh that if a CIA man saw a satellite picture of an Iraqi tank lying on one bank of a river, with its turret on the other, he'd still only note it down as 'possible damage'.

Even intelligence about a single Iraqi unit seemed to change all the time. Early in the air war, the Tawakalna division of the Republican Guard had moved south to protect the other seven Republican Guard divisions behind it. By the beginning of February, Tom King, the British Defence Secretary, declared that half the Tawakalna's weapons had been destroyed. By 16 February, US Army intelligence was saying that figure had risen to 72 per cent and that some of the Tawakalna's soldiers, brought in to replace those killed by the bombing, had only had three or four days' training. That was reassuring. But a week later, the night before the ground offensive, the estimate changed again. Intelligence was now saying the division had in fact only lost 33 per cent of its combat strength – unsettling news on the eve of battle.

Chuck Horner couldn't see what all the fuss was about and he was upset by what he called 'this big flap' over Battle Damage Assessment. He considered the success of the allied aircrews to be self-evident: 'Unfortunately, the bean-counters of the world absolutely demand accurate data.' As far as he was concerned, once he'd assigned his best planes, fitted with video-recorders, to picking off the Iraqi tanks and artillery, he knew he was destroying more than 150 every night. He could see from the recordings that he was 'hurting them', and he didn't care if the 'bean-counters' were sceptical.

Their fear though was that generals like Horner, anxious to prove the power of his aircraft, were in fact being conned by the Iraqis. Certainly Saddam's soldiers had long shown themselves to be expert in the techniques of deception, or 'maskirovka', as their Soviet advisers called it. Maskirovka took many forms. Tank crews were instructed to place pots of burning oil on their turrets to give the impression that they'd already been hit, or they'd put a spare track beside a tank as if it had been blown off. Fake artillery was created with stacks of old tyres and scaffolding. Bunkers and sand revetments were made to look empty when in fact ammunition stores lay hidden beneath them. The Iraqis also used inflatable dummy tanks, bought from Britain, France, Italy and eastern Europe. More than once they fooled allied pilots. During a night attack, the crews of British Lynx helicopters proudly thought their missiles had destroyed 13 tanks and personnel carriers in a 14-vehicle Iraqi convoy. 'Bingo, it's just like training,' they reported back. But with daylight, they made an embarrassing discovery: they had attacked British-made fakes of exactly the type they used for training back home.

To the allied war machine, the failure to establish an accurate Battle Damage Assessment was something of a humiliation – and one of the few Iraqi successes. The US Air Force had pensioned off many of its older reconnaissance aircraft – the only ones equipped to distinguish real from faked damage – leading one Pentagon official to complain that, 'the struggle for BDA was almost as bad as the fight with Iraq itself'.

Air commanders were forced to think of new tactics. 'We got a lot smarter as the war went on,' according to Major-General Moore, of a US Marines air wing. His approach though was hardly ingenious; it relied on brute force to eliminate any doubt in the minds of the 'bean-counters'.

If we found a battery of artillery out there or a tank battalion or a con-voy, we stayed on that thing and poured airplanes on top of it, until that thing was completely destroyed...just beating them to death until we were positive that not much was left of the outfit.

But most of the victims of this juggernaut approach were on the move and exposed, unlike the majority of Iraqis who remained dug in, under-ground. The unknown quantity was how well they would perform in battle.

Satellite pictures didn't seem to help very much. Many American divisions had their own fax-type machines for receiving these photographs almost directly from space. Technically, this 'down-linking' of hard copies of satellite images worked perfectly, and the pictures were then sent out to the units who needed them. But one young intelligence officer, serving with a US Army unit that would lead the allied advance, said he never received a single relevant satellite picture. The officer, a highly-motivated and ambitious captain, who would only be interviewed on the condition that he remained anonymous, listed a catalogue of failings.

Some of the first photographs he received had been processed in great detail by British analysts. Their arrival, he said, was very welcome but none covered the areas that would be reached by his unit's advance. Worse, two of the pictures turned out to look remarkably similar even though they had different coordinates. Close study showed they were of the same Iraqi army position – but one picture had apparently been pro-cessed upside down. 'I couldn't believe it when I realised what they'd done. The pictures were supposedly of different areas but I compared them. They were the same place, only one picture was the wrong way up. And this was supposed to be the hi-tech war!'

The captain and his commanders relied on their own reconnaissance and analysis to work out what lay ahead of them. They concluded that nothing much did and three times recommended to their headquarters that 'a little artillery and a little psy-ops' would see them through the handful of conscript Iraqi units standing between them and the Republi-can Guard. But the headquarters staff saw it differently. They sent the intelligence officer maps that showed 'whole divisions being ahead of us, maps with red squares all over them, when we knew that no one was there at all: everyone was going "oh my gosh" over nothing. According to them, we were fighting this 10-foot-tall enemy. We knew it was different'.

But the consensus among the allies was still that a ground war would be hard and bloody. As Captain Bob Ferguson, a company commander in the Desert Rats, was quoted as saying: 'People think it'll all last about five days but there's no way you can do that. We're talking about a profes-sional army. Christ, he's got a million men.'

However much the air chiefs protested, it was the caution of the 'bean-counters' that prevailed.

G eneral Colin Powell, the powerful chairman of the US Joint Chiefs of Staff, was among the most cautious of all. He'd long since decided that if the Iraqis had to be driven out of Kuwait, he wanted to do it with 'overwhelming force'. At one Pentagon briefing he announced: 'I've got a toolbox full of tools and I've brought them all to the party.' That meant attacks on the Iraqis would come not just from the air and from the ground – but from the sea as well. With 17 000 heavily-armed US Marines afloat in the Gulf, the assumption in the media – and in Baghdad – was that they would storm onto the beaches of Kuwait in a re-enactment of the Pacific landings of the Second World War.

In the event, that didn't happen – possibly because Schwarzkopf never had the choice. He said later that he decided not to allow the Marines to stage an amphibious landing, and he only kept them offshore to fool the Iraqis into thinking there'd be a sea-borne attack. However, our research shows that Schwarzkopf didn't have much alternative because of a row with the Royal Navy. Its five Hunt-class minehunters were probably the only vessels capable of clearing approaches through the Iraqi minefields that would allow landings to take place. But British commanders took the view that such an operation would be too dangerous – and they objected.

The Marines' plan was for the first assault to be by helicopter, and for the bulk of their heavy equipment to come by hovercraft or landing ship. It meant that mine-clearing would be essential – but the Royal Navy only heard of it late in the campaign. In a chance conversation between Royal Navy and US Marines officers, it became clear that the Marines had plans for up to five different landings – each of which required the British to clear the mines first. The Royal Navy were furious and, behind the scenes, there was now to be a bitter dispute.

According to the overall British commander, Sir Patrick Hine, the Marines wanted the Royal Navy to clear a long stretch of the Kuwaiti coast rather than a series of channels, which they feared might reveal the likely points of attack. The Marines also wanted the whole job done within 10 to 15 days. The Royal Navy thought this idea 'unrealistic' at best, and pointlessly 'dangerous' at worst. They said that the clearance work would not only take at least 30 days, but it would also put the

ALL NECESSARY MEANS

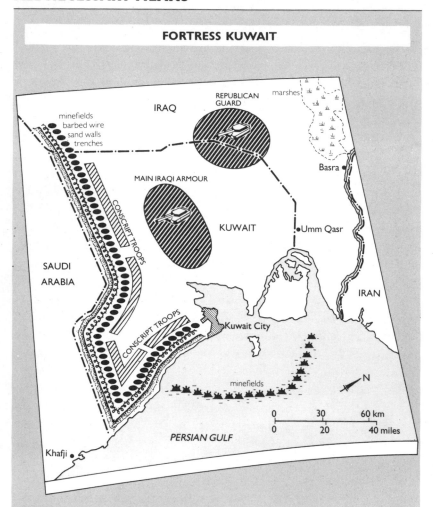

FORTRESS KUWAIT

Saddam hoped to defend Kuwait with a strategy described as 'old-fashioned' by many western generals. The huge minefields at sea and along the southern border were designed to slow the allied invasion and allow the main inland Iraqi tank units – particularly the Republican Guard – time to move into position to stage counterattacks. In the event, the allies were unable to invade by sea and outflanked Saddam by land.

minehunters at unacceptable risk. They would be in full sight of the Kuwaiti shore, day-in day-out, and defenceless against Iraqi artillery. Officers remember the Royal Navy commander, Commodore Christopher Craig, pointing this out in repeated radio-telephone conversations with Central Command in Riyadh.

The Marines didn't give up, though. They argued that all coalition forces should be prepared to expose themselves to the same degree of danger. The Marines said they were ready to suffer 10 per cent losses and the Royal Navy should be too. The Navy replied that, since its five minehunters were the best the coalition had, even the loss of one of them would have grave consequences. In the end, according to Hine, a high-level meeting was called. Experts were brought in, and the Marines reluctantly agreed that their plans were too hasty. 'It wasn't a case of us being made to look frightened,' says Hine. 'But we were conscious of the risks because they couldn't guarantee to suppress all the artillery and Silkworm missiles quickly enough.'

A liaison team of Marines, which had been on board one of the British warships, was unceremoniously put ashore. Navy commanders were relieved they'd eventually got their way – but many in the Marines thought their role in the Gulf War had been undermined. Although most allied commanders thought it was a sensible outcome, the Marines were angry and disappointed. After the war, Schwarzkopf himself admitted that his own country's minesweepers hadn't been up to the job – forcing him to rely on the Royal Navy. 'It had a serious impact,' he said, on the Marines' ability to stage beach landings. 'That's the capability that we just must have in the future if we are going to conduct amphibious operations.' Nevertheless, the pretence of a Marines force poised offshore was to continue.

It involved one of the most audacious missions of Desert Storm: a platoon of US Navy Seals (Sea, Air, Land commandos) faking a sea-borne attack on Kuwait. After slipping over the side of their Zodiac rubber dinghies, they laid buoys which, when later detected, were meant to look like the markers for a landing. Then they swam to the shore, with machine-guns slung across their backs, and planted timed explosives along the beach. These were scheduled to go off exactly three hours before the start of ground campaign. Just as planned, the explosions led Saddam's commanders to call in reinforcements, weakening their defences in the area of the planned allied attack.

The Seals' raid had been timed to coincide with a barrage of the Kuwaiti coast by US Navy warships. This was a useful role for an American fleet whose contribution, so far, had been relatively limited. There had been so many doubts about the accuracy of the Navy's Tomahawk cruise missiles that allied planners had assigned as many as 30 to a single target. The fact that the fleet's computers didn't match those of the US Air Force, which was co-ordinating the allied air campaign, didn't help either: each day's orders for the Navy's warplanes had to be delivered by courier rather than transmitted electronically. Now though came a chance for a spectacular role – the bombardment of Kuwait by the world's biggest battleships.

They were the showpiece of the US Navy's presence in the Gulf. The *Missouri* and the *Wisconsin*, Second World War veterans refurbished under Reagan's presidency, were 300 yards long and their shells were each the weight of a small car. The 16-inch guns could be heard for miles around. The battleships had first been used in Desert Storm to help drive Saddam's troops back from the border town of Khafji. They had sailed in close to the Saudi coast and shelled the Iraqi positions inland. Though their contribution was high-profile, it probably did not have much military significance. Of much more use to the allies would be having the battleships stationed within range of Kuwait. But that was easier said than done. Just as the US Marines would have been vulnerable to the Iraqi mines, the heavily-armoured *Missouri* and *Wisconsin* would be as well. The only way they could get close enough to the Kuwaiti shore would be with the help of the weakest vessels in the allied fleet, the tiny minehunters of the Royal Navy.

Navy commanders decided this operation was less risky than the plan suggested by the Marines: the minehunters wouldn't need to be so close to the shore. Even so, they insisted that, first of all, the conditions had to be right. The Iraqi Navy's missile-equipped patrol boats had to be destroyed; so did many of the enemy artillery and missile batteries along the coast. Allied bombers and Royal Navy helicopters armed with Sea

Skua missiles had already been in action against both these targets ceaselessly and by early February it was deemed safe to send the allied fleet north. The British minehunters received their orders to join the war on 11 February. They were given just under a fortnight to clear enough sea-space for the battleships to begin attacking Iraqi positions in Kuwait. According to General Schwarzkopf's master plan, the barrage had to begin by 23 February – to coincide with the ground offensive.

Allied policy before the war hadn't helped. Warships had been ordered to stay south of Kuwait, to avoid starting a confrontation too soon. But that gave the Iraqis a free hand in the northern Gulf for five months after the August invasion, and they used the time to lay a total of 1200 mines. By February, allied intelligence could only guess at the number and at their location. So it was with trepidation that the British minehunters gingerly set sail north, leading the two battleships and another dozen allied vessels. No one knew quite what to expect.

At first all went well. The fleet had crept up the edge of Iran's territorial waters, avoiding the currents in the centre of the Gulf in case they were carrying mines that had torn loose from their moorings. The US Navy had chosen an area for the battleships to fire from, a 12-mile by 4-mile 'fire-box' near the Kuwaiti coast, and the minehunters and American mine-sweeping helicopters quickly set about clearing it. It was perilous work. The little ships were well within range of Iraqi artillery and, worse, Iraqi Silkworm missiles. It was a time of constant tension and anxiety. Commander Jonathan Scoles, who was in charge of the British vessels, made a check radio call to one of the minehunters to ask how they were. 'Very alone, and very vulnerable,' came the reply.

Too soon they were spotted, either by a passing Iraqi boat or by the enemy troops on Faylakah island nearby. One of the many batteries of Silkworm missiles was ordered to prepare an attack – but that order was intercepted. The allied spy system heard that the minehunters were going to be the target and a message was flashed to the fleet. It was extraordinarily specific intelligence and could have come either from the satellites and planes listening to Iraqi radio traffic, or from the two Royal Navy submarines, *Otus* and *Opossum*, which had been secretly sent to the Gulf to join the eavesdropping effort.

ALL NECESSARY MEANS

The minehunters were immediately pulled back and, with the rest of the allied fleet, hurried well beyond missile range. For safety, they all stuck together and steamed away by exactly the same route they'd used to approach the coast. No one on board knew at the time, but by great good fortune that route happened to lie through the only gap in a vast, undiscovered belt of Iraqi mines. It was to remain undiscovered – until the following morning when the fleet turned around once more, headed back towards Kuwait and then struck disaster. Two US warships unwittingly steered straight into the mines.

The USS *Tripoli* was the first to be hit. A floating mine ripped a hole in its hull below the water-line and slightly injured four crewmen. The damage wasn't serious but the embarrassment was. The *Tripoli* was none other than the command ship of the American commodore in charge of mine-clearing. Hours later he and his staff were still shaken, as his vessel inched its way through a field of at least 20 mines bobbing all around them. Worse though was the fate of the warship USS *Princeton* an hour and a half later. The noise of its engines triggered the acoustic sensors of two more sophisticated and more powerful mines lying on the sea-bed. The warship was nearly split in two. Three sailors were injured, one of them seriously. It was the worst allied naval setback in the entire crisis. 'It was one hell of a Monday morning,' one British officer said later, not least because the pressure on the Royal Navy's minehunters was now greater than ever to get the battleships on station for the attack on Kuwait.

But it took at least three days for emergency repairs to be organised. Because the Iraqis had laid mines much further out to sea than the allies were expecting, it meant the approach lanes that needed to be cleared now had to be longer. The minehunters got to work and eventually opened a safe route 41 miles long. By 2p.m. on 23 February, the battleship *Missouri* was able to steam through and open fire over the minehunters' heads. The crews could feel the crack of the pressure-waves from the shells as they blasted above them. The deadline had been met, the allied ground offensive was just about to begin – but the Iraqis had not given up.

A Silkworm battery was again ordered to fire, but this time allied intelligence failed to intercept the command. To the horror of men on board the five minehunters, they spotted the bright exhaust plume heading their way. Their radar had been switched off to avoid detection, but the path of the huge missile was unmistakable to the human eye. They broke radio silence. 'They were really screaming,' according to an officer on another ship. 'It was another Monday morning, it couldn't have been worse; it's always a Monday morning.' Against a three-ton Silkworm, the tiny minehunters would not have a stood a chance. Armed only with light guns, there was nothing they could do as the weapon tore towards them. But it missed. It passed just a few feet above one of the minehunters, skimming its masts, and then rocketing on towards the main group of allied ships several miles beyond.

The target must have been the battleship *Wisconsin*. But other vessels were right beside her, including the minehunters' command ship, HMS *Herald*. Everyone was glued to their radar screens, watching the tiny blip approach them. It was still dark and the only defence was the Sea Dart missile system of HMS *Gloucester*. Two of the missiles were launched. The crews watched them streak towards the Silkworm, just as the Patriot missiles had so often been doing against Iraq's Scuds. The interception was successful and the Silkworm was destroyed – but only 200-300 yards from HMS *Herald*.

'There was just a big ball of fire, and then we felt the bang,' said one of those on board. 'It was quite a relief, I can tell you.' It was to be the last Iraqi attack on the allied fleet.

H ardly anybody knew about them and, if they did, they kept it quiet. But for months a special team of Royal Navy electronics experts had been at work preparing one of the biggest hoaxes of the war: an electronic lie about the location of the British 1st Armoured Division, the Desert Rats. Usually this team's role was to protect the Navy's communications from being intercepted. In the Gulf, it was given another vital task as well – to disguise the movement of the allies' heaviest forces. The British division was by now part of the giant American 7th Corps, which was to be General Schwarzkopf's main punch. It was essential to keep its location secret from the Iraqis.

ALL NECESSARY MEANS

That's why the Navy team, based in a high-technology radio suite on a British warship, played such an important part in Desert Storm. From their position just off the Saudi coast, they recorded every radio message transmitted by the British troops who were training not far inland. The signals were carefully stored on countless reels of tape. Then, as the tanks and troops began the 200-mile journey to their battle positions in the west, the tape-machines began to roll and the communications traffic of the last two months was played back over the airwaves. As far as Iraqi eavesdropping units could tell, the British division was staying put. 'Our commanders moved us physically up to the front,' said one British commander, 'but then electronically brought us all the way back again.'

To Saddam and his commanders, it looked as if the main allied invasion would be up through Kuwait. In fact, the coalition had long agreed that the thrust of their attack should be in southern Iraq – a huge left hook that would encircle the Republican Guard. On paper, it seemed the obvious strategy because, just as the Nazi Panzer divisions had swung past the French Maginot line in 1940, it would avoid the worst of the Iraqi obstacles along the border between Saudi Arabia and Kuwait. It sounded good in theory, but could it work? Some 350 000 soldiers, 2000 tanks and hundreds of thousands of tons of stores would have to be shifted along two highways leading out to the west. At the height of this massive manoeuvre, 4500 trucks were in use every day, one passing every three seconds. Schwarzkopf's orders were that nothing could be moved until the start of the air campaign – in case the Iraqis saw that the main strike would come from the west. That meant it would have to be done with astonishing speed. It cost 30 lives in accidents – one colonel called it 'the most frightening drive of my life'.

The move was executed by Lieutenant-General Gus Pagonis, Schwarzkopf's logistics chief. From his modest start back in August, when he'd hired a station-wagon for a bed and an office, his staff of three had expanded to 50 000 and his network of supply dumps had spread far to the west. 'We moved the equivalent of the state of Wyoming in 14 days,' he told us. It was an operation of extraordinary complexity; it had taken Pagonis four hours to brief General Powell and the American Defence Secretary, Dick Cheney, on all its details. They were 'flabbergasted' by

123

the scale of what he had to achieve and cross-examined him about whether he could really do it. 'How in the world are you going to work a trick like that on only two roads?' they asked.

Pagonis, a man who'd studied his predecessors, was confident he'd learnt their lessons. 'Napoleon lost his campaign against Russia for the lack of logistics; Hannibal pulled it off because he took them with him.' But his chief inspiration came while he sat in Dhahran reading Rommel's account of the desert war against the British. It showed Pagonis how Montgomery, even with inferior tanks, had won because he made sure his supplies kept up with his troops, each logistics base leap-frogging past the next. Pagonis decided to do the same.

Schwarzkopf gave him 21 days to complete the move. Secretly though, Pagonis set his own deadline – just 14 days. He thought the air war would be over quickly, and that it was better to be ready in case Schwarzkopf changed his mind. For Pagonis, it was the hardest fortnight of his life. 'If I had 30 minutes in a day without a problem, I had a good day.' But he met his own deadline, and he even found time to cheer up the troops by offering an alternative to their notorious pre-packed Meals-Ready-to-Eat. One of his team, Chief Warrant Officer Wesley Wolf, had suggested setting up mobile burger-and-chip vans for the battlefield. Pagonis liked the idea, and equipped 100 of his vehicles with ovens, deep-fryers and grills. He sent what soon became known as 'Wolfmobiles' off into the desert to follow the US Army deep into Iraq.

The fact that Britain's 1st Armoured Division joined the move west was only the result of yet another argument behind the scenes. British commanders had been putting relentless pressure on Schwarzkopf to allow the division to be switched from the US Marines' ground forces to come under the command of the US Army instead. The general didn't give way easily. The Desert Rats had started off with the Marines; they'd trained well together and their partnership seemed to suit the overall plan. The Defence Secretary, Tom King, had even visited them as they practised their desert manoeuvres in mid-November. But the truth was that ministers and commanders back in London were getting nervous:

they thought the Marines would take too many risks.

There was increasing British concern that the US Marines were 'utterly determined to win a slice of the glory in the war' to help their fight in Washington against spending cuts. The plan called for the Marines to tackle the Iraqi obstacles in Kuwait head-on. According to one of Britain's most senior defence chiefs, 'we could see them being particularly gung-ho and getting themselves in a charge up the coast, using us as the bludgeon'. The last thing Whitehall wanted was the British division caught in a brutal slogging match where heavy casualties would be the only certainty. The problem was making the switch, and it was only achieved after a series of awkward exchanges, none of which has been made public until now.

The first to raise it with Schwarzkopf was General Sir Peter de la Billière. Schwarzkopf was evidently unmoved because Whitehall then despatched the overall British commander, Air Chief Marshal Sir Patrick Hine, who flew out from High Wycombe to try his hand at persuasion. As he boarded his executive jet for Riyadh on 6 December, he knew that he had the Government's full backing to push hard for the change. British lives would be at risk if he failed.

Their meeting was neither 'acrimonious' nor successful. Hine first tried to convince Schwarzkopf that there would be advantages in allowing the British division to join the US Army's 7th Corps. He said the Desert Rats were ideally suited to the high-speed manoeuvre warfare everyone expected on the advance through the southern Iraqi desert. He also said the troops undertaking that long journey would need to be as strong as possible when they finally reached the Republican Guard. Hine went on to give Schwarzkopf the details of a major study he'd ordered into how the British division would support itself without calling on American help. It wasn't enough. Schwarzkopf knew that if the Desert Rats joined the US Army advance, they would have to keep themselves supplied along desert tracks the distance of Calais to Berlin. He wasn't sure the British could manage that, and he needed further persuading.

Hine began to think that the real reason for Schwarzkopf's objection was that he was under heavy pressure from the Marines. They were strongly opposed to losing their British support and, both in Riyadh and in Washington, they were lobbying hard to resist the change. Nevertheless, Hine continued his efforts. He quickly despatched a team of logistics experts to give Schwarzkopf a special briefing on the British division's plans for supporting itself. Only when they'd finished was the commander-in-chief satisfied – but even then he wouldn't approve the change.

The Marines kept up their pressure and it wasn't until the United Nations deadline had expired that Schwarzkopf was able formally to tell the British authorities that their two months of lobbying had paid off. The war was already under way by the time the 1st Armoured Division learnt that it could now join the US Army on its trip west. The Marines were sorry to see them go. One Marines officer even spent two days trying to find the new British positions so he could present a gift to his friend, Lieutenant-Colonel Rory Clayton of the Royal Artillery. It was a jagged piece of Iraqi shrapnel mounted on a plaque whose inscription read: 'God fights on the side with the best artillery.'

Though not in the best of taste, it was a reassuring gesture at a time when no one knew quite what to expect.

In allied headquarters in Riyadh, Schwarzkopf's job had never been more stressful – nor his temper worse. The atmosphere in the War Room was becoming increasingly uncomfortable. One of his staff, Brigadier-General Butch Neal, tried to make sure that 'the Bear' got enough sleep – 'so that it wouldn't impact on his disagreeability'. The problem wasn't just that with his explosive rage 'he'd eat major-generals for breakfast', as one British commander put it. It was more that his staff were becoming too frightened to tell him the truth. Schwarzkopf says he isn't proud of his temper, and told General de la Billière: 'I never get angry with people, I get angry with things.' But, as de la Billière points out, 'if you're the person managing the thing he's angry about, you can't help feeling it's a little bit personal'.

Schwarzkopf's own air commander, Chuck Horner, was particularly worried by his behaviour. He thought the tension Schwarzkopf generated was unhealthy because it meant that his subordinates never dared approach him with their problems. Horner, as mastermind of the bombing campaign, felt secure enough to offer advice to Schwarzkopf's staff: 'bring him solutions not problems, and know what you're talking about'. It was easier said than done, and soon officers adopted extraordinary tactics to raise important issues with their commander-in-chief. Instead of talking to him directly, they would ask Horner and Brigadier-General Buster Glosson to mention a topic on their behalf. 'Would you bring this up with the C-in-C?' they would whisper plaintively. It was a strange way to run a war.

But bringing the general bad news was even more difficult. Schwarzkopf's deputy, Lieutenant-General Buck Rogers, who had stayed behind to run Central Command's headquarters back in Florida, told us that his boss suffered from 'the old shoot-the-messenger syndrome'. He was alarmed at the way Schwarzkopf would shout at people who were only trying to help. 'You'd bring a problem to him and very likely you could wind up in a very unpleasant exchange of words. Any time you have that of course, you get people who just sit on bad news.' Rogers is scathing about the man given an honorary knighthood for his leadership of the allied campaign. 'Schwarzkopf was extremely hard to get along with. He was unforgiving.' He also accuses the general of an alarming failure to consult his own staff. 'There were times when I would be cut out,' Rogers recalls. 'I was not provided information and I had to go and scratch for it. I found that unnerving and unsatisfactory.'

Brigadier-General Neal was surprised at how often relatively trivial issues could ignite Schwarzkopf's temper, problems which Neal would classify as 'minor'. Sometimes he put it down to the general's fatigue or the burden of his enormous responsibility. As the man at the helm of the most improbable military coalition in history, Schwarzkopf had not only to be a general but also a diplomat. De la Billière, for one, praised his political awareness – his ability to judge the individual sensitivities of all the different national forces under his command. Yet he sometimes shocked his colleagues with his intolerance. During the day, he even objected to his staff watching television in the War Room – despite the fact that it sometimes provided the quickest source of news. Only when he was safely asleep down the corridor would they dare turn on the sets and watch CNN or the other American networks.

Chuck Horner noticed Schwarzkopf's exasperation at any delays. 'He would want the Republican Guard killed on the first day. Well, that's just not going to happen.' Horner worried too about the cast-iron guarantees Schwarzkopf sought from his staff. 'He'd try to get people to promise him things that it's inappropriate to promise.'

One issue that most angered Schwarzkopf was the presentation of his campaign: he was furious at the way his public affairs officers handled the daily news briefings. Television ensured these events were broadcast instantaneously around the world, giving them enormous importance in shaping public opinion. Initially the spokesmen were so reluctant to give anything away that, at one briefing, Lieutenant-Colonel Greg Pepin wouldn't even confirm details of that day's weather. Journalists soon began to joke that Pepin would also refuse to give the time on the grounds that it might 'breach operational security'. The less he said, the more hostile the press became and, in the end, the representatives of the key American news organisations went to Schwarzkopf to complain. He decided he had to make changes. In the War Room, and in Washington, there was already an acceptance that he was right: people squirmed in embarrassment at Pepin's performances. A kindly, bespectacled and rather awkward man, expert only in the artillery he'd made his career, he was pitied by Butch Neal as 'cannon-fodder'. Little did Neal realise that he'd soon be in the firing line himself.

Schwarzkopf tried out a few of the generals from his staff as replacements for Pepin. Finally, he chose Neal, the man who would appear on television screens around the world every day for the rest of the war. As the man who ran the War Room at night no one knew its workings more thoroughly – and he was free in the day to brief the media. It meant enduring long hours. Neal would only sleep from 10a.m. till 2p.m., when he'd have to catch up on the latest developments and prepare himself for the press. Though he always appeared looking fresh, relaxed and confident, he did more homework than his audience realised. Before each briefing, he sat down with a public affairs officer, Lieutenant-Colonel Mike Gallagher, who would pretend to be a journalist and fire the 35 most awkward questions of the day at him from across a table. Gallagher would have scanned the newspapers, faxed to him from the Pentagon, to find the likeliest lines of attack and so get Neal ready for the real thing.

Nothing worried military commanders more than the threat of 'unfavourable' stories circulating in the media at home. When President Bush talked about the Gulf campaign 'not being another Vietnam', the public relations staff took him to mean there'd be none of the unrestricted press access to combat units which had characterised that conflict. From commanders who believed that the American television networks had killed public support for the Vietnam war, there was a determination to control news-gathering as carefully as possible. Within 12 days of Saddam's invasion, Schwarzkopf's chief press adviser, Captain Ron Wildermuth, had drawn up a 10-page document, codenamed Annex Foxtrot, in which the key phrase was: 'news media representatives will be escorted at all times – repeat, at all times'. Only rarely did journalists successfully defeat the system. Some dressed in military clothing and one French photographer even smeared his car with a mixture of sand and sugar to make it look dirty and 'military'. But for the most part, the media controls meant that, in the age of global television, the most extensively-covered conflict in history was also one of the most censored.

Ironically, some of the best coverage of the war was being broadcast from Whitehall every day – in secret. At 8a.m. every morning, ministers and key staff would gather in special rooms in their various departments to watch their own private half-hour programme on closed-circuit television. Officials from the Defence Intelligence Service, the Foreign Office, the Ministry of Defence Operations Room and the Cabinet Office would each present their latest information. According to one insider, 'it meant that everybody knew everything by the start of the day'.

Then, at 9.30a.m. every day, the War Cabinet would gather in Downing Street for an even more detailed briefing by the Chief of the Defence Staff, Sir David Craig. Satellite photographs showing the results of allied bombing were spread out across the Cabinet table and highly-classified maps of Iraq and Kuwait were displayed as well. Little of this intelligence was ever shown to the full Cabinet. It was at the 9.30a.m. meetings that the Government would establish the 'line' for public consumption – the version of events that it would release to the press. From the earliest days of the crisis, a 'Media Handling Committee' had also been set up to influence political and public opinion through the newspapers and television. At first, its chairman, the Energy Secretary, John Wakeham, was anxious to anticipate potentially critical coverage. 'We took every aspect of policy we could think of and said, are we sure we've ironed out the bugs or are we going to get a story saying: "Widows to be thrown out of Army quarters and no chance of getting into a local authority home"?' Wakeham and his committee tried to prepare for all conceivable public relations pitfalls, even checking pension arrangements and how coroners' inquests would be handled. 'We worked out exactly what would happen so we could play the cards quickly when they had to be played.'

He played some of them in the House of Commons. One of Wakeham's fears was that during the war 'virtually any MP from either party could get on television' and, unless guided, could say 'something damaging to the war effort'. So he made sure that briefing papers on relevant news topics were available in Westminster in the hope that MPs, desperate for information as they dashed for the studios, would make use of them. One briefing paper, on the terms of the Geneva Convention, was quickly prepared when the first allied pilots were paraded on Iraqi television. 'It was surprising,' says Wakeham, 'how many MPs found it convenient to sound knowledgeable about the Convention, which they probably couldn't have done before they'd seen the bit of paper. It was good for them, they got it right; and it was good for us.'

Sometimes he performed the same service for his Cabinet colleagues. When Saddam began releasing oil into the Gulf, Wakeham thought to himself: 'I've got to get Michael Heseltine (the Environment Secretary) on the box.' He wanted to show the public that even a government at war cared about what was happening to the ecology of the Gulf. He acted quickly: 'I got the television cameras up to his house and I faxed him all the briefings papers so we could be seen to be saying that we cared.' In the event, such effort probably wasn't needed. Public opinion remained firmly behind the campaign in all key coalition countries. But the final phase, with the greatest risk of allied casualties, was still to come.

ALL NECESSARY MEANS

B y now G-day was set for 1a.m. London time on 21 February and the countdown had begun. The allies' heavy guns and rocket-launchers bombarded the Iraqi border positions with the biggest barrages since the Second World War. The tank units were being marshalled into position for their lunges into Iraq and Kuwait. The air attacks had never been more intense. And though the world could only guess, the land war was about to begin. Then, Schwarzkopf decided he needed more time to prepare and delayed G-Day to 1a.m. on 24 February. Unwittingly, that gave diplomacy a last-gasp chance because on 21 February, the day that allied troops should have begun their invasion, the Soviet Union announced that it had agreed an eight-point plan with Baghdad under which Iraqi forces would pull out within three weeks. President Bush appeared to have been put on the spot. He knew it would be hard to stop the countdown – not that he showed any sign of wanting to. But he did feel committed to treating the Gorbachev initiative with the respect due to one of the Big Five on the UN Security Council. He said he would 'consider' the plan overnight.

In reality though, there wasn't much to consider. He just had to be careful not to offend the Soviet Union. Moscow's support in the Security Council had given the allied campaign credibility in many otherwise sceptical countries, and the efforts of President Gorbachev's special envoy, Yevgeni Primakov, had, at least in Soviet eyes, borne fruit. Ten days earlier, after a hair-raising drive to Baghdad from Tehran, forced on him because of allied control of Iraqi airspace, Primakov had met Saddam and reported to Moscow: 'There are certain promising signs.' The Iraqis had indeed then announced their very first mention of a withdrawal from Kuwait – even though it was hedged with conditions. The Iraqi Foreign Minister, Tariq Aziz, travelled to Moscow and his talks with President Gorbachev produced the eight-point plan being 'considered' by President Bush. But by now it was all too late.

Just as the allies had worried before the campaign began that Saddam might stage a coalition-breaking 'partial withdrawal', President Bush and his advisers were now concerned that Saddam could not only drag out his departure but also survive with much of his army intact. One aide suggested setting a deadline for Iraq's withdrawal and giving it a week to get out. The idea was accepted, especially as the deadline chosen, noon Washington time on 24 February, was only a few hours before Schwarzkopf's secret G-Hour. The Americans knew that, even if Saddam tried to comply, it would be impossible for them to withdraw within seven days. Bush made his way out to the steps of the White House to issue his last ultimatum of the war.

In the murky, drizzling dusk, the allied armies lined up to recapture Kuwait. Thousands and thousands of tanks, armoured fighting vehicles and trucks loomed up onto the horizon, headlights on, and snaked their way over the muddy desert – 'like speeded-up film of a flower growing', according to one young British officer with the Queen's Royal Irish Hussars, stunned like everyone at the bewildering yet exhilarating scale of it all. His regiment alone stretched back nearly two miles in double-columns of tanks and trucks. 'It was the most incredible thing we'd ever seen.' It was also rather frightening because it meant that war was only a day or so away.

The greatest fear was still Saddam's chemical weapons potential. The intelligence warnings were as stark as ever – and the training in chemical protection had never been taken so seriously. It was particularly important for the American troops who, all through the autumn, had been alarmingly ill-prepared. A highly-classified report by the General Accounting Office, the investigative arm of the US Congress, had found that, even after they'd been in Saudi Arabia for several weeks, as many as one-third of the soldiers interviewed had never performed their usual jobs in full protective equipment. The report, which was to remain suppressed until after the war, concluded that three-quarters of the American combat units were not ready to survive in a chemical environment. But by the countdown to G-Day, the Pentagon believed it had put that right.

The British Army had started off better-prepared and stayed that way. All its troops had been given two painful injections against the deadly germs of anthrax, a biological weapon the Iraqis were known to have in their stocks. To the Defence Secretary, Tom King, this threat

ALL NECESSARY MEANS

suddenly seemed more menacing when a report reached his desk at 11p.m. one night saying some troops had fallen ill and sheep had been found dead in an area where anthrax had been detected. It would take five hours to check. 'I went to bed with every finger crossed,' says King. When he returned the next morning, he asked: 'What's the news?' The answer was that the report had been a false alarm: 'The chaps who looked as though they'd got anthrax in fact had flu, the American machines that identified the spores were now proved to be faulty, and somebody who'd had a closer look at the sheep found they'd had their throats cut.'

Nevertheless, the disease was still feared – but the antidote was debilitating. So much so that King decided to cancel the third and last in the series of anthrax injections, which was due a few days before G-Day, in case it made the soldiers ill at just the wrong moment.

Final preparations for war were now in full swing. Britain's Challenger tanks were fitted with special 'reactive' armour: brick-sized packages of explosive which, if struck by Iraqi missiles, would erupt and shear away the force of the incoming warheads. And anti-flash clothing had been distributed to protect the tanks' crews in case of fire. These were uncomfortably hot, especially when worn with chemical protection gear. But they did have one advantage: on the thigh of each flash suit was a perspex pocket and, in the last hours before battle, everyone busied themselves cutting out pictures of their families or girlfriends to fit inside. One officer, from the Queen's Royal Irish Hussars, a cavalry regiment proud to have taken part in the Charge of the Light Brigade, thought a picture of his horse more suitable. His driver had different priorities. He chose a photograph of a can of Tennents lager and, although the word was that the battle ahead might last three or four weeks, he was to enjoy one sooner than anyone imagined.

Chapter 6

THE 100-HOUR ROUT

> 'You saw the bomblets go off, like someone dancing a high-explosive fandango, right across the horizon . . . so anything in there was getting a pound of high explosive every three metres.'
>
> **Lt-Col Rory Clayton, Commander of 40 field Regiment Royal Artillery, June 1991.**

> **Rabir, survivor of the Iraqi Army's retreat from Kuwait, March 1991.**
>
> 'When the last plane had gone away people started moaning and screaming and calling out for help. The fires were raging and the tanks were exploding. It was the most dreadful sound I ever heard.'

The wind was so strong that the canvas walls of the British division's headquarters tent cracked against its frame with a noise almost like gunfire. An electric light was swinging wildly over the maps and documents that had been spread between General Rupert Smith and the staff officers gathered around him. The rain was beating down and, for the last planning meeting before this desert war began, they'd all dressed in the warmest clothes they could find. The general, wiry, witty and energetic, cursed the 'bloody cold' as he contemplated the most important moment of his campaign: the beginning. Even now, despite well over a month of bombing, he couldn't be sure what to expect from the enemy.

Nor could the men serving under him. 'We just didn't know,' said one colonel, 'that Saddam didn't have some magic factor we hadn't taken account of.' Only three weeks before, on a round of the regiments, General Smith had astounded a group of his officers by warning them that they might have to fight for as many as 60 days. A captain who listened with alarm later jotted down in his diary Smith's view that 'the idea of a

ALL NECESSARY MEANS

one-battle war looks less and less likely' – and that the general 'expected to get pretty severely mauled'. Smith had even read out the percentage losses he believed might be suffered. The captain nervously noted them down: 10 per cent of the fighting force would end up as casualities, and 20 per cent of those would be fatal. His audience were understandably chastened by the stark possibility that several hundred of them might die, and thousands might be wounded. But General Smith summed up his advice for dealing with bad losses and setbacks as FIDO: F---It, Drive On.

Luckily, although the troops knew extensive preparations had been made for dealing with casualties, they probably did not realise the expectations of officials in London. If they had, they might have been more anxious than they already were. Even at this late stage, Foreign Office officials in London were discreetly coaxing countries in Europe to provide extra hospital care. It wasn't made public at the time but the fear in Whitehall was that even the thousands of beds prepared at hospitals around Britain might not be enough.

Nevertheless, by G-Day on 24 February, General Smith was as ready as he could be. He had at his disposal an extraordinary array of firepower. At the spearhead were about 160 Challenger tanks, frequently scorned in peacetime as unreliable and slow to fire, but now, on the brink of war, well-maintained and effective. There were the Warrior armoured fighting vehicles, battle-taxis crammed with infantrymen, the heavy guns, and the new and untried Multiple Launch Rocket Systems. Supporting them were communications vehicles, helicopters, medical teams, repair units, and the fuel trucks and countless other lorries, all laden with food and ammunition to keep this mobile, town-sized force of 30 000 people supplied. With them were the teams of journalists and cameramen with a BBC Television News satellite dish.

It was a restless mass of humanity and hardware, occupying a huge block of sodden Saudi desert about 12 miles wide and a staggering 45 miles long. And it was only a fraction of the total allied force – one of at least a dozen allied divisions whose heavily-armed troops were fidgeting on the eve of battle.

According to the Schwarzkopf master plan, the British division was to serve as the hinge around which 250 000 American troops would swing clockwise in a vast wheeling movement into Iraq, first north and then east to cut off and attack the Republican Guard from behind. Schwarzkopf called it his 'Hail Mary', a winning move in American football. As he explained, the quarterback 'sets up behind the centre and all of a sudden, every single one of his receivers goes way out to one flank, and they all run down the field as fast as they possibly can into the end zone, and he lobs the ball'. Schwarzkopf's assessment was that the Iraqi army was 'on the verge of collapse', but still he didn't expect the campaign to be like a game. His own prediction was that the ground war might last anything from ten days to four weeks. So much was unknown, and so many different but interlocking units had to operate successfully together.

The French, with their fast, light vehicles, were on the far western rim of the Hail Mary, supported by America's 82nd Airborne Division, which had suffered terrible losses in another liberation campaign 47 years before – the battle to free France. To their right were the massed helicopters of the 'Screaming Eagles', the 101st Airborne Division, poised to spring north. Next was Schwarzkopf's blitzkrieg force, the half a dozen heavy tank divisions under the American 7th Corps, which had to lunge forward at high speed, deep into Iraq. On their right, and guarding against what they feared would be a counter-attack on their stretched supply lines, were the British.

All this was still a secret to Saddam. As far as he could tell, the main allied attack would come straight into Kuwait. There were indeed potent forces lined up along its southern border – the US Marines, the Egyptians, the Syrians, the Saudis and others – but their role was to rush for Kuwait City rather than try to defeat the Iraqi army. Though they had different aims, both halves of the campaign were linked. In the east, Schwarzkopf wanted to overwhelm the Iraqis in Kuwait itself – while, at the same time in the west, he wanted to smuggle in another force that could reach and destroy the mainstay of Saddam's regime, the Republican Guard, lurking just outside Kuwait in southern Iraq. At first British generals back in London had been concerned by the complexity of the plan, but eventually its sophistication had won them round. Now it was to be put to the test.

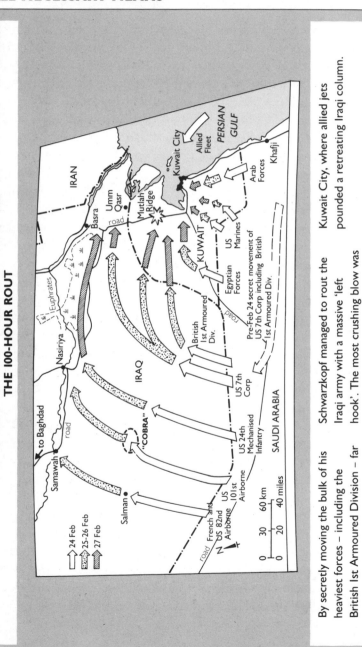

THE 100-HOUR ROUT

By secretly moving the bulk of his heaviest forces – including the British 1st Armoured Division – far to the west of Kuwait, General Schwarzkopf managed to rout the Iraqi army with a massive 'left hook'. The most crushing blow was struck at the Mutla Ridge, north of Kuwait City, where allied jets pounded a retreating Iraqi column.

THE 100-HOUR ROUT

In Schwarzkopf's War Room, they'd had formal approval from the President to proceed with the final phase of the campaign: Operation Desert Sabre. It was exactly 8p.m. on the evening of Saturday, 23 February and the deadline for Saddam to withdraw had passed that very minute. 'G-Hour' would be in eight hours' time, at 4a.m. The commander-in-chief and his senior aides were bunched for a final briefing around the oval table that stood in the centre of the room. The huge sliding wall-maps marked the positions of the allied armies and of the 'phase lines' – positions the various units were expected to reach by certain times. The first two phase lines for the British division had been labelled by an American planner, as 'Colorado' and 'New Jersey'. Just as in the final hours before the start of the air war, the atmosphere was becoming strained. The briefing was coming to an end and Schwarzkopf asked if anyone had any questions.

Yes, said the British commander, General Sir Peter de la Billière; he did have one thing. As the acknowledged master of the black arts of the Special Air Service, he was a figure regarded with awe by his coalition colleagues. They strained to hear what he'd have to say. To their surprise though, he remained silent and instead reached out to place a viewfoil on an overhead projector. Suddenly, emblazoned on the screen were words borrowed from American football: 'Iraq has won the toss and elected to receive.' It broke the ice. Several American generals were so amused they even copied the message into their diaries. Buster Glosson thought it was 'typically British, nicely done, and with class'. It was the last chart displayed in the room before the ground war started.

Amid the rush of the final preparations, Brigadier-General Neal found time to note down a few more lines that night:

Commander-in-Chief: emotional plea for prayer to support the 400 000 troops attacking tonight. Tension is mounting again. Several calls already about 'are we or are we not going?' C-in-C (Schwarzkopf) went to bed at 2200. I called Bill Keys and Mike Myatt (the two Marines division commanders) to wish them well. They are pumped up and confident. I envy them for what they are about to do. C-in-C arrives 0340.

ALL NECESSARY MEANS

In fact, Operation Desert Sabre was already under way in secret – long before the final briefing in the War Room and certainly well before the rest of the world knew about it. Though President Bush had declared the deadline to be noon Washington time, 8p.m. in the Gulf, on Saturday, 23 February, he didn't say that several thousand American forces were already in Iraq, preparing the way, not for an orderly Iraqi withdrawal in the unlikely event that Saddam should choose that option, but for a crushing Iraqi defeat.

It was actually on Friday, 22 February that the first major ground units crossed the border. The 2000 US Marines of Task Forces 'Grizzly' and 'Taro' breached the first of two lines of obstacles to speed the main advance that would follow later. Despite the operation's size, it was meant to be covert and stayed that way during the first rain-soaked night behind enemy lines. But the next day, the Marines had a bizarre encounter with some Iraqi soldiers. Rather than trying to drive the Marines out of Kuwait, the demoralised Iraqi troops surrendered without firing a shot and then showed the grateful Americans the lay-out of their minefields. While some thought this meant the going would all be easy, most commanders continued to fear the worst.

Much further west, American Army scouts were crossing the border in strength – well before the deadline. The classified official history of the US 3rd Armoured Division records that one unit had not only entered Iraq but also captured 200 prisoners by 4.55 p.m., three hours and five minutes before the deadline had passed. Another tough reconnaissance unit crossed the border – over six hours before Bush's ultimatum was up. This was 'Eagle' troop of the US Army's powerful 2nd Armoured Cavalry Regiment. The regiment's own private war diary records that once 'Eagle' had crossed, almost all of the rest of 2nd Armoured's tanks and Bradley fighting vehicles followed soon after. It meant that well over 1000 soldiers were about seven miles inside Iraq and it was still four and a half hours before the deadline was due to expire. They'd fired 500 shells in the space of just nine minutes at what they thought were Iraqi positions, only to find them empty, and had then awaited further orders. It didn't matter. Since the usual role of Armoured Cavalry Regiments is to lead the US Army into battle, there was clearly no holding back now, whatever

Saddam decided to do. The deadline was irrelevant. The ground war had begun.

T he weather couldn't have been worse. The blizzard of sand and rain that ripped through the allied columns was so dense that the soldiers could only just make out the shapes of each other's vehicles. But the hour had come at last and at 4a.m. Saudi time, 1a.m. in London, the French and American airborne units in the far west and the Marines in the east, charged north. Both immediately reported that they were making rapid progress. The French captured the small town of Salman; the 101st Airborne established a vast refuelling base, Firebase Cobra, well inside Iraq; and the Marines overcame the only serious resistance so far, plunging deeper into Kuwait. Almost all the allies' encounters with the enemy were ending the same way: in wholesale and rapid surrender.

Soon Lieutenant-General Gary Luck, the commander of the American XVIII Airborne Corps, in charge of the westernmost surge into Iraq, was able to call Schwarzkopf and report that the Euphrates valley, with its key highway connecting Baghdad with Kuwait, was now under his control, and that 3200 Iraqis were already prisoners. Schwarzkopf said 'Okay, fine', knowing the good news would be reported to him first. He then asked about the price of this stunning achievement, the number of allied casualties.

'Sir, to my knowledge, our casualties at this point are very low,' Luck replied.

Schwarzkopf pressed him: 'How low are they, Gary?'

'One report of one wounded soldier, sir.'

Schwarzkopf was incredulous and relieved. 'Gary!' he exclaimed, 'that's great!'

It encouraged Schwarzkopf to accelerate his campaign. Orders were immediately despatched to the rest of the force to start rolling some 12 hours sooner than planned. It meant that an already complicated plan had to be hurriedly reworked by all units, including the British division under General Rupert Smith. He knew that several miles ahead of him in the rain, the engineers of the American 1st Infantry Division, the 'Big Red

ALL NECESSARY MEANS

One', were already breaking through the belt of Iraqi obstacles along the border, and were marking the breaches with plastic tape and road-signs. General Smith's task was to organise the Desert Rats so that when they plunged through the 16 gaps created for them, leap-frogging their way into Iraq, they would arrive at the other side with their columns in the right order to fight an unpredictable enemy. He was agonising over whether the tanks should go first – but then be cut off from their supplies and artillery support; or whether it would safe enough for the latter to go through first, to give the tanks greater cover once they arrived. It all depended on the Iraqis and their reaction.

Privately he'd been weighing up three scenarios for what might happen in his sector. Either the Iraqis would counter-attack and prevent the Americans of the Big Red One from breaching the obstacles. The British would then have to rush to help. Or the Americans would penetrate the Iraqi defences but then be stopped from getting any further. That, too, would require the British to intervene earlier than expected. The third scenario was that the breaches were made successfully and there was no Iraqi response. In the event, that's what happened and when word reached General Smith, he decided to send his heavy guns into Iraq first so that they'd be ready to cover the advance of the Challenger tanks.

Just moving such an enormous force in foul conditions through another division's positions is regarded by military commanders as a feat in itself – so complicated that it had already been fully rehearsed. But another alarming problem arose. The commander of the US 7th Corps, under whom the British were operating, suddenly decided he wanted to send the bulk of the Big Red One into Iraq, ahead of the British division. It meant that its vast columns of tanks and trucks would have to cross the equally large British columns, all in the dark and rain. British commanders thought it was 'risky' at best. But they had to obey. Their solution was to send their main fighting units first, then pause to allow the Big Red One to pass through and, finally, nine hours later, to get the vital British supply trucks to come through as well. The tension was acute.

'The potential for this not going right,' one senior officer told us, 'was very great indeed.' No soldier likes being cut off from his supplies, least of all on his way into battle.

Their hatches were tight shut, they were fully dressed in their chemical protection suits and each of them was wondering: 'Who'll get hit first?' The Challenger crews of D squadron of the Queen's Royal Irish Hussars were rising towards a ridge in 'arrowhead' formation and they had no idea what was ahead of them. They were doing more than 30 mph, gliding smoothly over the sand, and for many 'it was pure adrenalin'. In one tank, a cassette player boomed with the stirring sound of 'I Vow to Thee My Country'. In others, there was silence, each member of the four-man crew straining through his sights for signs of the first battle. Major Toby Maddison, the squadron commander, announced over the radio: 'There's nothing friendly ahead of us. You're free to fire.' It was 3.15p.m. on Monday, 25 February and the first British tanks were pushing into Iraq. There was nervousness – and confusion.

Only a few hours before, the crews of D squadron had seen their first Iraqis. They were in a forlorn huddle in American custody. Some of the British troops felt reassured that, after all, the Iraqis 'weren't 10 feet tall'. But for most of them, it was the first, daunting glimpse of real war. The training was well and truly over, at a time when their nerves hadn't been helped by the latest intelligence. At dawn the previous day, D squadron had been sent a transparent plastic map marking the Iraqi positions in red, oval shapes – known as 'goose-eggs' in military jargon. To everyone's horror, the map was covered with them, 'just like measles'. In a gale and by torchlight, the young officers tried to copy the markings onto their own maps, struggling to keep the trace steady, and scarcely hiding the fact that they were 'shocked and frightened' by what they saw.

Now the tanks of D squadron were entering that nightmare, and they hadn't gone far when a radio message compounded their anxiety. From the battlegroup headquarters, Captain Andrew Cuthbert called out: 'Charlie Charlie One' – the instruction for all commanders to listen in. 'I do stress that this is an unconfirmed report,' he told them, 'but we've had indications that there are two enemy battalions closing from the northeast.' It seemed that the counter-attack everyone had dreaded was finally under way. The tank crews peered out nervously into the gloom until the next message came. That report on the two enemy battalions, it said, is now known to be bogus. There was relief but also fury. One tank commander felt badly let down by Intelligence and swore he'd never trust them again for the rest of the campaign. 'Everything we got from them turned out to be wrong and useless,' he said later. It was an unhappy start. And then the GPS satellite navigation system packed up.

It was the only way the tank commanders could pick their way through the featureless desert terrain. The system, highly praised by those fortunate enough to be issued with a unit, had one failing: for two hours every morning and another two every evening, the orbits of the satellites meant the entire Gulf region lost its cover. It slowed the pace of the advance. Lieutenant-Colonel Charles Rogers of the Staffords had already warned his men: 'There'll have to be great flexibility; in other words, nothing will go according to plan.'

Nothing did, least of all the first encounters with the enemy. They turned out to be completely one-sided – but no one knew if that would be the pattern for the rest of the campaign. The British tanks inched towards the Iraqi positions, fired a few shots at them and waited for a reaction. Usually there was some sporadic machine-gun fire in return, and then a 'mad waving of white flags, white underpants, white boards and scraps of paper'. Dozens of figures would loom out of the night and run wildly to try to give themselves up to their attackers. In the driving rain and the dark it was chaos. More than once, from one side of a set of Iraqi trenches, would come surrendering prisoners – and, from another, gunfire. Commanders faced the impossible choice of risking their men's lives to save others, or returning fire knowing that some would-be prisoners might get caught in the middle.

They took no chances with what they thought were their toughest Iraqi objectives, each of which General Smith had named after a metal. At objective 'Zinc', the only way commanders could find out the strength of the Iraqis there was to send in a patrol. At 10p.m. on the division's first night in Iraq, three tanks of the Queen's Royal Irish Hussars lumbered off into 'the worst weather we'd ever seen'. The mission, assigned to them by their colonel, Arthur Denaro, was either to draw fire or identify what was ahead of them. It was 11.30p.m. before their TOGS, the astonishingly powerful thermal observation night-sights, picked up some 'hot spots' half a mile away. But by then the division's huge array of artillery was lined up behind them. It had orders to saturate the area with shells and rockets at 1a.m. The patrol had to hurry back to safety. With only minutes to go, the three tanks were still on the wrong side of the 'Fire Support Line', the invisible boundary dividing friendly from hostile territory. One waiting captain leapt out of his tank and waved his torch frantically at the returning patrol to urge them to speed up. They made it at 12.58a.m.

Exactly two minutes later the horizon behind them lit up with an extraordinary ferocity. Hundreds of shells and rockets blasted into the air, vanished into the cloud and then reappeared beneath it several miles ahead, scattering thousands of tiny bomblets over the ground. The noise was deafening, the ground was shaking and there was never a moment when there weren't dozens of brilliant rays of light streaking through the night sky. The bombardment went on relentlessly for 27 minutes. Most of the 7th Armoured Brigade stopped to survey the scene before them. Tank crews opened their hatches and watched with astonishment. The brigade commander, Patrick Cordingley, even climbed out of his Challenger, mesmerised by a sight he found 'awe-inspiring'.

'It was like luminous rain,' one lieutenant said. 'It was the most staggering fireworks display,' said another. Thank God it's saving our lives, thought Lt-Col. Arthur Denaro, and thank God we aren't on the end of it.

One officer remembers: 'Out of the shit and the dust and the gloom came surrendering Iraqis running towards us.' But the true impact of the attack didn't become clear till daylight. The advancing units discovered that almost every piece of Iraqi equipment had been destroyed. Whole artillery emplacements had been reduced to smoking pits. At one position, the troops found a 15-year-old boy without his hands, a 52-year-old man missing a leg and others with their spines horribly exposed or their eyeballs dislodged. No one paused to count the dead.

An artillery officer who helped to co-ordinate the bombardment said:

Their whole world had been destroyed. The overpressure was so incredible. There was blood coming from their eyes and mouths. They had no will to do anything, their legs wouldn't work, they were paralysed. We'd see groups of soldiers who were aimless, ambling around, and you'd shout at them, but you wouldn't get through.

The injured were rushed back for treatment but for several it was already too late.

By now the frontline American units were about to find the Republican Guard. The tanks of 'Ghost' and 'Eagle' troops of the US Army's 2nd Armoured Cavalry Regiment were advancing cautiously through a sandstorm so intense they could hardly see ahead. All they knew was that sometime soon they'd encounter the formidable Tawakalna or 'Go with God' division whose role was to block the allies from reaching the rest of the Republican Guard. If there was to be a 'mother of all battles', Captain Mark Santiano and his crew were thinking, this would be the start of it. But the first encounter, when it eventually came, could hardly have been more frightening – for either side.

An American tank was climbing one side of a large embankment when the clouds of swirling dust suddenly parted to reveal, just 50 yards ahead, an Iraqi T-72 tank, one of their best, approaching up the other side. Both crews braked as hard as they could and reversed at high-speed. But the Americans were quicker off the mark and managed to fire two rounds which, amazingly, passed through the top of the sand embankment and destroyed the enemy tank the other side. The first big battle had begun and, however abject the collapse of the Iraqi forces elsewhere, the Iraqis here were coming out to fight.

'They were advancing all right,' says Santiano. 'I don't care what people say about the Iraqis not fighting because those guys we found had moved out and were looking for us.' One of the tank platoons under his command even found itself being outnumbered by T-72s swarming all around. The unit's confidential history admits the platoon was in danger of being 'overrun' and that it was only saved by a hurriedly-called artillery barrage of more than 2000 shells. But that was the exception: the rule quickly became that the crews in the American M1A1 tanks and Bradley fighting vehicles could not only see the Iraqis from farther away, but they also found it easier to hit them with their more powerful weapons.

'Each of us, it didn't matter whether we were in tanks or Bradleys, was taking out their tanks,' Santiano said. 'Even the control vehicle that was supposed to run the show joined in and took out six tanks and five APCs (Armoured Personnel Carriers). It was amazing.' He was stunned by the power of his weapons and had never expected them to be so much better than the Iraqis': 'We just got more and more confident knowing we couldn't be beat.'

The latest tank shells, made of extremely heavy depleted uranium, or 'DU', impressed them most. One lieutenant said:

> You wouldn't believe the sight of it. We'd put a DU round into a T-72 and you'd think for a second that nothing was happening, that maybe you'd missed and he was going to fire back, and then boom! the whole thing just explodes and immediately melts right to the ground before your eyes. Wow!

Like the allied pilots at the start of the war, they were almost hypnotised by the potency of their technology.

One young artillery controller, who was too busy to see the battle around him, couldn't believe the reports he was getting over the radio – that such a major engagement was being fought by his relatively small unit, with such success. After what seemed to him like hours of combat, his 'bladder was bursting' so he ordered his driver to stop and let him out. He was astounded by the sight of the fighting all around him: 'I was standing there turning right around and everywhere I looked there were things exploding, TOW anti-tank missiles shooting through the air, fires all around. The noise and light were incredible. I never did finish, I just leapt back inside for cover.'

The Iraqis were firing back where they could but either missed or failed to fire before being hit, or saw their shells land on target and, to their horror, only cause minimal damage. Some even seemed to bounce off the American armour.

By the time darkness fell, in this one engagement alone, 75 Iraqi tanks and armoured personnel carriers had been destroyed with unknown casualties, while, of the small American force, just one Bradley fighting vehicle had been badly hit and its driver killed; he was the only American

ALL NECESSARY MEANS

to die in this first encounter with what was supposed to be the élite of Saddam's army. It was a pattern to be repeated again and again as the allies advanced.

If the most forward Republican Guard units thought they were in trouble, the war was turning out to be a disaster for the rest of the Tawakalna division, following behind. Their move south had been detected by the radar of a J-STARS spy-plane, and orders were quickly sent to three B-52 bombers on their way from Spain to divert from their planned target and attack the Iraqi columns instead. Captain John Scott Ladner and his crew, 30 000 feet above the battlefield, spotted the dark shapes of the formations against the pale desert and, after checking with the nearest army units to make sure 'we didn't bomb our friendlies', they unloaded their huge sets of bombs with clinical ease. 'The Army guys called us back and said, "you did a good job, we enjoyed it".' What they were enjoying was a massacre.

As for the Republican Guard units who'd dug themselves into fixed positions in the sand, their fate was all but sealed. They were to be the victims of the heaviest American forces, including the 'Spearhead' 3rd Armoured Division. One of its battalion commanders was Lieutenant-Colonel John Kalb, an intimidating figure who wore sunglasses whatever the weather and always had a gnarled walking stick at his side. He'd planned his attack 'according to the textbook' and put it into effect almost effortlessly. His 14 Bradleys, each with TOW anti-tank missiles, and his 40 tanks approached as quietly as they could and lined up near the Iraqi positions. The Americans could see the turrets of the Iraqi tanks poking up out of the sand – but the Iraqis hadn't noticed them; some were later to say that they'd been told the allied armies were still five or six days away.

The Americans opened fire at once and could hardly miss. Their shells and missiles fell on the Iraqi tanks in a sudden, terrifying flash. The Iraqi crews who survived ran desperately for cover. According to Kalb, 'it was like a thousand tiny ants running all over the place completely surprised'. Any tanks that were seen trying to move into better protective positions 'we just blew away'. It was an onslaught that lasted only 10 minutes. 'I'm not kidding: in 10 minutes we'd killed 50 vehicles.'

For Kalb, it was a triumph of technology and training, and there was no need to feel much sympathy.

You don't want war to be fair. You want it to be as unfair as possible. It's not like ping-pong when you want the other guy to be able to hit the ball back. In war, you don't. Your job is just to focus as much extreme violence as possible with the single aim of winning. That's exactly what I did.

Wherever the allies could catch them, units of the Republican Guard were being crushed with a monotonous inevitability, and it made one wonder why Saddam's supposedly 'élite' troops had ever been held in such high esteem.

T hey swarmed wide-eyed around allied tanks and pleaded to be fed and driven to the camps; the rest of the Iraqi army too was in a state of collapse. Only some 36 hours into the ground offensive, on Monday, 25 February, Saddam had ordered his soldiers to withdraw. Kuwait, he declared, was no longer part of Iraq. Too late, allied leaders replied, as they watched his forces almost fall into their arms on a scale they could hardly believe. The troops, ravenously hungry after several days without supplies, were desperate to surrender – and they did so in countless different, often bizarre, ways.

In one place, dozens of Iraqis were found to have used their own barbed wire to build themselves a PoW camp and save the allies the trouble. Some even surrendered to a small unmanned reconnaissance plane that had been landed near by. Others rushed to help allied vehicles stuck in the mud, and then gave themselves up. For Schwarzkopf's troops, trying to advance at high speed, the sheer numbers became a burden. At least 120 Iraqis had 'attached' themselves to one British tank commander because they'd identified him as a friendly face. So when he sped off towards another group of Iraqi soldiers, the 120 sprinted after him across the desert, determined to remain in his custody. On another occasion, half a dozen Iraqi prisoners were perched on the top of a Warrior fighting

ALL NECESSARY MEANS

vehicle when the driver suddenly swerved to avoid machine-gun fire, throwing the soldier guarding the Iraqis off the turret. They leapt to his rescue, dusted him down and one even handed him back his gun so he could continue his watch over them.

Not all Iraqi troops surrendered immediately. A British Lance-Corporal, Ian Dewsnap, the driver of an earth-moving tractor, found himself entirely alone as about 30 Iraqi soldiers approached him. He realised they wanted to give themselves up so he herded them together and disarmed them, only to see another 60 to 70 Iraqis approaching more menacingly. Dewsnap, still alone and without a radio, fired over the heads and ordered them to lie down. They obeyed; one lightly-armed British soldier had taken control of up to 100 Iraqis. Dewsnap was awarded the Military Medal for his gallantry.

Other Iraqis were so eager to be taken prisoner that they complained if they were ignored. One stripped naked to get attention, while another sat down in front of a British tank in protest at being told to walk to the PoW camp. Two older conscripts even ended up as temporary recruits, after being won over by their first British Army breakfast of bacon and eggs. They seemed keen to stay, so the squaddies, who called them Bill and Ben because they couldn't master their names, taught them how to make the tea.

By this stage, the war had become a rout – and the Apache gunship crews, flying through the sky like swarms of killer bees, had never been busier. They called it 'working' the enemy, which was a euphemism for destroying them. 'They were out there having a heyday,' according to Lieutenant-Colonel Terry Johnson, the deputy commander of one Apache unit. 'I saw death and destruction everywhere,' said one of the pilots, Major Sam Hubbard. 'Dante's *Inferno* was all I could think of: I had a tank explode right under me. Coming back it was almost 10 kilometres wide of tanks burning and destroyed. As far as you could see there were tanks burning.'

It was the most extreme case of warfare-by-television. The pilots and navigators found their targets by adjusting an on-board night-vision camera and picking out the shape of a tank or truck on a blue-grey television screen in the cockpit. They would then line up the cross-hairs, launch a Hellfire missile or fire cannon and see their victim erupt in savage flame a split-second later. Backed by the most advanced technology, it couldn't have been easier. In fact, the attacks looked so one-sided, so like an arcade game, that only rarely were the Apaches' video-recordings released: they were too gruesome.

The BBC did manage to obtain one tape unofficially. It showed the chilling simplicity of an attack on an Iraqi convoy. Once the first few vehicles had exploded, the Apache's camera caught sight of dozens of Iraqi soldiers fleeing for their lives, tiny figures running from an enemy using weaponry of incomprehensible power. For the crews, it was all accomplished with the push of electronic buttons. The only physical sensation was the shuddering of the helicopter as it launched its missiles and shells.

The pace of the onslaught was now so rapid that the Apaches' support staff had to move forward in their own helicopters to keep them resupplied. One technician, Sergeant Bill Evans, couldn't help noting the pilots 'coming in dry, with no bullets – but with big smiles'. Some of the crews tried to distinguish between Iraqis who chose to fight, and those who tried to surrender. 'People with their hands up didn't get fired on,' according to Captain Mark Wilson, 'but ones firing or scurrying for vehicles got suppressed.' Other Apache crews 'suppressed' all the Iraqis they saw. 'The way I look at it,' said Captain Greg Vallet, 'if he'd seen me first, he would have killed me.' Even though it all seemed so easy, the allied troops didn't have much trouble motivating themselves. Regular reminders of what the war was supposed to be about helped to fire the crews with enthusiasm. Captain Wilson revealed to the US Army's newspaper that they were given briefings every night on the atrocities Iraq had committed in Kuwait, 'so every time we got out there, there was no holding back so Saddam can't do this again'.

The two British Scorpion reconnaissance vehicles were high on a ridge. It was 27 February, the last day of the war, and some of the

ALL NECESSARY MEANS

crewmen, from the Queen's Royal Irish Hussars, had got out to gather yet more prisoners. They had piled up the Iraqis' guns in the sand and one of the Scorpions was preparing to crush them. It was almost routine – until the attack started. Powerful and accurate rounds landed, wounding two of the crewmen, one of them badly. They all dashed for the cover of a sand dune as tank rounds and machine-gun fire sprayed all around them for an agonisingly long eight minutes. They were trapped and, with ghastly irony, the onslaught only stopped when they found and waved the same piece of white material that the Iraqis had used to signal their surrender only shortly before. It was then that they realised their attackers were American and that this was yet another incident of so-called 'friendly fire'. As a helicopter arrived to carry away the wounded, friendship was the last thought in British minds: one of the American rounds had even gone through the middle of the fluorescent identification sheet carried by all allied vehicles.

It wasn't only the Americans who made mistakes. A few hours later, Challenger tanks from the 14/20th King's Hussars fired on a pair of British Spartan air defence vehicles, injuring two soldiers; and only the day before, another Challenger, from the Scots Dragoon Guards, had shot at a Warrior infantry vehicle that served as part of the Staffords' Battlegroup headquarters, wounding an officer. But the worst British loss through friendly fire was on 26 February, when a company of the Royal Regiment of Fusiliers was mistaken for the enemy by American pilots. Nine men were killed and seven injured when, without any warning, two American A-10 tankbusters launched Maverick missiles at a pair of Warriors.

'We were more gutted than angry,' said one soldier, 'gutted that we had lost blokes for no reason.'

Everyone had anticipated such losses in the confusion of battle, especially in a multi-national force. Schwarzkopf himself had once been caught in an inaccurately co-ordinated raid by B-52s in Vietnam. But this mistake triggered immediate demands for an inquiry – and, almost as quickly, conflicting accounts emerged. After mounting pressure from relatives of the victims, the Ministry of Defence published the results of its investigation five months after the war. It said that the Warriors had been properly marked; they had not strayed outside their allotted sector; and the British air controller directing the A-10s had been misunderstood by the American pilots. In short, London believes that the Americans were to blame.

That isn't the way it's seen in the United States. Although President Bush told John Major, shortly after the war, that he was 'heartbroken' by the deaths, Lieutenant-General Chuck Horner claimed that the British air controller had been responsible. Horner criticised those campaigning for a full explanation. 'I think it's picking at a scab,' he told us in an interview. He also suggested that the pilots had looked for – and failed to see – the Warriors' friendly markings, the fluorescent sheets and the huge inverted 'V'. He asked us whether if he drove through 10 kilometres of dust, for example, he would have the correct markings. 'Yes, if I'm driving the vehicle,' he said, 'no, if I'm looking for it.'

His suggestion that the Warriors were too dirty to be correctly identified is flatly contradicted, not just by soldiers there at the time, but also by the British Board of Inquiry. It states that an American reconnaissance plane flying over the scene after the attack had managed to see that these were allied vehicles – from a higher altitude than the A-10 pilots who'd made two passes with binoculars before their attack. Why they then launched their missiles may never be known. Nor will the cause of the 35 American deaths through friendly fire – an alarming 25 per cent of all US combat fatalities.

R abir suddenly got new orders. Load up the truck with ammunition and supplies and leave Kuwait City – as fast as you can. For weeks he'd been desperate to get away, exhausted and frightened by the bombing, and aware that the allies were advancing every day. He'd only stayed because in his particular unit the officers were still very much in command. Now that he was allowed to leave, he knew he was in danger: the Iraqi army was in full retreat and at its most vulnerable. Everyone was frantic.

They clambered aboard anything with wheels: fire engines, tanks, self-propelled artillery, mini-buses, coaches, cars, and even bulldozers. On a normal day, the drive to the border should take only an hour and a

ALL NECESSARY MEANS

half. Now, many of them would never make it at all. Their progress was being watched and their destruction plotted.

The Kuwaiti Resistance broke the news first. Its members telephoned Central Command in Riyadh to report that the soldiers they hated so passionately were leaving their city at last. A Kuwaiti Air Force colonel who helped to lead the resistance was among those who now managed to get a call through to allied headquarters. A liaison officer was talking to him when Lieutenant-General Chuck Horner walked by. 'Do you want to talk to Kuwait City?' asked the officer.

Horner talked to the colonel who was looking out of his window and watching the Iraqis pull out: 'They're leaving!' the Kuwaiti said delightedly. 'These are evil people. These are the occupation forces – looters, rapists and torturers.'

Kuwait's seven-month ordeal was ending, and both Horner and the colonel started crying.

J-STARS airborne radar planes confirmed that huge columns were clogging the highways. And, at first light, a US Marine Corps pilot radioed back that the motorway interchanges were full of vehicles, all with their headlights on, using every lane to head north. He declared: 'The big bugout of Kuwait City is on.' His commander, Major-General Royal Moore, realised this was not a move to regroup and fight: 'It was obviously not a tactical deception, they were just getting out.' He needed guidance.

The man in charge of the War Room that night was Brigadier-General Neal, who realised that 'they were exiting Kuwait City big time'. In Neal's mind, there was no question of *not* attacking. In military jargon, the retreat of an enemy is called the 'exploitation phase' in which victory can be assured. So the only choice that night was where to attack the Iraqis and, in that, Neal believed he had two options. He knew that one suitable choke-point was the set of interchanges just outside the city, known as 'the clover leaf'; the other was near the border, at a narrow stretch of the highway where it rises to cross one of the few natural features in Kuwait: the Mutla Ridge. He decided against attacking the interchanges because that would probably keep the bulk of the fleeing Iraqis inside Kuwait City. 'That would have caused us to do city fighting, which would have destroyed the city and probably cost us a lot of casualties.'

Instead, he chose the Mutla Ridge and ordered mines to be dropped across the highway there. Military logic dictates that convoys are best hit from the front first to trap the others behind. It was one of the few times Neal felt that he had to wake General Schwarzkopf to get his approval. At two o'clock that morning he did so. 'I woke him up and he said, "That's the right decision", and he went back to bed.'

The most concentrated air attack of Desert Storm was set in motion. It became known as the 'turkey shoot' because the Iraqis offered virtually no resistance. Their best anti-aircraft weapons were either destroyed, abandoned or packed for the journey; only their smallest guns were available, but the allied jets easily stayed out of range.

Rabir and his colleagues heard the planes before they saw them, and knew they had absolutely no protection. 'There was nowhere to hide, we were trapped,' he recalls. 'The bigger vehicles were the first to get direct hits and explode. Everyone was running and screaming and trying to get away from the fires. Some cars at the back of the convoy crashed into others to get away.'

At first the Iraqis managed to continue their escape, picking paths through vehicles already destroyed. Chuck Horner was annoyed that some of them seemed to be getting away: 'We were having a lot of trouble stopping them because you blow up a vehicle and they pull off the road and pull around it and stuff like that.' The allies were attacking with 'extreme violence' but in Horner's view there was nothing wrong with that. 'We found in Vietnam that by trying to play games in war, all you do is extend it.'

But stormy weather and the smoke from the burning oil wells were hampering the attack, and the only aircraft that had a chance of accurately blocking the front of the convoy were F-15Es, with their infra-red and radar targeting devices. Their pilots had only just gone to sleep but a dozen of them were woken and given an hour and a half to get airborne with the most powerful cluster bombs available, CBU-87s. Each one carries 202 bomblets, all designed to spray lethal shrapnel and incendiary material for 50 feet around.

The pilots flew into a belt of thunderclouds and had to use their radar to find the Iraqi vehicles below them. The crew of one of the first F-15Es on the scene flew 'up to where the bottlenecks were, and we were able to do a lot of damage'. When they returned on another run they found it 'difficult to distinguish the burning vehicles from the oil fires' blazing near by. But by then the convoy had been stopped. Very quickly, the traffic backed up. The escape ground to a halt and the convoy stretched, at a standstill, more than three miles. 'Once we stopped it, it was a lot easier to deal with,' according to the chief of air staff, Buster Glosson. 'They couldn't move. If I could have killed every Iraqi in Kuwait City, I would have.'

With no risk of an Iraqi response, the biggest problem was air traffic control. 'We were wingtip-to-wingtip over there,' one pilot said. The normal practice of carefully planning each allied flight in advance had to be given up. Events were simply moving too fast. The solution, devised by the Marines 3rd Air Wing, which co-ordinated the attack, was to 'stack' the warplanes much as happens to passenger jets above crowded airports. Every 15 minutes a batch of eight freshly-armed jets would be allowed into the stack and held there until the batch ahead of them had dropped all of their bombs. When the airspace over the highway was clear, the next wave would be guided in. Three air controllers, aloft in their own jets, were always on hand to manage the flow. On average, there was an attack every 90 seconds.

Rabir saw some of his fellow Iraqis trying to run away across the sand-dunes only to be shot by aircraft fire or killed by setting off mines. 'Nobody tried to shoot back because we were so outnumbered. I leapt out of the cab and hid underneath the truck. It was hit but mercifully didn't explode. I saw hundreds killed and the attack seemed to go on for hours.'

In fact the Marines commander running the operation, Major-General Moore, decided to 'keep the flow going for almost seven hours, and all we did was pound those roads coming out of Kuwait City'. He only called a halt when the weather closed in and allied ground forces, including the British 1st Armoured Division, were due to approach the area from the west. By then, hundreds of trucks, buses, vans, tanks and armoured personnel carriers were lying wrecked. Probably around 400 Iraqis were killed. For Major-General Moore, 'it was our crowning glory'.

He also felt 'kinda bad that we hammered them like that' and he later justified the attack by claiming that the convoy could have threatened the advancing allied armies. But it was also vindicated, he told us, by what he saw on his first visit to Kuwait City: 'I saw that they were just thugs. They destroyed everything, cut out the carpet, desecrated buildings, took out light sockets, stole engines and tyres off cars, they stole TVs and raped and murdered through Kuwait City.' That convinced him the slaughter had been right: 'It was really kind of an execution.'

He was not the only American commander to see Mutla Ridge as a form of capital punishment. Buster Glosson regarded it as revenge for what the Iraqis had done during the occupation.

> The reason we were zeroing in on that area was because the people that had done all of the rape, pillage and murdering in Kuwait were the people that were trying to get out. I went after that convoy primarily because of the barbaric and ruthless way they had treated people in Kuwait. There were no worse people on the face of the earth.

In the view of some of those in Central Command, everyone driving out through Mutla Ridge that day was a war criminal and no trials were needed to prove it. In fact, many of the most senior Iraqi commanders may already have left, and it is possible that some Kuwaitis being taken to Iraq as hostages may have been among those killed. Although the United Nations had authorised the allies to use 'all necessary means' to liberate Kuwait, it is hard to see how the slaughter of rank-and-file Iraqi conscripts in retreat from the emirate could be judged 'necessary'.

Rabir and some other survivors ran until they collapsed on the roadside and fell asleep. 'When we woke and realised what had happened, we all broke down.'

A s the last planes left the Mutla Ridge on the evening of Wednesday, 27 February, President Bush summoned his top advisers to the Oval Office to take stock. The Iraqis had all but left Kuwait; their retreating columns were being bombed even after they had crossed into Iraq; and the US Army divisions were on the point of cutting them off. Bush wanted to call a halt immediately because he was worried that to continue the destruction of the Iraqi army would look vindictive. One adviser suggested announcing a ceasefire the following morning, to which Bush replied: 'I'd like to do it tonight.' But he added: 'Check it with Norm.'

General Colin Powell picked up the secure hotline to Schwarzkopf. Known as the 'Red Switch', it required both men to insert personal identification keys; this was one of the last times they would have to use it. Schwarzkopf agreed with Powell that hostilities should cease at midnight Washington time that night – 8a.m. the next day, 28 February, in the Gulf. It would mean that the ground war would have lasted 100 hours, a round number which appealed to Bush.

Schwarzkopf later claimed, in an interview with David Frost, that his recommendation had been to 'continue the march' because 'we could have completely closed the door and made it in fact a battle of annihilation'. That suggested he had disagreed with the decision of his president, and he was forced to apologise for a 'poor choice of words'. But Brigadier-General Butch Neal told us that he overheard that call: 'General Schwarzkopf participated in that decision and he agreed with the decision. I was right in there when he was talking to General Powell. It was a mutually-agreed upon decision.'

In another telephone conversation that day, with Britain's overall commander, Sir Patrick Hine, Schwarzkopf left the distinct impression that, while he went along with the President's decision in principle, he probably disagreed with its specific timing. 'He might have wanted to go on another 12 to 24 hours,' Hine recalls.

That's also what the British Government wanted – in secret. It has been confirmed to us by two members of the War Cabinet that John Major opposed Bush's decision to end the war as too hasty. The assessment reaching Downing Street from British intelligence analysts was that less Iraqi weaponry had been destroyed, and more was escaping, than the Americans claimed. Above all, it was Whitehall's view that the big American divisions should be given time to complete their swing east through Iraq – to block the escape of the Republican Guard. 'We thought it was better to get the Iraqi forces completely encircled before stopping,' according to one member of the War Cabinet.

But the advice Bush got from General Powell was clear. 'By tonight, there really won't be an enemy there; if you go another day, you're basically just fighting stragglers.' In London, it was recognised that 'it was not in the nature of the American army to go around shooting people in the back'. There was concern none the less that a significant number of the enemy were withdrawing to Basra. The Foreign Policy Adviser, Charles Powell told us: 'This slightly unfortunate outbreak of chivalry on the part of the US military was 24 hours too early because what they hadn't done was close the loop, bottled up all the Iraqi forces and disarmed them before they left.' The Prime Minister, John Major, 'queried whether it wouldn't have been better to go on for another 24 hours'.

According to another member of the War Cabinet, Major 'pressed hard' for Washington to agree. He instructed Powell to convey his view to the White House. Downing Street officials believed they were much better prepared than their American counterparts to judge the consequences of the timing of the end of the war. They had already drawn up contingency plans for how to handle the final moments of Desert Storm. Powell used the pre-set dialling on his secure phone line to call up the President's National Security Adviser, Brent Scowcroft, and told him that, in London's opinion, 'it might be better to go on a bit longer and tie it all up'. The same message was delivered by the Foreign Secretary, Douglas Hurd, who was in Washington that day. None of this lobbying worked. It was an American-led campaign and the President had made his decision.

Word reached the troops of the British division in the early hours of Thursday, 28 February. Their orders had changed several times during the night and now, finally, they were told to race to the Kuwait–Basra road and block it before the fighting stopped at 8a.m. It meant a high-speed dash across the desert, so fast that two Challenger tanks failed to spot Iraqi bunkers ahead of them and fell through their corrugated-iron roofs. But, by 7.25a.m., the most advanced British units had reached the road and closed it. They were the first to see the aftermath of the attack.

ALL NECESSARY MEANS

Twelve hours after the last air attack, many of the vehicles were still burning amid the sea of devastation. There were bodies on the ground, blown out of their cars and trucks, and limbs scattered everywhere. One officer peered into the back of a lorry and saw ten Iraqi soldiers sitting 'looking normal, but all dead', killed by the tiny fragments of a cluster bomb. The pall overhead from the burning oilfields added to the 'dismal and unhappy feeling' of many of the troops there. After the long wait in the desert, and the anxiety of combat, ending the campaign amid such a scene of unrestrained destruction was 'an unpleasant anti-climax'. It was also the first chance in 100 hours to catch some sleep. The order to stop fighting was only minutes away.

The message to suspend all hostilities was written in the War Room in Riyadh. Butch Neal made a note in his diary of the time Schwarzkopf signed it: 3.30a.m. He also jotted down part of what it said. 'When we suspend offensive operations, take all measures necessary to ensure your troops' safety. If attacked, attack. If not, defend.'

The news spread almost instantaneously – on the ground, at sea and in the air. First Lieutenant Terry Abel was flying an American tanker over Iraq when, at 8a.m., 5a.m. in London, he heard an AWACS control plane suddenly call out: 'Attention all players, attention all players! This is Bulldog on guard. Effective immediately, all offensive activity to cease.' The message was repeated, then several times more, as pilot after pilot radioed in asking to hear it again. It took a while to sink in. 'Then people just started yelling on the radios,' Abel said. The airwaves exploded with jubilant voices.

The war was over and Central Command staff in Riyadh were watching President Bush on television declare: 'Kuwait is liberated. Iraq's army is defeated. Our military objectives are met.' It was a triumphant address – but it was interrupted by the frenzied alert of a Scud attack. The euphoria in the War Room evaporated. It looked as though Saddam was firing a final salvo. When it turned out to be a false alarm, Neal wiped his brow in relief and wrote one last entry in his diary: 'Phew!'

Chapter 7
WHO HAD WE
L BERATED?

'Tonight, the Kuwaiti flag once again flies above the capital of a free and sovereign nation.' President George Bush, 27 February 1991.

US Senator Ernest Hollings, June 1991. **'Down in Kuwait, the torture and rape continue under the emir.'**

mid the sound of laughter and victorious gunfire, Kuwaiti children were clambering over Iraq's abandoned defences along the shore of their capital city. The tanks, trenches and bunkers had become a huge adventure playground, a final humiliation for what had been the fourth largest army in the world. On the heady morning of liberation, Kuwaitis were so relieved that their terror was over, so busy celebrating, that they hardly gave a thought to the danger of their children playing on a seafront still littered with mines. But it wasn't only the children who were exploring the abandoned Iraqi fortifications; everyone from allied generals to the first western reporters were intrigued to discover what life had been like for Iraqi conscripts, who had spent so many months gazing at the Gulf, wondering when it would all be over.

It felt uncomfortable, exploring these deserted bunkers. They were no more than underground hovels but they were recognisable enough as people's homes for the prying to seem intrusive. Still scattered inside were the soldiers' unwashed clothes, battered helmets and filthy mattresses, riddled with lice and beetles. Small cooking fires were left

ALL NECESSARY MEANS

alight, kettles, teacups, shaving brushes and pathetic collections of tins and packets beside them. In the rush to get away, one Iraqi had left a letter half-written on the upturned crate that had been his desk. Pinned to the walls were a few adornments: looted curtains and photographs of scantily-dressed models and sports cars torn from magazines. Some of the bunkers had makeshift electric lighting, others had little niches cut in the sand walls for paraffin lamps. In the most opulent city in the world, the bulk of the Iraqi army had been living in squalor.

The commanders of this brutal occupation force looked after themselves rather better. On the edge of the city, by its Seventh Ring Road, one of the authors stumbled on a huge, and much more sophisticated, network of Iraqi bunkers, which sprawled for miles. It was like a little town. Built of reinforced concrete and supplied with power and water, this was a defence complex untouched by allied bombing. Some of the bunkers were still furnished with tables, wardrobes and carpets but most had already been stripped bare – by Kuwaitis. After being looted themselves for seven months, they had decided it was now their turn. Soon, the tortured would also do some torturing.

Although Kuwait had just been liberated by the allies, western reporters, including one of the authors, still had a struggle getting in, even in a press convoy under British Army escort. Cautiously, the cars wound their way through dozens of burnt-out tanks and trucks creating an obstacle course along the main road from the border. Negotiating it in the total darkness caused by the raging oil fires required constant concentration. For one journalist, it was too much; his car rammed into a tank turret, somehow managing to impale itself on the long barrel of the gun. But then came the biggest barrier of all – an officious Saudi colonel who decided to refuse to let this particular press party into Kuwait City. The only reason, it turned out, was injured pride; no one had bothered to ask for his permission, not even the British army major escorting the reporters. The two officers had a long, bitter argument while the convoy sat immobilised for several hours.

Eventually, a BBC satellite telephone was set up in the middle of the road so that the major could appeal to higher authorities. When the Saudi colonel realised what was happening, he ordered his troops to prepare to open fire on the telephone, without any regard for its cost, let alone its value to the reporters who depended on it. It was the most extraordinary display of petulance and suddenly one wondered how the allies had ever managed to stay together long enough to win the war. In the end, the colonel had to relent though only after extracting a grovelling apology. By the time the convoy eventually arrived in Kuwait City, it was what would have been rush-hour almost anywhere else in the world, yet nothing stirred. Although the Iraqis had gone, many of the Kuwaitis hadn't yet come out; nervously, they were staying in their homes – still waking up from their long nightmare.

When they took to the streets, the celebrations began, with scenes reminiscent of Europe's liberation in 1945. Colonel Jesse Johnson, commander of America's Special Forces, listened with pride as the crowd chanted 'Bush, Bush, Bush!' Johnson laughed when they also tried to shout 'Schwarzkopf, Schwarzkopf, Schwarzkopf!' only to discover his name was too awkward to pronounce. It was a grateful nation and a grateful city, thought Johnson, as vast columns of allied tanks trundled through the cheering crowds and as the balmy air filled with the stuttering chatter of machine-gun fire. The shooting was in joy, not anger, but it was frightening none the less. 'What goes up must come down,' one allied officer warned, as young Kuwaitis sprayed bullets into the sky. Indeed, there were reports later of several people being killed as a result; it seemed ridiculous that anyone who had survived the horrors of the Iraqi occupation should now have to die so unnecessarily. Privately, American officers were furious with the ill-disciplined Arab troops who were so trigger-happy, but this was a party no one, not even liberators, dared stop.

Come and see!' said a Kuwaiti gleefully. By the American embassy, a platoon of US Marines was sitting around a campfire, wearing Rambo headbands and listening to the blare of heavy metal music from their portable hi-fi. They looked like they'd just stepped off the set of a film about the Vietnam war. In fact, the Marines had made a remarkable

162

ALL NECESSARY MEANS

discovery, which they were eager to share with us. In a school, tucked away behind the embassy, they had stumbled across a vast sandpit covering most of the floor. It was a detailed model of how the Iraqis would defend Kuwait. The sandpit had been created with meticulous care. The sea was painted blue and the shoreline was marked with miniature barbed wire. Inland, cut-out pieces of card, clumps of Lego, and miniature guns marked the positions of Iraqi battalions, minefields and artillery units. Two carved wooden sticks represented the city's famous water towers. More menacingly, little flags with the image of two crossed spoons marked the locations of chemical weapons.

The Marines perched themselves on the sandpit's walls and speculated that Saddam Hussein himself might have come here to ponder this elaborate plan. He was certainly filmed visiting Kuwait shortly before the war and, quite possibly, chose this room to be briefed by his generals on their strategy for its defence. If Saddam did come, he never realised they were preparing for the wrong sort of war. The model, with three bright red cardboard arrows placed on the sea and pointing to the coast, depicted the Iraqis' obsessive fear of an amphibious attack. It was a miscalculation that forced them to commit no fewer than 28 battalions to defending the shore, each unit marked with a loop of blue ribbon. Overnight, as the allies swung in from the opposite direction, the sandpit had become a monument to Iraqi strategic naïvety. Outside, where the plan had been put into effect, there were intricately-laid minefields, antiquated artillery pointing out to sea, and sandbagged pillboxes on every street corner. It was all evidence of how thoroughly Saddam had misunderstood allied thinking. While he had hoped for a long and bloody ground war, General Schwarzkopf had outgunned and outpaced him. The Marines found the sandpit so amusing they laughed out loud.

The helicopter bringing Britain's ambassador back to Kuwait landed on a dusty football pitch next to the embassy. 'It's absolutely tremendous to be back!' shouted Michael Weston over the roar of the rotor blades. It was early evening, and a light, oily drizzle was falling over liberated Kuwait. Weston seemed startled by the size of the reception awaiting him. After five months under siege in the embassy compound, he could have been forgiven for never wanting to set foot inside the place again. In fact, he was as happy as the Kuwaitis lining up to shake his hand. His way had been cleared by British Marines launching a spectacular, if rather over-dramatic, operation to search the embassy for mines and booby-traps – 85 of them had abseiled from helicopters in a show that looked suspiciously media-oriented. Weston even admitted, as he was showing one of the authors around, that the damage to his embassy had been caused, not by the Iraqis, but by overzealous Marines blasting their way into the building.

The ambassador was keen to point out the grounds where he and his consul, Larry Banks, had lived off the land until 16 December – a gesture of British defiance against Saddam's order to close the embassy down, which had so irritated the Americans. 'Larry created this vegetable patch while the siege was going on,' the ambassador explained, 'but the siege continued long enough for us both to enjoy the fruits of his garden.' The two diplomats had also constructed a makeshift shower by piercing a pipe running from the embassy well.

With all that behind him now, Weston watched the Union flag being raised once more, albeit rather incompetently. A gusty wind wrapped the flag around the pole and it took several minutes for the British troops to hoist it to the top. Still, it served as a symbol of victory and Lieutenant-General Sir Peter de la Billière remarked proudly how British diplomats had been the last to leave Kuwait and were now among the first to return. But the celebrations were muted. Everyone was still shocked by what they were discovering of Kuwait's agony.

It can never be easy for the victim of torture to return to where he was made to suffer. But Mohammed al-Rakas, a quiet young man who had worked with the Kuwaiti Resistance, was anxious to show us where he had been put through almost unimaginable pain. In brilliant midday sunshine, he walked into Nayef Palace, a sprawling building, which under the Iraqis had become a chamber of horrors. Straightaway he knew where to take us. It was still there in the courtyard – the simple metal frame that looked like it might once have had a child's swing attached to it. But this one was for another purpose. Calmly, he demonstrated how the Iraqi secret police, the Mukhabarat, locked him in handcuffs, which they then hooked onto the frame's crossbar. There, he said, he hung as the interrogators set to work. Usually they would run a cable, still lying on the ground, from a power point to the metal frame. Mohammed said that he was electrocuted until his body was numb with the pain:

> You could stand 20 to 30 seconds, and then you'd just black out. At the same time they'd be hitting you with all sorts of things, like lumps of wood or strips of rubber. Sometimes, even when you'd done nothing, you'd still want to say 'yes, yes, yes I did it'.

The dead told their tales of terror almost as eloquently as the living. In Mubarak hospital, mutilated corpses lay in metal drawers or under blankets. Dr Abdul Behbehani pulled out the body of a father of four, whose legs had been horribly burned with acid and who had died from a bullet which entered his brain through the left ear. Another man had had his skull smashed and his eyes gouged out, as well as being shot at close range. The doctor noticed how the Iraqis liked to experiment with their victims. 'They didn't just kill people in one way, they were trying to make it a work of art.'

Amnesty International, which conducted a lengthy investigation, listed no fewer than 38 types of torture devised by the Iraqis, including 'prolonged beating all over the body, breaking of limbs, extinguishing cigarettes on the body and in the eyes, gouging out of the eyes, electric shocks, sexual assault and mock executions'.

Dr Behbehani, who had continued to work at the hospital throughout the occupation, saw the victims of every kind of atrocity. On each shift, he would expect to receive between three and seven bodies, with the numbers rising soon after the Iraqis arrived and shortly before they left. 'Their first crime was that they were Kuwaiti,' he said of the corpses in his morgue. 'Their second crime was that they left their houses.'

Yet not all the alleged atrocities which had so shocked the world turned out to be true – though many Kuwaitis regarded it as a near-her-

WHO HAD WE LIBERATED?

esy to say so. Two wealthy young Kuwaitis, Mubarak and Ahmed, who generously offered us food and accommodation, were outraged at the suggestion. They were considerate, compassionate people – the very best kind of Kuwaitis, who had stayed on after the invasion helping to organise food distribution. Now they wanted to help the BBC to tell the outside world how they had suffered. At dinner one evening, a Kuwaiti guest asked why the allegations of Iraqi atrocities had always been reported by British television as claims, rather than as facts. When the explanation was offered that we couldn't be sure that the allegations were true without independent corroboration, another Kuwaiti guest spoke up. He said the BBC had been right to be cautious because Kuwaitis had exaggerated the amount of killing, perhaps as much as ten times. 'We had to do it,' he confessed, 'to get the world's attention.'

It wasn't only Kuwaitis who had exploited Iraq's atrocities for propaganda. Leaders of the alliance did so too, in particular President Bush. Amnesty International's general secretary, Ian Martin, could hardly believe the hypocrisy. For years, he and his colleagues had been denouncing the abuses committed by Iraq only to be ignored. 'Just months before the invasion of Kuwait,' Martin recalled, 'the United Nations Human Rights Commission decided not to take action.'

After 2 August, it was all very different. The telephones at Amnesty's London headquarters were jammed with inquiries about Iraq's record on human rights, and copies of the organisation's past reports on Iraq were in huge demand. Amnesty's reaction was scathing. 'There were many people in and out of government at the end of 1990 who had reason for deep shame, and sometimes self-interested regret, at their failure to stand up against human rights violations.' The American, British and French governments had also turned a blind eye to atrocities in some of the regimes that were now partners in the coalition against Saddam. Ian Martin noticed how abuses committed by enemies were exploited as propaganda, while those committed by allies 'were lost in the silence'.

Most emotive of the accusations levelled against the Iraqi occupation force was that troops had thrown premature babies from their hospital incubators and removed the machines to Baghdad. It was an allegation much repeated by President Bush and, although at one cemetery officials reported finding the bodies of about 120 babies buried since Saddam's invasion, there was nothing to prove a connection with the seizure of the incubators. One of the authors visited Kuwait's maternity hospitals for evidence of this atrocity and heard the same, negative answer from doctors and nurses alike. 'Yes, it was terrible,' one said, 'but, no, it wasn't here; it was somewhere else down the road.' Investigators from Amnesty were also trying to substantiate the allegation. After exhaustive enquiries, they concluded: 'the story did not stand up'. A Kuwaiti doctor told us that the Iraqis had, at one stage, planned to steal the incubators but then thought better of it. So many babies had died prematurely, he said, because there were simply too few medical staff to care for them: most had fled after the invasion. He didn't blame them for escaping yet he looked ashamed.

Like any other country after liberation, many in Kuwait were racked with guilt for not doing enough to resist the occupation. Publicly, they all boasted that they were heroes. At a petrol station one afternoon, the attendant was describing the horror of Iraqi rule when we asked: 'Were you in the Resistance?' Defensively, he replied: 'Everyone was in the Resistance.'

Kuwaitis weren't the only ones to suffer. Iraqis died under the regime as well. Ironically, the most vivid evidence of this came from the firm of American public relations consultants hired by the Kuwaiti government to improve its image. The consultants had obtained an amateur videotape, secretly filmed during the occupation, which showed the execution of three men by firing squad. Copies of the tape were rapidly distributed to all the television correspondents in Kuwait, most of whom assumed the three victims were Kuwaitis. They were seen dying on a patch of waste ground where executions were an almost daily routine. The tape showed a small crowd and a child cycling nonchalantly by as the six-man firing squad took aim and shot for some 30 seconds. Afterwards, the onlookers drifted away while an army ambulance collected the bodies. It was a terrifying glimpse of the brutal reality of occupied Kuwait. But for the public relations consultants, the release of the tape caused severe embarrassment because the victims turned out to be Iraqi, not Kuwaiti. It was later discovered that they were soldiers who had been caught stealing. Rather than illustrating the murderous nature of Saddam's regime and Kuwait's noble endurance of it, the incident showed that at least one element of the Iraqi army was trying to keep its troops in order, even though the Iraqi regime itself was committing theft, and worse, on a far larger scale.

Now, as Kuwait celebrated with parties and parades, the little country was consumed with a new terror – mutual suspicion and recrimination. The atmosphere soon became sinister. At night, with no electricity to power the street lights, landmarks seemed to disappear and it was frighteningly easy to get lost. The only illuminations were the torches of the Kuwaiti militiamen at road-blocks. If drivers failed to spot them and slow down, they would find themselves peering through the dark at machine-guns. Once the militiamen recognised you as a western reporter, there were words of welcome to Kuwait and thanks for the allied victory. If you looked like a Palestinian, it was very different.

'Death to Palestinian Traitors!' read graffiti on a wall in Hawalli, the predominantly Palestinian area of Kuwait City. It was here that many resistance fighters turned their guns on suspected collaborators. Of the 400 000 Palestinians in Kuwait before the invasion, some inevitably came to work with the Iraqis. But all of them were under suspicion because the PLO leader, Yasser Arafat, openly supported Saddam. After the rape of Kuwait, there was little patience for justice in the quest for retribution; little evidence would be required in the subsequent martial law trials, and little mercy shown. One Palestinian was sentenced to 15 years in prison for wearing a Saddam Hussein T-shirt, and six other defendants were sentenced to death for working on *Al-Nida*, a newspaper set up by the Iraqis during their rule. Twenty-nine people in all were condemned to death – for which Kuwaiti leaders were condemned to harsh international criticism.

Amnesty, which only months before had highlighted Iraq's human-rights abuses in Kuwait, now turned the spotlight on Kuwait, declaring: 'Unfair trials are bad enough in cases where defendants face penalties of imprisonment but they are absolutely intolerable where the penalty is death.'

Such was the outcry from the West that the Kuwaiti government had

ALL NECESSARY MEANS

to change tack. The kangaroo courts were stopped, the death sentences commuted and martial law lifted in a belated attempt to improve Kuwait's reputation. But, by then, many more Palestinians had been punished without any trial at all: they were simply taken from their homes, blindfolded and driven away to interrogation centres. At Sabah al-Salem police station, Palestinians said that there were three different rooms where they were tortured. In what the police nicknamed 'the party room', they beat their suspects. In 'the barbecue room', they administered electric shocks and cigarette burns, and in 'the juice drinking room' they forced Palestinians to drink sewage. Sometimes they were simply executed on the spot. The body of one Palestinian, gagged, tied up and shot three times, was found under a road bridge in full view of the traffic. Allegations of atrocities were usually met with indignant denials but one Kuwaiti police captain was honest enough to attempt to explain the campaign of violence against the Palestinians: 'If one of your neighbours told the Iraqis where your friends were hiding, you would find that neighbour and you would kill him. Even if you had no weapon you would use your hands and you would beat him to death.'

President Bush refused to be troubled by the activities of those he had risked so much to free. The people of liberated France, he said, 'did not take kindly to those that had sold out to the Nazis'. Bush said that it was 'expecting a little much' to ask the people of liberated Kuwait to treat collaborators differently from the French before them. The investigators from Amnesty International though were appalled and depressed by what they saw on their visit to post-war Kuwait. They appealed to the emir to stop the killing. In a report published in April 1991, the human rights group said:

These violations are continuing and appear to be largely unchecked. Their scale and persistence threaten to leave an indelible stain on Kuwait's human-rights record. This is all the more lamentable in the light of hopes that the kind of violations that occurred under the Iraqi occupation would be a thing of the past.

Kuwait, liberated in the name of a revitalised United Nations seeking

WHO HAD WE LIBERATED?

to end dictatorship and establish a 'new world order', was supposed to be behaving more honourably.

In the early days of liberation, before the emir and most of his ministers returned from exile in Saudi Arabia, there was near anarchy and vigilante groups thrived. But when the killing and harassment of Palestinians continued after the ruling family's return, it became clear that it was giving its support, at least tacitly, to the new cycle of torture and murder. Indeed, those who had lived abroad during the months of occupation appeared to be the most aggressive and vengeful.

The homecoming was an embarrassing flop. On the drive out to Kuwait International Airport to film the return of the emir, something seemed wrong. Then it dawned on us: there were no jubilant Kuwaitis lining the roads waiting to wave to the motorcade of their returning leader, as they had to the advancing allied armies. Instead, around the airport, there were hundreds of security men, as if the Kuwaiti leadership expected an assassination attempt, rather than a show of affection.

Few could understand why the emir had stayed away so long, apparently preferring the antiseptic luxury of the Sheraton Hotel in Ta'if, in southern Saudi Arabia, to his supposedly beloved homeland. Now, almost three weeks after liberation, he finally kissed the Kuwaiti tarmac. On his way into the city, a few hundred of his supporters did turn out to greet him. But the emir's subjects had changed. Many had been radicalised by the occupation and had become bolder in their demands for the restoration of parliament and free elections. Those who had suffered under the Iraqis regarded themselves as different, even superior, to those who had fled (and no one had forgotten that the first to flee had been the emir). They had learned to organise themselves, putting together a resistance network and a food-distribution system. There was a new sense of unity, born of government without the al-Sabahs. Now the chaotic lack of planning further tarnished the royal family's image.

Although the emir, his crown prince and his cabinet had had seven months in which to prepare for the reconstruction of their country, they returned with no ideas. Astonishingly, even the minister for planning, Suleiman Mutawa, admitted: 'I have not yet begun to plan. I have not even opened a planning document. You have to realise that nobody is thinking about anything except the immediate present.' But even the present was an embarrassing failure for the leadership. For weeks – or months in some districts – people had to cope with only occasional power, erratic telephones, and not much food. Even in the ornate palace of the crown prince, there was no running water for weeks after the war.

On his visit there, the Prime Minister, John Major, was amazed at having to use bottled Evian water to wash his hands. It was the kind of chaos everyone expected for a few days, perhaps a fortnight, but as it dragged on, Kuwaitis increasingly blamed their rulers for laziness. The American ambassador was so frustrated that he started distributing food himself, trying to shame the government into action. Needless to say, it didn't work. Months after liberation, though the burnt cars had been cleared away, the air in many side-streets still stank of festering rubbish. Some thought that the al-Sabahs wanted to preserve the mess as a lingering reminder to the world of what they had suffered. Others came to realise the explanation was far more simple: incompetence.

The emir's portrait might have been displayed across the country but his popularity plummeted as conditions failed to improve. The leaders of Kuwait's fledgling, and frequently imprisoned, opposition parties were gaining new support from normally more loyal Kuwaitis. But the opposition had to tread carefully. The al-Sabahs had turned on them several times in the past and the fear was that once the foreign media left they would do so again. While meeting with Kuwaiti friends one evening, we mentioned plans to cover the burgeoning opposition to the al-Sabahs in a news report. There was an embarrassed hush. It turned out that one of the guests was a son of the crown prince. He took the host aside and firmly told him, 'there is no opposition now'. He was wrong.

A few days after the liberation, Dr Abdul Aziz Sultan sat back in his garden chair and casually embarked on a venomous denunciation of the al-Sabah family. In many Arab countries it would have been enough to have him shot. Post-war Kuwait was different. The ruling family found itself having to tolerate criticism, especially from its well-connected subjects. There was none more so than Dr Aziz Sultan, a handsome man with prematurely greying hair; as chairman of the Gulf Bank and frequent guest on the embassy cocktail-party circuit, he was a pillar of the Kuwaiti establishment. Yet, in a BBC interview, he thought nothing of calling for, in effect, revolution. 'I think the present government is completely incompetent to lead and manage Kuwait. I think their government in the last ten years was completely incompetent. I think because of that we have had many a crisis.' He pointed a finger of blame directly at the emir, the crown prince and their cabinet for allowing the country to be invaded. 'I think the people associate the collapse of Kuwait, in the first two minutes of the attack, with the incompetence of the government.'

Kuwaitis were gathering almost every night for 'Diwaniyas', informal evening meetings of anything between a few dozen and a few hundred citizens for the debate of public affairs. Before the invasion, many of the more overtly political gatherings had been broken up by the police. Now, their participants felt far more confident about their fundamental demand – for the constitution to be restored. It had been a model for democracy in the Arab world when it was introduced in 1962. But it was a fragile creation. When the parliament had tried to investigate leading members of the al-Sabah family in 1986, the emir decided to close it down. He suspended the constitution on the pretext of the tension caused by the Iran–Iraq war when there'd been a spate of bombing attacks in Kuwait and an attempt on his life. The country was returned to autocratic rule.

After Iraq's invasion, the emir and his critics had set aside their differences for the sake of national unity. Now though, the opposition were demanding free elections in months, not years. Eventually the al-Sabahs came up with the date of October 1992 and, in the meantime, they set up a 'National Council'. This was a toothless pseudo-parliament, with no power to make any laws, and with a third of its 75 members appointed by none other than the emir. 'We can only suggest things to the government, which can ignore us as it chooses,' one of its deputies, Khalifa al-Kazani, admitted sadly. The opposition denounced it as a sham: 'It reveals the insistence of the regime on maintaining their monopoly of power.'

Washington has gently tried to nudge the al-Sabahs towards political reform but has felt constrained by a fear of upsetting its far more important, and more conservative, ally, King Fahd of Saudi Arabia. President Bush chose to appear unconcerned. 'The war wasn't fought about democracy in Kuwait,' he correctly pointed out. 'The war was fought about aggression against Kuwait.' But the British Government was more insistent on the need for reform. The ambassador in Kuwait, Michael Weston, was instructed to press the al-Sabahs 'to be exemplary', although Downing Street realised this message was unwelcome.

Even when Kuwait's opposition demanded 'democracy', they were only talking about votes for a few; not necessarily for women, and certainly not for 'second-class citizens' – those who couldn't trace their Kuwaiti ancestry back beyond 1920. The reality was that the country operated a form of apartheid: immigrants do all the work for relatively good money but no political rights. In the elections of 1985, only 90 000 out of a total population of 1 695 000 in Kuwait were allowed to vote. In the event, the parliament they elected was dissolved a year later.

Whatever the clamour for democracy, Kuwait's rulers decided after the war to change the balance of their population. Native Kuwaitis no longer wanted to be a small minority in their own country. This was most easily achieved by refusing to allow non-Kuwaitis to return – even those taken away by the Iraqis. On the northern border at Safwan, where allied commanders agreed the terms of the ceasefire with Iraq, a pitiful sight soon developed of Palestinians, Sri Lankans, Sudanese, Egyptians and countless others attempting to return to the country they had been forced to leave. Many had lived in Kuwait for years and some had even been born there. They had expected a welcome home but when they crossed the border, they were rounded up, put in a bus, and dumped back in Iraq; never mind that they had walked barefoot to escape from Saddam's forces and that they were the very people who had laboured so hard to make Kuwait the successful state it was before the war. Privately, American troops patrolling the area told us they were infuriated. Some thought it was a despicable display of inhumanity but there was nothing they could do about it.

The second stage of the population 'solution' was to make life difficult for thousands of unwanted citizens. Some of the stateless *Bedouns* (literally those without) suddenly found themselves being classified as Iraqis and dismissed from their jobs. Many Palestinians, hounded in the country they had made their home, decided their only choice was to emigrate, some leaving for Jordan. As for the 100 000 Iraqis living in Kuwait, there was little hope, even if they had been there all their lives. Many were deported. 'We have begun the purification of evil elements in this country,' said the Crown Prince, Sheikh Saad. It led to heart-rending scenes as families were driven into Iraq, screaming at the border 'the Iraqis will kill us'. It violated the Geneva Convention which says that no one can be forcibly repatriated to a hostile country if they have reasonable grounds to doubt their safety. But even for those who stayed, there was the constant fear of being thrown out of work or into jail. In the country the world had taken pity on, mercy was in short supply.

O n bad days, the smoke would drift in through open windows and scatter tiny droplets of oil across the furniture. The sky would be so blanketed by the dense smog that daybreak never seemed to come. Even at noon, cars used their headlights and everywhere you could hear the sound of coughing. Many visitors, including BBC news teams, wore facemasks as a precaution. Saddam's most damaging legacy was hanging over Kuwait. He had wanted the emirate for its oil-wealth and when that was denied to him, he did his best to destroy it. Six million barrels of oil were going up in smoke every day. All along the horizon, as far as the eye could see, huge orange flames spewed into the air with the roar of jet-engines. The oilfields themselves were everyone's vision of Hell. Whichever way you turned, there was yet another cluster of fires. The heat could be felt even through the closed windows of a car or a helicopter.

It was feared that the fires would unbalance the earth's climate, disrupting the monsoons and spreading starvation in the Third World. The warnings have proved alarmist so far, although droplets of Kuwaiti oil did fall as far afield as the Himalayas. In Kuwait itself, doctors reported an increase in the number of patients with asthma and bronchitis, and the lungs of slaughtered animals were found to have been blackened. But, efforts to help became entangled in Kuwaiti bureaucracy.

ALL NECESSARY MEANS

First on the scene were the famous fire-fighters of Texas. The Kuwaiti government had haggled over how much to pay them and, only after a delay, accepted offers of help from Red Adair, Boots and Coots, and other firms. By late March they began assessing what would be needed, not just to extinguish the fires, but also to cap the wrecked wellheads and stop unburnt oil seeping into the ground. The Texans were charging hundreds of millions of dollars for their services but, as one of them put it, 'if you think experts are expensive, try calling an amateur'. One amateur did rather well in fact: an American sergeant, Forrest Irvin, plugged one leaking oil well with his bare hands. Covered from head to toe in 'oil and gunge', he spun a control wheel that stemmed the flow.

It had originally been thought that there were about 500 oil fires but the firefighters discovered that often where satellite pictures had shown a single well burning, there were sometimes at least three. The total turned out to be 737. Extinguishing them had never seemed a more daunting task than during the first attempt a month after the war. While Red Adair's team tried to plug leaking wells, his erstwhile rival, Boots Hansen, a taciturn figure in stained white overalls, agreed to start on the fires. Little seemed to go his way. At one stage, Kuwaiti border officials had impounded much of his equipment (even though the fires which it was designed to put out were within sight of their offices). The machinery was eventually released, but its first use was a spectacular failure. Hansen's plan was to lower a huge metal tube over the fire to channel the flames, and then inject thousands of gallons of water 'to snuff them out'. As Hansen and his team advanced behind heat-reflecting corrugated tin sheets, all seemed to go well. Against the full force of the flames, a crane lowered the metal tube into position and the water pumps were switched on. There was a loud hissing and vast clouds of steam appeared. But nothing else happened; the fire raged on. 'I need more water', Hansen shouted. The pumps were already working at full stretch. The plan hadn't worked.

Later, better techniques were devised and by spring the fires were being put out at a rate of two a day. Even so, it would take many months to extinguish Saddam's inferno. Kuwait's memory of its time as his nineteenth province would last far longer.

Chapter 8
AFTER THE STORM

'Now, we can see a new world coming into view . . .

there is the very real prospect of

a new world order.'

President
George Bush,
7 March 1991.

Prince Khaled bin
Sultan,
May 1991.

'Saddam Hussein will not last a month,

but then again that's what I said two months ago.'

Schwarzkopf didn't want to humiliate the eight Iraqi officers who had come to discuss the terms of the ceasefire. Still, they had to be searched before they went into a tent set up on the Kuwaiti border. The most senior of the Iraqis, apparently failing to recognise Schwarzkopf, said rather pompously: 'The only person that's going to search me is my counterpart.'

'What do you mean by your counterpart?' said Schwarzkopf.

'The person that's going to negotiate,' replied the Iraqi general, who then looked at Schwarzkopf and said: 'Who are you?'

'I'm General Schwarzkopf.'

If nothing else, it was proof of just how poor the Iraqi army's intelligence about its enemy had been. Schwarzkopf joked that he wasn't very famous in Iraq. Within a few minutes though he was sitting at a table with a can of Diet Pepsi at his side, ready to talk.

Behind Schwarzkopf sat Britain's General de la Billière, who was determined that this should be 'a telling session, not a negotiating session'. His first priority was to secure the release of captured British soldiers, including those of the SAS. The Iraqis reported that they were holding 41 prisoners of war, and they asked how many the allies had. 'As of last night we had 60 000, but we're still counting,' said Schwarzkopf, to the obvious amazement of Iraq's deputy chief of staff, Sultan Hasheem Ahmad, and its 3rd Corps Commander, Salah Abbud Mahmud. Then they tried to argue that their forces had voluntarily withdrawn from Kuwait, which Schwarzkopf refused to accept.

'You know,' he told them, 'we could probably argue here until sunset as to whether or not what you were doing was withdrawing.'

Two hours later, the Iraqis had agreed to all allied demands. Schwarzkopf, though, made one mistake, with dramatic repercussions. Although he told the Iraqis that they couldn't fly their warplanes, he was 'suckered' into making an exception for their helicopters. Saddam pretended he wanted them for for 'rebuilding and administration', but they were to become a key weapon in the civil war that was already erupting and threatening his survival.

Never had Saddam seemed so vulnerable. As demoralised troops trudged home from the front, they quickly spread word of their catastrophic defeat. Some had deserted, others had escaped from the allied killing fields outside Kuwait City, and together they helped to foment insurrection. No longer were they heroes of the state, but 'traitors and mercenaries', according to one Iraqi newspaper. 'All of them shall regret it.' Undaunted, Shiites in the south stormed jails and Ba'ath party buildings, carrying portraits of their mentor, Ayatollah Bakr al-Hakim, whose group, the Supreme Assembly of the Islamic Revolution in Iraq, was based in Tehran. Thirsting for vengeance, there was frenzied killing in Basra and other cities. For a few heady days, it seemed that the oppressed of Iraq might finally overthrow their oppressor. But Saddam was far from finished, and he could still rely on his old protector, the Republican Guard.

At the last allied checkpoint in southern Iraq, we tried to gauge who had the upper hand by foraging for scraps of information from refugees who had fled from the fighting. On the afternoon of 6 March, a pick-up

AFTER THE STORM

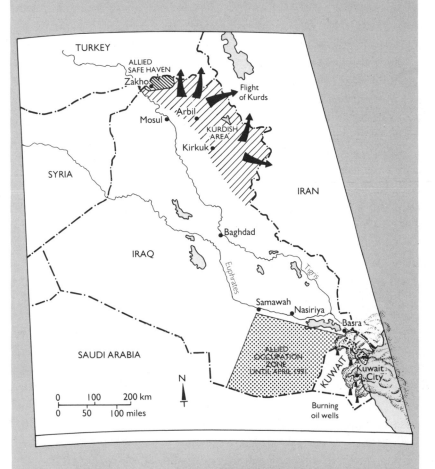

Although the allies succeeded in liberating Kuwait, the impact of the oil fires and the crushing of the Shiite and Kurdish uprisings will be felt for years to come.

ALL NECESSARY MEANS

truck headed towards us on the road from Basra. Crammed in the back were perhaps twenty dark and frightened faces but peeping out from amongst them was a white one. It turned out to be Brock Matthews, a Briton who'd been kidnapped from his home in Kuwait City in January, dragged off to Iraq and thrown into a cell. He climbed out of the truck, dusted down his shirt, and delivered an account of his ordeal.

After two months in jail near Basra, Matthews had almost given up hope, when Shiite rebels broke into the prison. 'We ran and walked as fast as we could,' he recalled, still scarcely believing his good fortune. He had taken shelter with rebel sympathisers. 'They gave us food, something to eat, a wash. We hadn't had a bath for two months.' There had been no water in the building where he was incarcerated, and his daily diet had been a bit of stale bread and half a tomato. When Matthews had finished his story a fast car took him home to Kuwait City for a hot shower, and later that week we saw him enjoying the delights of a gin and tonic at a British embassy party. But his thoughts were with the rebels who had become his friends. He sensed that victory was slipping away from them. 'They've had a good beating for the last two or three days,' he told us. 'The army have really beaten hell out of them.'

Someone else who watched the Shiites' fate just as helplessly was Captain Daniel Miller of the American 2nd Armoured Cavalry Regiment. He and his men had been among the first allied units to fight their way into Iraq, yet, now they were there, they weren't allowed to stop Saddam's soldiers crushing the rebellion. Captain Miller ran his regiment's northernmost observation point on the outskirts of Samawah, which was only 150 miles from Baghdad and was the last of the rebel towns in the south to fall to Saddam. Now, with their binoculars and night-vision goggles, Miller and his colleagues were simply spectators as the Iraqi army set about recapturing Samawah. It was a difficult military operation because the town lies on the southern bank of the Euphrates and the allies had bombed the bridge leading to it. But the army attacked first with artillery and then with helicopter gunships and, after two days, they crossed the river in rafts to take the town for Saddam.

Miller felt helpless. 'We saw the flashes of gunfire and we could hear it all, almost as if we were taking part – but sadly, we weren't.' He told us that he believes that any male over the age of 12 was shot if he was from a suspected rebel family. 'We saw dumper trucks and earthmovers being brought into position for what can only have been one purpose – to dig mass graves.'

It was while the remnants of the Republican Guard were busy putting down this insurrection, that the Kurds in the north saw their chance and seized it. Towns fell to them even without a battle; *Peshmerga* guerrillas would send messages that they were approaching as a signal that the revolt should start. In Arbil, about 60 miles north of Kirkūk, it began at seven o'clock in the morning and was all over three hours later. For a while, Kurdish leaders like Dr Mahmoud Osman were elated. 'We really didn't attack anyone. People simply rose up and handed the cities to us.'

But the insurgents were fighting under a false assumption – that they enjoyed Western support. When George Bush had called on the people of Iraq to 'take matters into their own hands' and force their dictator to 'step aside', they had made the mistake of reading the President's lips. What he actually wanted, it later transpired, was a palace coup – to keep the regime but change its leader. It was a subtle distinction, which was lost on the rebels and most of the world as well. Bush didn't want the Sunni Muslim minority to lose power in Baghdad because they blocked the spread of Shia fundamentalism from Iran. And, in any case, what if the Kurds should succeed in winning themselves an independent Kurdistan? Would they then also press their claims for self-rule in Syria, Turkey and the Soviet Union – all of which had been good allies during the war? Despite Bush's rhetoric about the new world order, he wanted the old borders to remain and so did little to hamper the defeat of an inconvenient revolt.

Bush had always promised the American people that they wouldn't get bogged down in another quagmire like Vietnam. He didn't want to tarnish his swift success in the Gulf or to dent his post-war popularity ratings, now soaring into the nineties. But the policy of 'non-interference' meant there were some tough questions for the White House from commentators and congressmen alike. Was it right to bomb a country and then abdicate responsibility for its future? Why allow Saddam to survive, after insisting he was 'worse than Hitler'? Had the allies deliberately let him keep enough of his army to crush his enemies inside Iraq? In fact, intelligence officials told us one of the Republican Guard's two big tank divisions, the Hammurabi, escaped from Desert Storm with much of its weaponry intact, and, altogether, some 800 tanks and 800 artillery pieces got away – far more than General Schwarzkopf claimed.

Bush's spokesman, Marlin Fitzwater, complained that critics couldn't have it both ways. 'One day people say we should have stopped the fighting; the next they say we didn't go far enough.' But the truth was more complicated. Unofficially, allied policy had been to inflict only a 'sustainable defeat' on Saddam, which meant beating him but not so completely that it would disrupt the balance of power in the Middle East. Among Britain's most senior military commanders, Sir Patrick Hine firmly believed that Iraq should be left with a big enough army to hold its own against Syria or Iran – and also to keep the country from falling apart. Hine's view was that it was in the best interests of the West to prevent Iraq being sliced up into a new Lebanon. It wasn't a bad thing, he thought, that Iraq had come out of the war with its national identity still intact. 'The Shiites and the Kurds chanced their arm. They thought the Iraqis were weaker than they were and got their comeuppance.'

When it dawned on the Kurds that they were alone and beaten, they decided to flee en masse, almost overnight it seemed. They were running from death, but some of them were also running towards it as they headed for the frozen mountain tops of the border with Turkey and Iran. Our BBC colleague, Tom Carver, fled with them and delivered an account of the journey that helped to awaken the world from its post-war complacency:

> In the bitter wind on the summit, I saw a legless man being bumped along in a wheelchair; a woman, her face twisted by the agony of childbirth, crouching for shelter among the rocks; old women dressed only in the nighties and dressing gowns they had left in.

There was no sign of Bush's 'new world order' high up on Turkey's border in early April 1991. At Isikveren, a desolate, desperate refugee camp, one of us was immediately surrounded by hundreds of miserable people all clamouring to tell their own tale of tragedy. One victim stuck out from the crowd: a 12-year-old boy whose face had been burned in a napalm attack. His cheeks and forehead were covered in tiny black blisters but he bore the pain calmly, standing in front of his family's tent – one more witness to the crimes of Saddam Hussein.

These particular refugees had managed to get further into Turkey than most of their compatriots, setting up camp on a plateau below the mountains they had risked everything to cross. But if they thought they had reached a promised land, they were much mistaken. They could see fresh running water in a stream next to their tents, only to have Turkish troops form a human barrier to stop them getting to it; the Turks did not want these refugees and were not inclined to make life any easier for them.

We listened to a Turkish major tell them that they would have to move back up the mountain the following day, to a position right next to the border. He promised life would be better up there, that they would find mobile hospitals and plentiful food supplies. The refugees were sceptical and understandably appalled at the prospect of climbing back up the steep slopes they had just descended. Some of them threatened to resist but the next day we arrived at the camp to see them filing pathetically up the mountain, the great unwanted.

The elderly panted loudly on this second arduous ascent in a week; even fitter men and women, drenched in sweat, collapsed by the side of the path. Some panicked, beseeching us to reassure them that they were not being taken back to Iraq. Others consoled themselves with naïve optimism; that soon they might be able to leave this place and make a new life in Europe as politicial refugees – France, Germany or Holland, they said; they didn't mind which.

At the end of this draining trek, nobody was greatly surprised that conditions on the mountain-top were little better than those down below. They may even have been worse because the trucks that were beginning to deliver bread had to drive much further now, up the perilous, muddy mountain track. Often vehicles going down got stuck, obstructing

ALL NECESSARY MEANS

vehicles that were coming up. If a consignment of loaves did get to the top, an hysterical mob would chase the truck in a whirlwind of dust and dirt. It was the survival of the fittest, Kurds scrambling over each other to get some small scrap of bread, or literally crumbs. In the face of this undignified desperation, the two or three guards on the back of the lorry would end up whipping or beating those they had come to feed.

Perhaps they had little alternative; nothing is more terrifying than a stampede of famished humanity. We saw a middle-aged mother, who had suffered a deep gash above her eye, in the midst of this chaos. She was one of the many losers. Worse, there was no fresh water here; refugees were reduced to grabbing handfuls of snow and melting it. The snow was filthy and the water it produced unhygienic. The Turks began delivering fresh water by tanker – drawing it from the stream where the Kurds had originally settled. Ludicrously, the authorities had to drive thousands of gallons of it all the way up a mountain they had just forced the Kurds to climb. Moving them had been a pointless cruelty – the latest injustice to a long-suffering people.

A few days later, when we were trying to drive to another camp, at Cukurca, the road was blocked by landslides. Instead we stopped at another, much smaller settlement that superficially looked rather pleasant. It was a gloriously sunny day and, on the rich green grass, the Kurds had pitched their tents next to a river which, at that spot, marks the border between Turkey and Iraq. The women were doing their washing in the water, and for a few moments the refugees here seemed to enjoy a far better quality of life than most of their counterparts. But as we got closer we noticed scuffles on a small bridge across the river; Kurds coming over it were being challenged and stopped by Turkish troops, under orders to prevent these wretched people moving from one bank to the other – because that meant crossing from one country to the other. Huge piles of food – including pasta, potatoes and tinned fruit – were lying uselessly on the Turkish side, only a few dozen yards from the Kurds, but tantalisingly out of reach to people suffering from pneumonia, diarrhoea and gastro-enteritis. In every tent, we found someone lying on the floor, usually too tired even to moan or cry with the pain.

On behalf of the Kurds here, Idrees Salih, an engineer who had escaped from Zakho and who spoke remarkably good English, used our television camera to make an appeal to the leaders of the western world:

> We want Mr Bush and James Baker and John Major . . . to save us from this condition and to help us, because we are suffering. We feel angry with them now. We don't know what will happen to us, where we will go.

To his astonishment, a few minutes later, Salih was able to watch one of those three men passing overhead in a helicopter – James Baker, on his way to see Cukurca camp for himself. It was a tense visit, which lasted only seven minutes – long enough for one refugee to reproach the Secretary of State for his country's inconsistency. Afterwards, Baker admitted that the plight of the Kurds was 'almost beyond belief', and, back in Washington, an aide at the White House had to agree. 'We wrote the civil war off,' he said, 'but we can't write off the refugees.'

The Americans were perfectly prepared to sympathise, but not to do very much. When John Major came up with a plan to create 'safe havens' for the Kurds, there was an embarrassed silence at the White House, and in many parts of Whitehall. Privately, one of the Prime Minister's most senior advisers at Number Ten thought that Major 'was being panicked by newspaper headlines'. This aide shared the Prime Minister's compassion for the refugees but had no sympathy for the Kurdish cause. He told us later: 'The most awful things had been going on inside Iraq against the Kurds and the Shiites for a very long time. What happened after the war wasn't actually very different in scale from what had been done before.' This adviser even compared the Kurdish leaders to the worst elements in Saddam's regime. 'The Iraqis are exceptionally brutal, vengeful people, as indeed are the Kurds, who have a record of violence and unpleasantness which is probably second to none.'

Near by, at the Foreign Office, there was the same cynicism. Why, a high-ranking official asked us, was there such a romantic affinity with the Kurds anyway? 'The British seem to have a bit of a thing about them,' he

ALL NECESSARY MEANS

complained, bewildered that his ministers had received a record amount of mail about the refugees. 'Can it really be that the Great British Public, in some curious way, remembered that we were responsible for not giving the Kurds a state of their own?' He was thinking back to the Kurdish revolts earlier in the century which Britain had helped to suppress.

While the Whitehall mandarins might dismiss the public's concern, they had to take a share of the blame for failing to predict this human catastrophe. We discovered that as early as the beginning of December 1990, officials from London had travelled to Washington for a critical meeting to agree policy on the aftermath of a war with Iraq. The four-man British delegation came from the Foreign Office, Cabinet Office and Ministry of Defence, but neither they, nor their Bush administration colleagues, had thought to consider the future of the Kurds and the Shiites. They looked ahead to almost everything else – arms sales, regional security and Israel – but the possibility of civil war and an exodus of refugees wasn't foreseen. With hindsight, it was an extraordinary lapse.

Now foreign policy had to follow public opinion. Mrs Thatcher was applauded, even by her critics, for demanding from the pavement outside her home that 'something must be done'. In fact, something was already being done by her successor. John Major had asked the Foreign Office to come up with ideas about how to help the Kurds. They suggested what became the 'safe haven' plan. The Prime Minister decided not to tell the Americans about it just yet. The Downing Street view was that Bush and his advisers were so 'petrified about another Vietnam' that they would not support it. Instead, Major decided to push his proposals through the European Community. There was a frantic effort to get them ready in time for an EC summit about to be held in Luxembourg, and even on the flight out the plan was still being finalised. Major's press secretary, Gus O'Donnell, was hurriedly trimming down a 'wordy' draft from the Foreign Office into something 'which could be sold' to the outside world.

While he was on the aircraft, the Prime Minister was advised that, without American support, the 'safe haven' idea might well fall flat on its face. He decided to press ahead anyway. This was Britain going it alone for once, and a conscious decision was taken not to tell Washington until Major was actually in Luxembourg. Once the aircraft had landed, a call was made to Britain's ambassador at the United Nations, Sir David Hannay, who was due to have lunch that day with the UN Secretary General, Javier Perez de Cuellar. It meant that Major's plan could get his early approval. Finally, the Prime Minister's new foreign affairs adviser, Stephen Wall, telephoned the White House. Brent Scowcroft, the man who was effectively his opposite number, wasn't there so he had to leave a message. It made a nice change for the British to be letting the Americans know about an initiative, rather than the other way round.

The reaction was hostile. 'It's a wild idea, it's not well thought out,' said Iraq's ambassador to the UN, Abdul Amir al-Anbari. Privately, the Bush administration agreed – in a rare show of unanimity with Baghdad. Yet the President had James Baker telling him of the intense diplomatic pressure in favour of intervention. Bush was forced to fall into line with Major. His officials worried about the effect it might have on the President's post-war image. 'He was seen as undisputed leader all through the Gulf War, but now he's clearly trailing behind the Europeans,' one of them murmured disconsolately. In Downing Street, there was quiet satisfaction, that while the United States had led the world against Iraq, 'after the war, we were leading America'.

The Prime Minister and President smoothed things over in a 20-minute phone call. The White House soon devised a plan for troops to be sent to help the Kurds. Defence Secretary Dick Cheney and General Colin Powell were unhappy with the decision but Bush had to consider which would do him most damage – American troops lingering in Iraq, or Kurds dying every day on prime-time network television news. Yet even as the President despatched his forces, he was determined to pull them back as soon as he could. That would be made easier for him by the Kurds' talks with Saddam. When one Kurdish leader, Jalal Talabani, embraced and kissed the Iraqi president on both cheeks, it looked to the world as if he was treating the man who had murdered thousands of his people as a long-lost brother. Saddam promised that he was ready to discuss Kurdish autonomy, and this unlikely reconciliation helped to give Bush and other allied leaders the excuse to withdraw their soldiers. That, in turn, weakened the Kurds' bargaining position with Saddam. By the middle of July 1991, the last coalition forces had left northern Iraq and a

ALL NECESSARY MEANS

'rapid reaction force' was set up over the border in southern Turkey, ready to go back in should Saddam try once more to intimidate the Kurds. In place of Operation Provide Comfort, Operation Poised Hammer was born.

The Kurds pleaded with the soldiers to stay. Their banners were written in polite English for the cameras: 'we are insecure,' they read, and 'the Kurds are exposed.' There was no animosity, only gratitude for what the troops had done and nervousness for the future. 'They helped us at the right time,' said Tawfiq Abu, a guerrilla leader. 'If they hadn't come we would all be dead.' It was a tribute to John Major, but many British soldiers were reluctant to leave, fearing that their departure would turn out to be an act of betrayal.

Two months after the war, Saddam Hussein was able to throw a fifty-fourth birthday party. There was not much to celebrate except his own survival, yet coloured lights and streamers adorned public buildings and portraits of the president. In Tikrit, a town close to his birthplace, there was a special ceremony. Schoolgirls waved garlands of flowers and sang, 'the birthday of Saddam is the birthday of Iraq'. But most Iraqis were cursing him, not celebrating, and, amid the misery of those who'd fled, it was easy to forget the horrendous suffering of the bulk of the Iraqi population. Relief agencies said that the infant mortality rate had doubled from its pre-war rate of 40 per 1000. According to a team from the United Nations International Children's Emergency Fund (UNICEF), 'malnutrition, which had not been seen in Iraq for at least the last decade, is now widely reported'. The UN's envoy, Prince Sadruddin Aga Khan, who visited Iraq, came away predicting a human catastrophe unless the economic blockade was eased: 'Sanctions were not designed to make the people of Iraq suffer the way they are suffering now.'

In Basra, one woman was no stranger to suffering. Her name was Leila and she sat at the bedside of her dying three-year-old son, contemplating what she had to show for all the months of turmoil Saddam Hussein had inflicted on her and millions of others. Her little boy was suffering from severe malnutrition and suspected cholera, one of many patients in the dilapidated al-Tahrir hospital where there was not enough medicine to treat him. Another of her children had already died – a baby who she hadn't even been able to get to a doctor. Her grandmother was seriously ill. Leila, too, was suffering from malnutrition – her face under the black veil was gaunt and pale because she had given up her food so the children could have it instead. The doctors told her that she was lucky; by not eating she might have avoided getting the cholera. Leila couldn't help looking back to what life had been like before 2 August 1990. Her house had been cramped with 18 people living there, including her own five children and her husband's relatives, but they had coped. With sanctions, however, they had to survive on only a little rice and flour and then, when the bombing began, there was no electricity or water. She knew she shouldn't, but Leila used water from the Shatt-al-Arab river.

> It was green and tasted very bad. I knew it would make us sick and I tried to keep the children from drinking too much of it. I had to use it to cook the little rice we had. The baby got sick first, and within a few days she died. I wished I had died instead of my baby. Maybe I will.

Once again the people of Iraq were being punished more than their leader but Bush insisted that he would not end the pain until Saddam had gone. 'I will not have our people voting to lift sanctions while he is in power,' said the President. But, later, the allies let Iraq sell some of its oil and use the proceeds, controlled by the UN, to buy food and medicine.

At one stage after the war, it seemed that Saddam had been humbled. He appeared to do as he was told by the UN and some people even started calling him a 'yes-man'. His parliament had rubber-stamped acceptance of the punitive UN ceasefire, which demanded the payment of reparations to Kuwait. And he tried to create a more forgiving image, promising democracy and announcing an amnesty for draft-dodgers and political opponents. But it was all a sham; he was just buying himself time while he regained his strength and rebuilt his power-base. As though everyone should simply forget all that had happened, he even asked why sanctions were still in place, 'when the war is over and Kuwait is back to the borders it had before 2 August?'

ALL NECESSARY MEANS

One reason that the embargo was maintained soon became clear. Saddam was making a mockery of the UN's demand that he should abandon his secret nuclear research programme. Despite 42 days of bombing during Desert Storm, some of the Iraqis' nuclear technology had been successfully protected and now they were busy concealing what they'd salvaged. There was an almost farcical game of hide-and-seek with a team of UN inspectors, which culminated in shots being fired over their heads when they got too close. The investigators, armed only with video cameras, still managed to film some of Saddam's uranium enrichment equipment, to the delight of an American official. 'This is bingo,' he said in relief. 'We've really caught them with their pants down.'

It supported the claims by a defecting Iraqi engineer that his country still had a flourishing nuclear weapons programme. In fact, the Americans were suddenly finding out how little they had known; that the Iraqis had at least four more nuclear research centres than had been thought, and the calutron system for enriching uranium. The defector might have been exaggerating, 'to pay for his ticket' as the intelligence community say, but he also reported that Saddam wanted to develop his first nuclear device by the end of 1991.

In familiar style, Bush accused his old enemy of 'lying and cheating'. He threatened to unleash a fresh wave of bombing on a war-weary Iraq; a list of 100 targets was drawn up by the Pentagon. Once again, the UN Security Council gave the Iraqis a deadline; this time it was 25 July 1991, by which they had to come clean about their nuclear programme or 'face the consequences'. Only six months after the war, it was back to the brinkmanship of Bush against Saddam – of who would blink first. In the event, the Iraqis became increasingly open. But as long as Saddam Hussein was still in power, the Gulf War was not really over.

The allies were all too aware that it was their defence contractors who'd helped to create the monster of Iraq's military machine. Now they were talking about trying to make sure it never happened again. President Bush – determined as always to show that a better world could emerge from the Gulf crisis – made arms control in the Middle East a priority. But, as ever, war was followed by an arms race and the White House, despite its noble vision, didn't seem to be doing very much to stop it. Countries which had helped in the coalition against Baghdad had to be rewarded and, the day after Bush announced his proposals to stop proliferation in the Middle East, the Defence Secretary, Dick Cheney, was in Jerusalem unveiling a new package of military aid to Israel, including 10 F-15 fighters. The White House said that it was also hoping to sell billions of dollars worth of weapons to Saudi Arabia, Egypt, the United Arab Emirates, Bahrain and Turkey.

America's defence industry, facing cuts in orders by its own government, has tried to cash in on a surging demand for weapons which bear the label 'as seen in the Gulf'. The war had been like a world trade fair for the arms industry, and many Middle Eastern countries became keener than ever to acquire smart bombs, Apache helicopters, and the American M1A1 (Abrams) tanks. They wanted high-tech weapons, even if they didn't have the skills and training to make effective use of them.

Washington had been chastened by the prospect of taking on an enemy with weapons of mass destruction and Bush proposed banning them from the Middle East. But often more threatening have been the conventional arms which, historically, are more likely to be used in the region's wars. John Major came up with the idea of a 'register' of the sales of such weapons, which would bring the shady dealings of both buyer and seller out into the open. Embarrassingly for his government, a fortnight after he had secured support for the idea from the 'G7' Economic Summit in London, new details emerged of exports of British arms technology to Iraq. The Department of Trade and Industry admitted that it authorised the sale of plutonium, uranium and other materials to Iraq until three days after Saddam's invasion of Kuwait. So huge are the potential profits from the arms trade that, despite the hopes of John Major and others, they may never succeed in curbing it.

Certainly Arab customers are unlikely to cut their military budgets as long as Israel still has an advanced nuclear programme. Only a diplomatic breakthrough in the interminable Arab–Israeli stalemate could stop a spiral of spending in the post-war arms bazaar. Once the guns in the Gulf had fallen silent, that was the job to which the American Secretary of

ALL NECESSARY MEANS

State, James Baker, was assigned. He and Bush had always rejected Saddam's claim of 'linkage' between the Kuwaiti and Palestinian crises. At the same time, they consistently spoke about the prospect of a new peace initiative once Saddam was defeated – linkage by another name. 'Our commitment to peace in the Middle East does not end with the liberation of Kuwait,' said the President. It was a pledge that led James Baker to undertake six trips to the region in six months. By the summer of 1991, Baker had managed to set up a peace conference. The breakthrough came when Syria's President Assad suddenly agreed to talk to his old enemy, Israel. The Israeli Prime Minister, Yitzhak Shamir, agreed to attend but insisted he would not give up 'land for peace'. Even so, Baker believed that he could see a 'window of opportunity', though many in Israel and the Arab world were just waiting to slam it shut.

For many Americans, the Gulf War was all wrapped up by their victory parades and the avalanche of ticker-tape that tumbled from the tower blocks of New York onto troops returning from the front. The people of the United States felt good about themselves and that meant they felt good about their President. Indeed, it sometimes seemed that the point of the war had been not only to restore the al-Sabahs but also to restore American self-confidence. On 4 July, American Independence Day, George Bush joined a parade through the small rural town of Marshfield, Missouri. There he told the American people that they no longer needed to feel self-doubt or shame because of Vietnam; the troops in the Gulf had changed all that:

> These young men and women went to the desert and brought honour to our nation . . . they liberated a nation abroad and transformed a nation at home . . . the real miracle took place not in the sands of Kuwait, it unfolded in the American heart.

Vietnam was a burden lifted, a psychological scar erased. There were more celebrations that day by the US troops protecting the Kurds in northern Iraq. They let off fireworks and then had to reassure the civilians around them that these weren't bombs that were bursting above them. 'There's no cause for alarm,' blared the loudspeakers in Zakho. 'The fireworks are to celebrate a traditional American holiday.' The party was perhaps a little insensitive, but the winners of this war didn't always think too much about the losers.

Neither did they want to talk about how many Iraqis might have died during Desert Storm. It was the great, dark secret of the war. American officials were as reluctant to give 'body counts' when it was over, as they had been during it. In all our interviews with senior military commanders, only one was prepared to hazard a guess at the enemy death toll. Schwarzkopf's deputy commander-in-chief, Lieutenant General Buck Rogers, told us that he believed it may have been as high as 200 000. Officially, Central Command had calculated that 100 000 Iraqi soldiers had been killed. But intelligence officers stressed that this was a purely mathematical exercise: they had subtracted prisoners of war and deserters and assumed a 'mortality rate' for those troops still on the battlefield. The Iraqis produced a higher estimate. They said that as many as 110 000 of their troops and 45 000 civilians had died.

However many Iraqis had been killed, President Bush was troubled by the fact that one in particular was not only alive but prospering. 'I would guess Saddam Hussein will be in power after George Bush leaves office,' predicted one Republican Senator. Getting rid of Saddam had never been a stated war aim, but, like the capture of General Noriega in Panama, it would have made victory all the more complete. Bush grew increasingly sensitive to criticism from those who were casting doubt on his triumph. 'Some are moving the goalposts,' he snapped five months after the ceasefire. 'Some are trying to redefine what the war was about . . . Was it the total demise of Saddam Hussein? It wasn't.' But his old ally, Mrs Thatcher, later implicitly criticised Bush for failing to bring Saddam to trial before agreeing to a ceasefire.

After the initial euphoria, questions were even being asked about how much of an achievement it had been to defeat Iraq. Military experts began to suggest that perhaps it was not, after all, the victory to heal a superpower's injured pride, but rather a 'no-contest walkover'. A contributor to the authoritative *Jane's Intelligence Review* went as far as to say that, 'in real terms, Desert Storm was not a war'. With hindsight, it seemed that predictions of impenetrable minefields and of chemical retaliation had been unduly, perhaps even deliberately, pessimistic, and the strength of Iraq's troop numbers was greatly exaggerated. 'I think we overestimated their capabilities,' said Major-General Paul Funk of the US Third Armoured Division. And what of the great deception plan? The Iraqis, Funk pointed out, 'could have looked into any of our manuals and figured out that we weren't going to attack straight ahead'. Even US Under Secretary of Defence Frank Kendall had to admit that not much could be gleaned from this curiously one-sided war. 'What we did not learn was how to defeat a modern, well-trained, well-motivated, well-led force in a dynamic environment.'

To some extent, while Schwarzkopf's cunning won the war, Saddam's stupidity lost it. The dictator surely made one of modern history's most colossal blunders when he refused to withdraw from Kuwait just before, or even just after, the UN deadline. It would have left intact his huge army, his oil revenues and his respect in the Arab world. He would also have proved a point to the Kuwaitis. When it was all over, Saddam as usual found fault with everyone except himself and he began a familiar purge of his Ba'ath party officials and senior military commanders. He was said to have had fourteen of them executed, after they were told to come to collect medals for their service in Kuwait.

In one notable speech though, Saddam did have the grace to shoulder at least some of the blame for the Gulf War. 'Each of us should quickly take stock of his mistakes. When we say we were inattentive, we must guard against being caught unawares again. When we say that we were confused, we must make sure not to lapse into perplexity again.' It sounded uncomfortably like a leader trying to learn lessons from one war in preparation for the next.

While Saddam had got all his calculations wrong, it was hard to deny that George Bush had got most of his right. Against expectations, he had succeeded in holding together a fragile coalition of some 30 nations, and he had kept Israel out of the war. He had gambled on getting the authority of both the United Nations (against Mrs Thatcher's advice) and Congress, and it had paid off; this was a very 'legal' war. He had struggled to convince his people that Kuwait was a cause worth dying for, and that this was about something more than cheap oil; in the end though, they had believed him. He had promised it would not be another Vietnam, and it wasn't. The Pentagon had ordered 16 099 body bags to be sent out to the Gulf, and only 148 of them were used to bring back bodies of American servicemen killed in action.

Saddam knew he could never beat America and her allies, but he did think he could turn public opinion against the war. He misread the West, just as it misread him in the days before 2 August when Norman Schwarzkopf sat in Florida and laughed at the idea that the Iraqis would invade Kuwait.

Bibliography

ANDERSON, J. and VAN ATTA, D.
Stormin' Norman: An American Hero
Zebra Books, Kensington Publishing Corp., New York, 1991.

DARWISH, A. and ALEXANDER, G.
Unholy Babylon: The Secret History of Saddam's War
Gollancz, 1991.

INTERNATIONAL INSTITUTE FOR STRATEGIC STUDIES
Strategic Survey 1990–91
Brassey's, 1991.

KHALIL, S.
Republic of Fear: Saddam's Iraq
Hutchinson, 1991.

MILLER, J. and MYLROIE, L.
Saddam Hussein and the Crisis in the Gulf
Times Books, New York, 1991.

PYLE, R.
Schwarzkopf: The Man, the Mission, the Triumph
Mandarin, 1991.

RAF Yearbook Special: Air War in the Gulf
RAF Benevolent Fund's International Air Tattoo Publishing Unit, 1991.

SALINGER, P. with LAURENT, E.
Secret Dossier: The Hidden Agenda Behind the Gulf War
Transl: H. Curtis, Penguin, 1991.

WOODWARD, B.
The Commanders
Simon & Schuster, 1991.

Index

Index

Index

Index